THE DEAD LETTER

AN AMERICAN ROMANCE

SEELEY REGESTER

Edited, with an introduction and notes,
by Leslie S. Klinger

LIBRARY LIBRARY OF CONGRESS

Poisoned Pen PRESS

Published by Poisoned Pen Press, an imprint of Sourcebooks,
in association with the Library of Congress
P.O. Box 4410, Naperville, Illinois 60567-4410
(630) 961-3900
sourcebooks.com

This edition of *The Dead Letter* is based on the edition in the Library of
Congress's collection published in 1867 by Beadle and Company. The original,
unsigned illustrations were engraved by Nathaniel Orr & Company.

Library of Congress Cataloging-in-Publication Data

Names: Victor, Metta Victoria Fuller, author. | Klinger, Leslie S, editor.
Title: The dead letter : an American romance / Seeley Regester;
  with an introduction and notes by Leslie S. Klinger.
Description: Naperville, Illinois : Poisoned Pen Press, [2021] | Series:
  Library of Congress crime classics | Published in association with
  the Library of Congress. | Includes bibliographical references.
Identifiers: LCCN 2020053767 (print) | LCCN 2020053768
  (ebook) | (trade paperback) | (epub)
Subjects: GSAFD: Mystery fiction.
Classification: LCC PS3129.V58 D4 2021 (print) | LCC PS3129.V58 (ebook) |
  DDC 813/.4--dc23
LC record available at https://lccn.loc.gov/2020053767
LC ebook record available at https://lccn.loc.gov/2020053768

Printed and bound in the United States of America.
SB 10 9 8 7 6 5 4 3 2 1

CONTENTS

Foreword   vii

Introduction   ix

PART I.   1

CHAPTER I.
  The Letter.   3

CHAPTER II.
  Events of a Night.   6

CHAPTER III.
  The Figure Beneath the Trees.   18

CHAPTER IV.
  Moreland Villa.   29

CHAPTER V.
  Mr. Burton, the Detective.   45

CHAPTER VI.
  Two Links in the Chain.   68

CHAPTER VII.
  Eleanor.   82

CHAPTER VIII.
The Haunted Grave.   91
CHAPTER IX.
The Spider and the Fly.   111
CHAPTER X.
The Anniversary.   129
CHAPTER XI.
The Little Guest and the Apparition.   151
CHAPTER XII.
The Night in Moreland Villa.   173
CHAPTER XIII.
The Shadow Assumes Shape.   186

PART II.   197

CHAPTER I.
The Letter.   199
CHAPTER II.
Our Visits.   212
CHAPTER III.
The Confession.   229
CHAPTER IV.
Embarked for California.   244
CHAPTER V.
On the Trail.   253
CHAPTER VI.
At Last—At Last.   262
CHAPTER VII.
Now for Home Again.   278
CHAPTER VIII.
The Ripe Hour.   283

CHAPTER IX.
   Joining the Missing Links.   296
CHAPTER X.
   The New Life.   305

Reading Group Guide   310
Further Reading   312
About the Author   314

FOREWORD

Crime writing as we know it first appeared in 1841, with the publication of "The Murders in the Rue Morgue." Written by American author Edgar Allan Poe, the short story introduced C. Auguste Dupin, the world's first wholly fictional detective. Other American and British authors had begun working in the genre by the 1860s, and by the 1920s we had officially entered the golden age of detective fiction.

Throughout this short history, many authors who paved the way have been lost or forgotten. Library of Congress Crime Classics bring back into print some of the finest American crime writing from the 1860s to the 1960s, showcasing rare and lesser-known titles that represent a range of genres, from cozies to police procedurals. With cover designs inspired by images from the Library's collections, each book in this series includes the original text, reproduced faithfully from an early edition in the Library's collections and complete with strange spellings and unorthodox punctuation. Also included are a contextual introduction, a brief biography of the author, notes, recommendations for further reading, and suggested discussion questions. Our hope is for these books to start conversations, inspire further research, and bring obscure works to a new generation of readers.

Early American crime fiction is not only entertaining to read, but it also sheds light on the culture of its time. While many of the titles in this series include outmoded language and stereotypes now considered offensive, these books give readers the opportunity to reflect on how our society's perceptions of race, gender, ethnicity, and social standing have evolved over more than a century.

More dark secrets and bloody deeds lurk in the massive collections of the Library of Congress. I encourage you to explore these works for yourself, here in Washington, DC, or online at www.loc.gov.

—Carla D. Hayden, Librarian of Congress

INTRODUCTION

Crime writing in America did not begin in books or stories. In fact, crime writing was first undertaken by clergy in the seventeenth century who wrote sermons for their congregations, sometimes based on the evidence given against notorious criminals, sometimes embellished. This writing was soon secularized, and the "broadsides"—penny newspapers that were published on, among other occasions, the eve of public hangings—became widely popular. The first important American work that was admittedly fiction was the trio of stories by Edgar Allan Poe about the amateur detective, the Chevalier C. Auguste Dupin—"The Murders in the Rue Morgue" (1841), "The Mystery of Marie Rogêt" (1842), and "The Purloined Letter" (1844). These had a great vogue in Europe, where Poe's genius was lauded, but apparently made little impression in America, where no one took up Poe's mantle of well-crafted tales. Poe himself moved on to other subjects after this brief experiment.

Three forms of American crime fiction did flourish in the mid-nineteenth century: the dime novels, the casebooks, and the city-mysteries. Dime novels, the American version of the "penny dreadfuls," were cheap, poorly written but lurid tales of crime and detection, published in the form of pulp magazines (typically eight to ten sheets) or as inexpensive "yellowback" (paperback) editions. The earliest of these date from the late 1830s, and they thrived through the turn of the new century. Many were written by anonymous or pseudonymous authors, and they covered a wide gauntlet of stories—historical adventures featuring pirates, highwaymen, bandits, detectives, cowboys, and the like. At the same time, American authors began to pen what were termed "casebooks," purporting to be genuine accounts of the activities of detectives. Some of the earliest of these are James Holbrook's *Ten Years among the Mail Bags: or, Notes from the Diary of a Special Agent of the Post-Office Department* (1855), a collection of probably partially true stories, and the stories of John Babbington Williams collected in *Leaves from the Note-Book of a New York Detective* (1865).* A third thread of crime writing, known as city-mysteries, began in Europe with the success of Eugène Sue's *The Mysteries of Paris* (1840–41) and George W. M. Reynolds's *The Mysteries of London* (1844) but was soon copied in America by George Lippard in his 1844–45 Philadelphia novel, *The Quaker City; or, The Monks of Monk-Hall,* and Ned Buntline's *The Mysteries and Miseries of New York: A Story of Real Life* (1847–48).† Lippard and Buntline both wrote in depth of criminals, gamblers, prostitutes, and other creatures of the streets as well as the businessmen who preyed on them. American versions focused on the "mysteries and miseries" of such disparate locales as San Francisco, New Orleans, Cincinnati, and St. Louis, as well as smaller "cities" like Troy, New York; Fitchburg, Massachusetts; Nashua, New Hampshire; and Pottsville, Pennsylvania.

---

* The stories originally appeared in *Ballou's Dollar Monthly Magazine* in 1862.

† Edward Zane Carroll Judson, who wrote as "Ned Buntline," was a prolific author of books and dime novels. He came to fame primarily in connection with his promotion of the myths of Buffalo Bill.

By the 1860s, the public—and this included much of the middle classes—was reading "sensation" novels (called by one critic "novels with a secret"*). Certainly, the most popular was *The Woman in White* by Wilkie Collins (1859), the protagonist of which becomes an amateur detective. Other extremely successful examples of the new genre were Ellen (Mrs. Henry) Wood's *East Lynne* (1861) and Mary Elizabeth Braddon's *Lady Audley's Secret* (1862). In this same decade, however, three novels appeared that shifted attention from secrets to professional detectives solving crimes.† The first two were English: *The Trail of the Serpent* (1860) by Mary Elizabeth Braddon and *The Notting Hill Mystery* (1862) by Charles Felix.

The Trail of the Serpent, originally titled *Three Times Dead; or, The Secret of the Heath*, focuses on Jabez North (Ephraim East in the original version), a criminal who changes his identity three times, and Mr. Peters (Waters in the original), an unrelenting, mute police detective. The story, like so many sensation novels before it, is filled with coincidences that ultimately bring about the clever villain's capture. *The Notting Hill Mystery* is another remarkable work, set apart from Braddon's book by an assemblage of crime scene reports, maps, depositions, and commentary by the detective, an insurance investigator. Julian Symons hailed it as an important forerunner of twentieth-century police procedurals, with a style very different from its sensational forerunners.‡ However, the means of murder—sympathetic

---

* Kathleen Tillotson's introduction to Wilkie Collins's *The Woman in White* (1859) in the Riverside edition (Boston: Houghton, Mifflin, 1969).

† Admittedly, Charles Dickens had depicted Inspector Bucket in some depth in *Bleak House* (1852–53), but no one took his lead.

‡ Julian Symons, *Bloody Murder: From the Detective Story to the Crime Novel* (New York: Viking, 1981), 52.

commands via mesmerism—is so outlandish and dependent on near-mystical ideas as to make the novel more like a Gothic romance than a detective novel.

The third true mystery novel to appear was distinctly American: *The Dead Letter* (1866)* by "Seeley Regester."† *The Dead Letter* was a significant step away from the sensational toward the rational. The principal detection is done by Mr. Burton, a professional associated with the New York City Police Department. Burton has only been a detective for a few years, but he is middle aged, having discovered his talents for detection after he himself was a victim of arson. Burton is described as "intelligent, even educated, a gentleman in language and

---

* There is some confusion about the publication date. The editor of *Beadle's Monthly*, in which the story was published in 1866, expressly states that it was first published "two years previously." (See "About the Author," page 317, second note.) However, details of the mysterious 1864 "first publication" are missing. The novel was serialized in *Beadle's Monthly* beginning with the January 1866 issue and was completed in the September 1866 issue. While many sources indicate that the book itself was first published in 1867 (for example, Chris Steinbrunner and Otto Penzler's *Encyclopedia of Mystery & Detection* and Rosemary Herbert's *Oxford Companion to Crime & Mystery Writing*), the *New York Tribune* for September 15, 1866, clearly states (in an advertisement) that the book was "published this morning." The 1866 edition was a mere 120 pages long, with very small type; the 1867 edition, with the same text, was more than 300 pages long. Both versions included the illustrations that appeared in the initial magazine publication. Curiously, the first four chapters were also published (presumably as a marketing device) in *Harper's Weekly* on February 10, 1866, with the following at the end of the fourth chapter: "For a continuation of this remarkable story, see BEADLE'S MONTHLY for February, now ready and for sale by all Booksellers and Newsdealers; or sent, post-paid, on receipt of the price. TWENTY-FIVE CENTS, Beadle & Co. Publishers, 118 William Street, New York—Advertisement." The same four chapters, with the same advertisement, also appeared in the February 3 and February 10, 1866, issues of *Frank Leslie's Illustrated Newspaper*.

---

† It is now known that this was a pseudonym of Metta Victoria Fuller Victor. The magazine appearances of the novel did not list the author's name on any of the nine segments of the story. In the table of contents for the publisher's bound volume of the January–June 1866 issues of *Beadle's Monthly*, the author's name is given as "Seeley Regester"; in the bound volume for July–December 1866, the author's first name is given as "Seely." In the first book publication in 1866, it appears as "Seeley Register," while the 1867 publication—on which this volume is based—spelled her last name "Regester."

manner." He is "a quite different person" from that which the narrator "expected from a member of the detective-police."* While the principal discoveries are facilitated through the psychic talents of Burton's daughter, here, for the first time, an American author created an American crime story to be solved by an American detective. Many of Burton's ideas about means of detection were ahead of his time, including handwriting analysis and careful sifting of crime scene evidence, and his tenacity and incorruptibility convey a positive impression of the police, at a time not long after the introduction of official police forces around America.

The Dead Letter is an important landmark in the history of American crime fiction. It is not only the first American crime fiction written by a woman; it is the first American crime novel. Though Anna Katharine Green would come to be known as "the mother of detective fiction," Victor deserves full credit for setting America on the path of crime writing at least as good as that coming out of England. Victor also made it possible for women like Green and lesser-known writers like Emma Murdoch Van Deventer, Bessie Turner, and eventually Mary Roberts Rinehart to make (in the words of scholar Kate Watson) "women writing crime become almost commonplace in America."† But *The Dead Letter* should not be remembered principally for the gender of its author. Rather, its uniquely literate and extended treatment of the American crime story should be appreciated. Though there was an abundance of American tales of rogues,

---

* In fairness, it should be remembered that the New York Police Department was in turmoil, with a little war ongoing between the "Municipals" (the police appointed by the city) and the "Metropolitans" (those controlled by the state government) as recently as 1857. The populace was the victim of rioting, in which many of the police participated, and the NYPD was wracked with corruption as Tammany Hall sought to control it.

† Kate Watson, *Women Writing Crime Fiction, 1860–1880: Fourteen American, British and Australian Authors* (Jefferson, NC: McFarland, 2012), 130.

criminals, and detectives told by men, it was not until Earl Derr Biggers, Ellery Queen, S. S. Van Dine, and Dashiell Hammett began writing in the 1920s that American male crime writers were producing work as notable as *The Dead Letter*.

—Leslie S. Klinger

PART I.

THE DEAD LETTER.

CHAPTER I.

THE LETTER.

I paused suddenly in my work. Over a year's experience in the Dead Letter office[*] had given a mechanical rapidity to my movements in opening, noting and classifying the contents of the bundles before me; and, so far from there being any thing exciting to the curiosity, or interesting to the mind, in the employment, it was of the most monotonous character.

Young ladies whose love letters have gone astray, evil men whose plans have been confided in writing to their confederates, may feel but little apprehension of the prying eyes of the

---

[*] Although the US postal system traces its roots to 1737, when Benjamin Franklin was the postmaster of Philadelphia in the colony of Pennsylvania, an official "dead letter office" was not opened until 1825, though postal records going back to 1777 detail "dead letters." James H. Bruns, writing for the Smithsonian National Postal Museum, explained that clerks handled three types of "mystery mail": "Misdirected letters, which were those which had all of the right information necessary to get them delivered, but for some reason were sidetracked, largely either because they weren't handled correctly by postal employees or had been abandoned at the designated post office; 'Blind Readings,' so called because to the average postal worker the address would appear as though it was read blindfolded; and prank mail." "Remembering the Dead," *EnRoute* (Newsletter of the National Postal Museum), 1, no. 3 (July–September 1992). The eponymous "Dead Letter" here, we will learn much later, is in the first category.

Department;* nothing attracts it but objects of material value—sentiment is below par; it drives attention only to such tangible interests as are represented by bank-bills, gold-pieces, checks, jewelry, miniatures, et cetera. Occasionally a grave clerk smiles sardonically at the ridiculous character of some of the articles which come to light; sometimes, perhaps, looks thoughtfully at a withered rosebud, or bunch of pressed violets, a homely little pin-cushion, or a book-mark, wishing it had reached its proper destination. I can not answer for other employees, who may not have even this amount of heart and imagination to invest in the dull business of a Government office; but when I was in the Department I was guilty, at intervals, of such folly—yet I passed for the coldest, most cynical man of them all.

The letter which I held in my paralyzed fingers when they so abruptly ceased their dexterous movements, was contained in a closely-sealed envelope, yellowed by time, and directed in a peculiar hand to "John Owen, Peekskill, New York," and the date on the stamp was "October 18th, 1857"—making the letter two years old. I know not what magnetism passed from it, putting me, as the spiritualists say, *en rapport* with it;† I had not yet cut the lappet;‡ and the only thing I could fix upon as the cause of my attraction was, that at the date indicated on the envelope, I had been resident of Blankville, twenty miles from Peekskill—and something about that date!

Yet this was no excuse for my agitation; I was not of an

---

* The Post Office Department, that is, the head of which became a cabinet position in 1872. It wasn't until 1970 that the US Postal Service was established as an independent agency.

---

† A sharing of feelings or thoughts. Spiritualism, the pseudoscientific "religion" that maintained that the spirits of the dead remained in contact with the living and had spiritual "lives" after death, relied on the medium or liaison between the living and the dead to be *en rapport* with the spirits, often through tangible objects belonging to the dead.

---

‡ The flap of an envelope.

inquisitive disposition; nor did "John Owen" belong to the circle of my acquaintance. I sat there with such a strange expression upon my face, that one of my fellows, remarking my mood, exclaimed jestingly:

"What is it, Redfield? A check for a hundred thousand?"

"I am sure I don't know; I haven't opened it," I answered, at random; and with this I cut the wrapper, impelled by some strongly-defined, irresistible influence to read the time-stained sheet inclosed. It ran in this wise:

"DEAR SIR—It's too bad to disappoint you. Could not execute your order, as everybody concerned will discover. What a charming day!—good for taking a picture. That old friend I introduced you to won't tell tales, and you had not better bother yourself to visit him. The next time you find yourself in his arms, don't feel in his left-hand pocket for the broken toothpick which I lent him. He is welcome to it. If you're at the place of payment, I shan't be there, not having fulfilled the order, and having given up my emigration project, much against my will; so, govern yourself accordingly. Sorry your prospects are so poor, and believe me, with the greatest possible esteem,

"Your disappointed NEGOTIATOR."

To explain why this brief epistle, neither lucid nor interesting in itself, should affect me as it did, I must go back to the time at which it was written.

CHAPTER II.

EVENTS OF A NIGHT.

It was late in the afternoon of a cloudy, windy autumn day, that I left the office of John Argyll, Esq., in his company, to take tea and spend the evening in his family. I was a law-student in the office, and was favored with more than ordinary kindness by him, on account of a friendship that had existed between him and my deceased father. When young men, they had started out in life together, in equal circumstances; one had died early, just as fortune began to smile; the other lived to continue in well-earned prosperity. Mr. Argyll had never ceased to take an interest in the orphan son of his friend. He had aided my mother in giving me a collegiate education, and had taken me into his office to complete my law studies. Although I did not board at his house, I was almost like a member of the family. There was always a place for me at his table, with liberty to come and go when I pleased. This being Saturday, I was expected to go home with him, and stay over Sunday if I liked.

We quickened our steps as a few large drops were sprinkled over us out of the darkening clouds.

"It will be a rainy night," said Mr. Argyll.

"It may clear away yet," I said, looking toward a rift in the west, through which the declining sun was pouring a silver stream. He shook his head doubtfully, and we hurried up the steps into the house, to escape the threatened drenching.

Entering the parlors, we found no one but James, a nephew of Mr. Argyll, a young man of about my own age, lounging upon a sofa.

"Where are the girls?"

"They haven't descended from the heavenly regions yet, uncle."

"Dressing themselves to death, I expect—it's Saturday evening, I remember," smiled the indulgent father, passing on into the library.

I sat down by the west window, and looked out at the coming storm. I did not like James Argyll much, nor he me; so that, as much as we were thrown together, our intercourse continued constrained. On this occasion, however, he seemed in excellent spirits, persisting in talking on all kinds of indifferent subjects despite of my brief replies. I was wondering when Eleanor would make her appearance.

At last she came. I heard her silk dress rustle down the stairs, and my eyes were upon her when she entered the room. She was dressed with unusual care, and her face wore a brilliant, expectant smile. The smile was for neither of us. Perhaps James thought of it; I am sure I did, with secret suffering—with a sharp pang which I was ashamed of, and fought inwardly to conquer.

She spoke pleasantly to both of us, but with a preoccupied air not flattering to our vanity. Too restless to sit, she paced up and down the length of the parlors, seeming to radiate light as she walked, like some superb jewel—so lustrous was her countenance and so fine her costume. Little smiles would sparkle about her lips, little trills of song break forth, as if she were unconscious of observers. She had a right to be glad; she appeared to exult in her own beauty and happiness.

Presently she came to the window, and as she stood by my side, a burst of glory streamed through the fast-closing clouds, enveloping her in a golden atmosphere, tinting her black hair with purple, flushing her clear cheeks and the pearls about her throat. The fragrance of the rose she wore on her breast mingled with the light; for a moment I was thrilled and overpowered; but the dark-blue eyes were not looking on me—they were regarding the weather.

"How provoking that it should rain to-night," she said, and as the slight cloud of vexation swept over her face, the blackness of night closed over the gleam of sunset, so suddenly that we could hardly discern each other.

"The rain will not keep Moreland away," I answered.

"Of course not—but I don't want him to get wet walking up from the depot; and Billy has put up the carriage in view of the storm."

At that moment a wild gust of wind smote the house so that it shook, and the rain came down with a roar that was deafening. Eleanor rung for lights.

"Tell cook to be sure and have chocolate for supper—and cream for the peaches," she said to the servant who came in to light the gas.

The girl smiled; she knew, in common with her mistress, who it was preferred chocolate and liked cream with peaches; the love of a woman, however sublime in some of its qualities, never fails in the tender domestic instincts which delight in promoting the comfort and personal tastes of its object.

"We need not have troubled ourselves to wear our new dresses," pouted Mary, the younger sister, who had followed Eleanor down-stairs; "there will be nobody here to-night."

Both James and myself objected to being dubbed nobody. The willful young beauty said all the gay things she pleased, telling us she certainly should not have worn her blue silks, nor puffed her hair for us—

"—Nor for Henry Moreland either—he never looks at me after the first minute. Engaged people are so stupid! I wish he and Eleanor would make an end of it. If I'm ever going to be bridemaid, I want to be—"

"And a clear field afterward, Miss Molly," jested her cousin. "Come! play that new polka for me."

"You couldn't hear it if I did. The rain is playing a polka this evening, and the wind is dancing to it."

He laughed loudly—more loudly than the idle fancy warranted. "Let us see if we can not make more noise than the storm," he said, going to the piano and thumping out the most thunderous piece that he could recall. I was not a musician, but it seemed to me there were more discords than the law of harmony allowed; and Mary put her hands over her ears, and ran away to the end of the room.

For the next half-hour the rain came down in wide sheets, flapping against the windows, as the wind blew it hither and thither. James continued at the piano, and Eleanor moved restlessly about, stealing glances, now and then, at her tiny watch.

All at once there occurred one of those pauses which precede the fresh outbreaking of a storm; as if startled by the sudden lull, James Argyll paused in his playing; just then the shrill whistle of the locomotive pierced the silence with more than usual power, as the evening train swept around the curve of the hill not a quarter of a mile away, and rushed on into the depot in the lower part of the village.

There is something unearthly in the scream of the "steam-eagle," especially when heard at night. He seems like a sentient thing, with a will of his own, unbending and irresistible; and his cry is threatening and defiant. This night it rose upon the storm prolonged and doleful.

I know not how it sounded to the others, but to me, whose imagination was already wrought upon by the tempest and by the presence of the woman I hopelessly loved, it came with an effect perfectly overwhelming; it filled the air, even the perfumed, lighted air of the parlor, full of a dismal wail. It threatened—I know not what. It warned against some strange, unseen disaster. Then it sunk into a hopeless cry, so full of mortal anguish, that I involuntarily put my fingers to my ears. Perhaps James felt something of the same thing, for he started from the piano-stool, walked twice or thrice across the floor, then flung himself again upon the sofa, and for a long time sat with his eyes shaded, neither speaking nor stirring.

Eleanor, with maiden artifice, took up a book, and composed herself to pretend to read; she would not have her lover to know that she had been so restless while awaiting his coming. Only Mary fluttered about like a humming-bird, diving into the sweets of things, the music, the flowers, whatever had honey in it; and teasing me in the intervals.

I have said that I loved Eleanor. I did, secretly, in silence and regret, against my judgment and will, and because I could not help it. I was quite certain that James loved her also, and I felt sorry for him; sympathy was taught me by my own sufferings, though I had never felt attracted toward his character. He seemed to me to be rather sullen in temper, as well as selfish; and then again I reproached myself for uncharitableness; it might have been his circumstances which rendered him morose—he was dependent upon his uncle—and his unhappiness which made him appear unamiable.

I loved, without a particle of hope. Eleanor was engaged to a young gentleman in every way worthy of her: of fine demeanor, high social position, and unblemished moral character. As much as her many admirers may have envied Henry Moreland, they could not dislike him. To see the young couple together was to feel that theirs would be one of those "matches made in heaven"—in age, character, worldly circumstances, beauty and cultivation, there was a rare correspondence.

Mr. Moreland was engaged with his father in a banking business in the city of New York. They owned a summer villa in Blankville, and it had been during his week of summer idleness here that he had made the acquaintance of Eleanor Argyll.

At this season of the year his business kept him in the city; but he was in the habit of coming out every Saturday afternoon and spending Sabbath at the house of Mr. Argyll, the marriage which was to terminate a betrothal of nearly two years being now not very far away. On her nineteenth birthday, which came in December, Eleanor was to be married.

Another half-hour passed away and the expected guest did not arrive. He usually reached the house in fifteen minutes after the arrival of the train; I could see that his betrothed was playing nervously with her watch-chain, though she kept her eyes fixed upon her book.

"Come, let us have tea; I am hungry," said Mr. Argyll, coming out of the library. "I had a long ride after dinner. No use waiting, Eleanor—he won't be here to-night"—he pinched her cheek to express his sympathy for her disappointment—"a little shower didn't use to keep beaux away when I was a boy."

"A *little* rain, papa! I never heard such a torrent before; besides, it was not the storm, of course, for he would have already taken the cars* before it commenced."

---

* Railroad cars or streetcars, that is; we will see later that Moreland used the rail. Streetcars were typically horse drawn in the city, but the suburbs were early adopters of electric cars. The railroads were of course steam driven.

"To be sure! to be sure! defend your sweetheart, Ella—that's right! But it may have been raining down there half the day— the storm comes from that direction. James, are you asleep?"

"I'll soon see," cried Mary, pulling away the hand from her cousin's face—"why, James, what is the matter?"

Her question caused us all to look at him; his face was of an ashy paleness; his eyes burning like coals of fire.

"Nothing is the matter! I've been half asleep," he answered, laughing, and springing to his feet. "Molly, shall I have the honor?"—she took his offered arm, and we went in to tea.

The sight of the well-ordered table, at the head of which Eleanor presided, the silver, the lights, the odor of the chocolate overpowering the fainter fragrance of the tea, was enough to banish thoughts of the tempest raging without, saving just enough consciousness of it to enhance the enjoyment of the luxury within.

Even Eleanor could not be cold to the warmth and comfort of the hour; the tears, which at first she could hardly keep out of her proud blue eyes, went back to their sources; she made an effort to be gay, and succeeded in being very charming. I think she still hoped he had been delayed at the village; and that there would be a note for her at the post-office, explaining his absence.

For once, the usually kind, considerate girl was selfish. Severe as was the storm, she insisted upon sending a servant to the office; she could not be kept in suspense until Monday.

She would hardly believe his statement, upon his return, that the mail had been changed, and there was really no message whatever.

We went back to the parlor and passed a merry evening.

A touch of chagrin, a fear that we should suspect how deeply she was disappointed, caused Eleanor to appear in unusually high spirits. She sung whatever I asked of her; she played some delicious music; she parried the wit of others with keener and brighter repartee; the roses bloomed on her cheeks, the stars rose in her eyes. It was not an altogether happy excitement; I knew that pride and loneliness were at the bottom of it; but it made her brilliantly beautiful. I wondered what Moreland would feel to see her so lovely—I almost regretted that he was not there.

James, too, was in an exultant mood.

It was late when we retired. I was in a state of mental activity which kept me awake for hours after. I never heard it rain as it did that night—the water seemed to come down in solid masses—and, occasionally, the wind shook the strong mansion as if it were a child. I could not sleep. There was something awful in the storm. If I had had a touch of superstition about me, I should have said that spirits were abroad.

A healthy man, of a somewhat vivid imagination, but without nervousness, unknowing bodily fear, I was still affected strangely. I shuddered in my soft bed; the wild shriek of the locomotive lingered in my ears; *something besides rain seemed beating at the windows.* Ah, my God! I knew afterward what it was. It was a human soul, disembodied, lingering about the place on earth most dear to it. The rest of the household slept well, so far as I could judge, by its silence and deep repose.

Toward morning I fell asleep; when I awoke the rain was over; the sun shone brightly; the ground was covered with gay autumn leaves shaken down by the wind and rain; the day promised well. I shook off the impressions of the darkness, dressed myself quickly, for the breakfast-bell rung, and descending, joined the family of my host at the table. In the midst of our cheerful repast, the door-bell rung. Eleanor started; the thought that her lover might have stayed at the hotel adjoining the depot on account of the rain, must have crossed her mind, for a rapid blush rose to her cheeks, and she involuntarily put up a hand to the dark braids of her hair as if to give them a more graceful touch. The servant came in, saying that a man at the door wished to speak with Mr. Argyll and Mr. Redfield.

"He says it's important, and can't wait, sir."

We arose and went out into the hall, closing the door of the breakfast-room behind us.

"I'm very sorry—I've got bad news—I hope you won't"—stammered the messenger, a servant from the hotel.

"What is it?" demanded Mr. Argyll.

"The young gentleman that comes here—Moreland's his name, I believe—was found dead on the road this morning."

"Dead!"

"They want you to come down to the inquest. They've got him in a room of our house. They think it's a fit—there's no marks of any thing."

The father and I looked at each other; the lips of both were quivering; we both thought of Eleanor.

"What shall I do?"

"I don't know, Mr. Argyll. I haven't had time to think."

"I can not—I can not—"

"Nor I—not just yet. Sarah, tell the young ladies we have come out a short time on business—and don't you breathe what you have heard. Don't let any one in until we return—don't allow any one to see Miss Eleanor. Be prudent."

Her frightened face did not promise much for her discretion.

Hastening to the hotel, already surrounded by many people, we found the distressing message too true. Upon a lounge, in a private sitting-room, lay the body of Henry Moreland! The coroner and a couple of physicians had already arrived. It was their opinion that he had died from natural causes, as there was not the least evidence of violence to be seen. The face was as pleasant as in slumber; we could hardly believe him dead until we touched the icy forehead, about which the thick ringlets of brown hair clung, saturated with rain.

"What's this?" exclaimed one, as we began to relieve the corpse of its wet garments, for the purpose of a further examination. It was a stab in the back. Not a drop of blood—only a small triangular hole in the cloak, through the other clothing, into the body. The investigation soon revealed the nature of the death-wound; it had been given by a fine, sharp dirk or stiletto. So firm and forcible had been the blow that it had pierced the lung and struck the rib with sufficient force to break the blade of the weapon, about three-quarters of an inch of the point of which was found in the wound. Death must have been instantaneous. The victim had fallen forward upon his face, bleeding inwardly, which accounted for no blood having been at first perceived; and as he had fallen, so he had lain through all the drenching storm of that miserable night. When discovered by the first passer-by, after daylight, he was lying on the path, by the side of the street, which led up in the direction of Mr. Argyll's, his traveling-bag by his side, his face to the ground. The bag was not touched, neither the watch and money on his person, making it evident that robbery was not the object of the murderer.

A stab in the back, in the double darkness of night and storm! What enemy had Henry Moreland, to do this deed upon him?

It is useless now to repeat all the varying conjectures rising in our minds, or which continued to engross the entire community for weeks thereafter. It became at once the favorite theory of many that young Moreland had perished by a stroke intended for some other person. In the mean time, the news swept through the village like a whirlwind, destroying the calmness of that Sabbath morning, tossing the minds of people more fearfully than the material tempest had tossed the frail leaves. Murder! and such a murder in such a place!— not twenty rods from the busiest haunts of men, on a peaceful street—sudden, sure, unprovoked! People looked behind them as they walked, hearing the assassin's step in every rustle of the breeze. Murder!—the far-away, frightful idea had suddenly assumed a real shape—it seemed to have stalked through the town, entering each dwelling, standing by every hearthstone.

While the inquest was proceeding, Mr. Argyll and myself were thinking more of Eleanor than of her murdered lover.

"This is wretched business, Richard," said the father. "I am so unnerved I can do nothing. Will you telegraph to his parents for me?"

His parents—here was more misery. I had not thought of them. I wrote out the dreadful message which it ought to have melted the wires with pity to carry.

"And now you must go to Eleanor. She must not hear it from strangers; and I can not—Richard!—you will tell her, will you not? I will follow you home immediately; as soon as I have made arrangements to have poor Henry brought to our house when the inquest is over."

He wrung my hand, looking at me so beseechingly, that, loth as I was, I had no thought of refusing. I felt like one walking with frozen feet as I passed out of the chamber of horror into the peaceful sunlight, along the very path *he* had last trodden, and over the spot where he had fallen and had lain so many hours undiscovered, around which a crowd was pressing, disturbed, excited, but not noisy. The sandy soil had already filtered the rain, so as to be nearly dry; there was nothing to give a clue to the murderer's footsteps, whither he went or whence he came— what impress they might have made in the hard, gravelly walk had been washed out by the storm. A few persons were searching carefully for the weapon which had been the instrument of death, and which had been broken in the wound, thinking it might have been cast away in the vicinity.

CHAPTER III.

THE FIGURE BENEATH THE TREES.

As I came near the old Argyll mansion, it seemed to me never to have looked so fair before. The place was the embodiment of calm prosperity. Stately and spacious it rose from the lawn in the midst of great old oaks whose trunks must have hardened through a century of growth, and whose red leaves, slowly dropping, now flamed in the sunshine. Although the growing village had stretched up to and encircled the grounds, it had still the air of a country place, for the lawn was roomy and the gardens were extensive. The house was built of stone, in a massive yet graceful style; with such sunshiny windows and pleasant porticoes that it had nothing of a somber look.

It is strange what opposite emotions will group themselves in the soul at the same moment. The sight of those lordly trees called up the exquisite picture of Tennyson's "Talking Oak":

> *"Oh, muffle round thy knees with fern,*
> *And shadow Sumner-chace!*

> *Long may thy topmost branch discern*
> *The roofs of Sumner-place!"**

I wondered if Henry had not repeated them, as he walked with Eleanor amid the golden light and flickering shadows beneath the branches of these trees. I recalled how I once, in my madness, before I knew that she was betrothed to another, had apostrophized the monarch of them all, in the passionate words of Walter.† Now, looking at this ancient tree, I perceived with my eyes, though hardly with my mind, that it had some fresh excoriations upon the bark. If I thought any thing at all about it, I thought it the work of the storm, for numerous branches had been torn from the trees throughout the grove, and the ground was carpeted with fresh-fallen leaves.

Passing up the walk, I caught a glimpse of Eleanor at an upper window, and heard her singing a hymn, softly to herself, as she moved about her chamber. I stopped as if struck a blow. How could I force myself to drop the pall over this glorious morning? Alas! of all the homes in that village, perhaps this was the only one on which the shadow had not yet fallen—this, over which it was to settle, to be lifted never more.

Of all the hearts as yet unstartled by the tragic event was that most certain to be withered—that young heart, this moment so full of love and bliss, caroling hymns out of the fullness of its gratitude to God for its own delicious happiness.

Oh, I must—I must! I went in at an open window, from a portico into the library. James was there, dressed for church, his prayer-book and handkerchief on the table, and he looking over

---

* "The Talking Oak" is an 1842 poem by Alfred, Lord Tennyson, in which the lover confides his feelings to an oak in the woods, which repeats the confession. A "chace" is a green lane leading up to a farm or house.

---

† "Walter" is the narrator of Tennyson's poem.

the last evening's paper. The sight of him gave me a slight relief; his uncle and myself had forgotten him in the midst of our distress. It was bad enough to have to tell any one such news, but any delay in meeting Eleanor was eagerly welcomed. He looked at me inquiringly—my manner was enough to denote that something had gone wrong.

"What is it, Richard?"

"Horrible—most horrible!"

"For heaven's sake, *what* is the matter?"

"Moreland has been murdered."

"Moreland! What? Where? Whom do they suspect?"

"And her father wishes me to tell Eleanor. You are her cousin, James; will you not be the fittest person?" the hope crossing me that he would undertake the delivery of the message.

"*I!*" he exclaimed, leaning against the case of books beside him. "I! oh, no, not I. I'd be the last person! I'd look well telling her about it, wouldn't I?" and he half laughed, though trembling from head to foot.

If I thought his manner strange, I did not wonder at it—the dreadful nature of the shock had unnerved all of us.

"Where is Mary?" I asked; "we had better tell her first, and have her present. Indeed, I wish—"

I had turned toward the door, which opened into the hall, to search for the younger sister, as I spoke; the words died on my lips. Eleanor was standing there. She had been coming in to get a book, and had evidently heard what had passed. She was as white as the morning dress she wore.

"Where is he?" Her voice sounded almost natural.

"At the Eagle Hotel," I answered, without reflection, glad that she showed such self-command, and, since she did, glad also that the terrible communication was over.

She turned and ran through the hall, down the avenue toward

the gate. In her thin slippers, her hair uncovered, fleet as a vision of the wind, she fled. I sprung after her. It would not do to allow her to shock herself with that sudden, awful sight. As she rushed out upon the street I caught her by the arm.

"Let me go! I must go to him! Don't you see, he will need me?"

She made an effort to break away, looking down the street with strained eyes. Poor child! as if, he being dead, she could do him any good! Her stunned heart had as yet gone no further than that if Henry was hurt, was murdered, he would need her by his side. She must go to him and comfort him in his calamity. It was yet to teach her that this world and the things of this world—even she, herself, were no more to him.

"Come back, Eleanor; they will bring him to you before long."

I had to lift her in my arms and carry her back to the house.

In the hall we met Mary, who had heard the story from James, and who burst into tears and sobs as she saw her sister.

"They are keeping me away from him," said Eleanor, pitifully, looking at her. I felt her form relax in my arms, saw that she had fainted; James and I carried her to a sofa, while Mary ran distractedly for the housekeeper.

There was noisy wailing now in the mansion; the servants all admired and liked the young gentleman to whom their mistress was to be married; and, as usual, they gave full scope to their powers of expressing terror and sympathy. In the midst of cries and tears, the insensible girl was conveyed to her chamber.

James and myself paced the long halls and porticoes, waiting to hear tidings of her recovery. After a time the housekeeper came down, informing us that Miss Argyll had come to her senses; leastwise, enough to open her eyes and look about; but she wouldn't speak, and she looked dreadful.

Just then Mr. Argyll came in. After being informed of what had occurred, he went up to his daughter's room. With uttermost tenderness he gave her the details of the murder, as they were known; his eyes overrunning with tears to see that not a drop of moisture softened her fixed, unnatural look.

Friends came in and went out with no notice from her.

"I wish they would all leave me but you, Mary," she said, after a time. "Father, you will let me know when—"

"Yes—yes." He kissed her, and she was left with her sister for a watcher.

Hours passed. Some of us went into the dining-room and drank of the strong tea which the housekeeper had prepared, for we felt weak and unnerved. The parents were expected in the evening train, there being but one train running on Sunday. The shadow deepened over the house from hour to hour.

It was late in the afternoon before the body could be removed from the hotel where the coroner's inquest was held. I asked James to go with me and attend upon its conveyance to Mr. Argyll's. He declined, upon the plea of being too much unstrung to go out.

As the sad procession reached the garden in front of the mansion with its burden, I observed, in the midst of several who had gathered about, a woman, whose face, even in that time of preoccupation, arrested my attention. It was that of a girl, young and handsome, though now thin and deadly pale, with a wild look in her black eyes, which were fixed upon the shrouded burden with more than awe and curiosity.

I know not yet why I remarked her so particularly; why her strange face made such an impression on me. Once she started toward us, and then shrunk back again. By her dress and general appearance she might have been a shop-girl. I had never seen her before.

"That girl," said a gentleman by my side, "acts queerly. And, come to think, she was on the train from New York yesterday afternoon. Not the one poor Moreland came in; the one before. I was on board myself, and noticed her particularly, as she sat facing me. She seemed to have some trouble on her mind."

I seldom forget faces; and I never forgot hers.

"I will trace her out," was my mental resolve.

We passed on into the house, and deposited our charge in the back parlor. I thought of Eleanor, as she had walked this room just twenty-four hours ago, a brilliant vision of love and trium-phant beauty. Ay! twenty-four hours ago this clay before me was as resplendent with life, as eager, as glowing with the hope of the soul within it! Now, all the hours of time would never restore the tenant to his tenement. Who had dared to take upon himself the responsibility of unlawfully and with violence, ejecting this human soul from its house?

I shuddered as I asked myself the question. Somewhere must be lurking a guilty creature, with a heart on fire from the flames of hell, with which it had put itself in contact.

Then my heart stood still within me—all but the family had been banished from the apartment—her father was leading in Eleanor. With a slow step, clinging to his arm, she entered; but as her eyes fixed themselves upon the rigid outlines lying there beneath the funeral pall, she sprung forward, casting herself upon her lover's corpse. Before, she had been silent; now began a murmur of woe so heart-rending that we who listened wished ourselves deaf before our ears had heard tones and sentences which could never be forgotten. It would be useless for me, a man, with a man's language and thoughts, to attempt to repeat what this broken-hearted woman said to her dead lover.

It was not her words so much as it was her pathetic tones.

She talked to him as if he were alive and could hear her. She was resolved to make him hear and feel her love through the dark death which was between them.

"Ah, Henry," she said, in a low, caressing tone, pressing back the curls from his forehead with her hand, "your hair is wet still. To think that you should lie out there all night—all night—on the ground, in the rain, and I not know of it! I, to be sleeping in my warm bed—actually sleeping, and you lying out in the storm, dead. That is the strangest thing! that makes me wonder—to think I *could!* Tell me that you forgive me for that, darling—for sleeping, you know, when you were out there. I was thinking of you when I took the rose out of my dress at night. I dreamed of you all night, but if I had known where you were, I would have gone out barefooted, I would have stayed by you and kept the rain from your face, from your dear, dear hair that I like so much and hardly ever dare to touch. It was cruel of me to sleep so. Would you guess, I was vexed at you last evening because you didn't come? It was that made me so gay—not because I was happy. Vexed at you for not coming, when you could not come because you were dead!" and she laughed.

As that soft, dreadful laughter thrilled through the room, with a groan Mr. Argyll arose and went out; he could bear no more. Disturbed with a fear that her reason was shaken, I spoke with Mary, and we two tried to lift her up, and persuade her out of the room.

"Oh, don't try to get me away from him again," she pleaded, with a quivering smile, which made us sick. "Don't be troubled, Henry. I'm *not* going—I'm *not!* They are going to put my hand in yours and bury me with you. It's so curious I should have been playing the piano and wearing my new dress, and never guessing it! that you were so near me—dead—murdered!"

The kisses; the light, gentle touches of his hands and forehead, as if she might hurt him with the caresses which she could not withhold; the intent look which continually watched him as if expecting an answer; the miserable smile upon her white face—these were things which haunted those who saw them through many a future slumber.

"You will not say you forgive me for singing last night. You don't say a word to me—because you are dead—that's it—because you are dead—murdered!"

The echo of her own last word recalled her wandering reason.

"My God! murdered!" she exclaimed, suddenly rising to her full hight,* with an awful air; "who do you suppose did it?"

Her cousin was standing near; her eyes fell upon him as she asked the question. The look, the manner, were too much for his already overwrought sensibility; he shrunk away, caught my arm, and sunk down, insensible. I did not wonder: We all of us felt as if we could endure no more.

Going to the family physician, who waited in another apartment, I begged of him to use some influence to withdraw Miss Argyll from the room, and quiet her feelings and memory, before her brain yielded to the strain upon it. After giving us some directions what to do with James, he went and talked with her, with so much wisdom and tact, that the danger to her reason seemed passing; persuading her also into taking the powder which he himself administered; but no argument could induce her to leave the mute, unanswering clay.

The arrival of the relatives was the last scene in the tragedy of that day. Unable to bear more of it, I went out in the darkness and walked upon the lawn. My head was hot; the cool air felt grateful to me; I leaned long upon the trunk of an oak, whose dark shadow shut out the starlight from about me; thought was busy with recent events. Who was the murderer? The question

---

* An alternate, now obsolete, spelling of *height*.

revolved in my brain, coming uppermost every other moment, as certainly as the turning of a wheel brings a certain point again and again to the top. My training, as a student of the law, helped my mind to fix upon every slightest circumstance which might hold a suspicion.

"Could that woman?"—but no, the hand of a woman could scarcely have given that sure and powerful blow. It looked like the work of a *practiced* hand—or, if not, at least it had been deliberately given, with malice aforethought. The assassin had premeditated the deed; had watched his victim and awaited the hour. Thus far, there was absolutely no clue whatever to the guilty party; bold as was the act, committed in the early evening, in the haunts of a busy community, it had been most fatally successful; and the doer had vanished as completely as if the earth had opened and swallowed him up. No one, as yet, could form any plausible conjecture, even as to the *motive*.

In the name of Eleanor Argyll—in the name of her whom I loved, whose happiness I had that day seen in ruins, I vowed to use every endeavor to discover and bring to punishment the murderer. I know not why this purpose took such firm hold of me. The conviction of the guilty would not restore the life which had been taken; the bloom to a heart prematurely withered; it would afford no consolation to the bereaved. Yet, if to discover, had been to call back Henry Moreland to the world from which he had been so ruthlessly dismissed, I could hardly have been more determined in the pursuit. In action only could I feel relief from the oppression which weighed upon me. It could not give life to the dead—but the voice of Justice called aloud, never to permit this deed to sink into oblivion, until she had executed the divine vengeance of the law upon the doer.

As I stood there in silence and darkness, pondering the matter, I heard a light rustle of the dry leaves upon the ground, and felt, rather than saw, a figure pass me. I might have thought it one of the servants were it not for the evident caution of its movements. Presently, where the shadows of the trees were less thick, I detected a person stealing toward the house. As she crossed an open space, the starlight revealed the form and garments of a female; the next moment she passed into the obscurity of shadows again, where she remained some time, unsuspicious of my proximity, like myself leaning against a tree, and watching the mansion. Apparently satisfied that no one was about—the hour now verging toward midnight—she approached with hovering steps, now pausing, now drawing back, the west side of the mansion, from one of the windows of which the solemn light of the death-candles shone. Under this window she crouched down. I could not tell if her attitude were a kneeling one. It must have been more than an hour that she remained motionless in this place; I, equally quiet, watching the dark spot where she was. For the instant that she had stood between me and the window, her form was outlined against the light, when I saw that this must be the young woman whose strange conduct at the gate had attracted my attention. Of course I did not see her face; but the tall, slender figure, the dark bonnet, and nervous movement, were the same. I perplexed myself with vain conjectures.

I could not help connecting her with the murder, or with the victim, in some manner, however vague.

At last she arose, lingered, went away, passing near me with that soft, rustling step again. I was impelled to stretch out my hand and seize her; her conduct was suspicious; she ought to be arrested and examined, if only to clear herself of these circumstances. The idea that, by following her, I might trace her to some haunt, where proofs were secreted, or accomplices hidden, withheld my grasp.

Cautiously timing my step with hers, that the murmur of the

leaves might not betray me, I followed. As she passed out the gate, I stood behind a tree, lest she should look back and discern me; then I passed through, following along in the shadow of the fence.

She hurried on in the direction of the spot at which the murder had been committed; but when nearly there, perceiving that some persons, though long past midnight, still hovered about the fatal place, she turned, and passed me. As soon as I dared, without alarming her, I also turned, pursuing her through the long, quiet street, until it brought her to a more crowded and poorer part of the village, where she went down a side street, and disappeared in a tenement-house, the entrance-hall to which was open. I ought to have gone at once for officers, and searched the place; but I unwisely concluded to wait for daylight.

As I came up the walk on my return, I met James Argyll in the avenue, near the front portico.

"Oh, is it you?" he exclaimed, after I had spoken to him. "I thought it was—was—"

"You are not superstitious, James?" for his hollow voice betrayed that he was frightened.

"You did give me a confounded uneasy sensation as you came up," he answered with a laugh.—How can people laugh under such circumstances?—"Where have you been at this hour, Richard?"

"Walking in the cool air. The house smothered me."

"So it did me. I could not rest. I have just come out to get a breath of air."

"It is almost morning," I said, and passed on into my chamber.

I knew who watched, without food, without rest, in the chamber of death, by whose door my footsteps led; but ache as my heart might, I had no words of comfort for sorrow like hers—so I passed on.

CHAPTER IV.
MORELAND VILLA.

Several minor circumstances prevented my going in search of the woman who had excited my suspicions on the previous day, until about nine o'clock of the morning, when I engaged an officer, and we two went quietly, without communicating our plans to any one else, to the tenement-house before spoken of.

Although Blankville was not a large village, there was in it, as in nearly every town blessed with a railroad depot, a shabby quarter where the rougher portion of its working people lived. The house stood in this quarter—it was a three-story frame building, occupied by half a dozen families, mostly those of Irish laborers, who found work in the vicinity of the depot. I had seen the strange girl ascend to the second floor, in the dim light of the previous night, so we went up and knocked at the first door we came upon. It was opened by a decent-appearing middle-aged woman, who held the knob in her hand while she waited for us to make known our errand; we both stepped into her apartment, before we spoke. A rapid glance revealed an innocent-looking room with the ordinary furniture of such a place—a cooking-stove, bed, table, etc.; but no other inmate. There was a cupboard, the door of which stood open, showing its humble array of dishes and eatables—there were no pantries, nor other places of concealment. I was certain that I had seen the girl enter this room at the head of the stairs, so I ventured:

"Is your daughter at home, ma'am?"

"Is it my niece you mean?"

I detected an Irish accent, though the woman spoke with but little "brogue," and was evidently an old resident of our country—in a manner *Americanized.*

"Oh, she is your niece? I suppose so—a tall girl with dark eyes and hair."

"That's Leesy, herself. Was you wanting any work done?"

"Yes," answered the officer, quickly, taking the matter out of my hands. "I wanted to get a set of shirts made up—six, with fine, stitched bosoms." He had noticed a cheap sewing-machine standing near the window, and a bundle of coarse muslin in a basket near by.

"It's sorry I am to disappoint you; but Leesy's not with me now, and I hardly venture on the fine work. I make the shirts for the hands about the railroad that hasn't wives of their own to do it—but for the fine bussums"—doubtfully—"though, to be sure, the machine does the stitches up beautiful—if it wasn't for the button-holes!"

"Where is Leesy? Doesn't she stop with you?"

"It's her I have here always when she's out of a place. She's an orphan, poor girl, and it's not in the blood of a Sullivan to turn off their own. I've brought her up from a little thing of five years old—given her the education, too. She can read and write like the ladies of the land."

"You didn't say where she was, Mrs. Sullivan."

"She's making the fine things in a fancy-store in New York—caps and collars and sleeves and the beautiful tucked waists—she's *such* taste, and the work is not so hard as plain-sewing—four dollars a week she gets, and boarded for two and a half, in a nice, genteel place. She expects to be illivated to the forewoman's place, at seven dollars the week, before many months. She was here to stay over the Sunday with me—she often does that; and she's gone back by the six o'clock train this mornin'—and she'll be surely late at that by an hour. I tried to coax her to stay the day, she seemed so poorly. She's not been herself this long time—she seems goin' in a decline like—it's the stooping over the needle, I think. She's so nervous-like, the news of the murder yesterday almost killed her. 'Twas an awful deed that, wasn't it, gintlemen? I couldn't sleep a wink last night for thinkin' of that poor young man and the sweet lady he was to have married. Such a fine, generous, polite young gintleman!"

"Did you know him?"

"Know him! as well as my own son if I had one!—not that ever I spoke to him, but he's passed here often on his way to his father's house, and to Mr. Argyll's; and Leesy sewed in their family these two summers when they've been here, and was always twice paid. When she'd go away he'd say, laughing in his beautiful way, 'And how much have you earned a day, Miss Sullivan, sitting there all these long, hot hours?' and she'd answer, 'Fifty cents a day, and thanks to your mother for the good pay;' and he'd put his hand in his pocket and pull out a ten-dollar gold-piece and say, 'Women aren't half paid for their work! it's a shame! if you hain't earned a dollar a day, Miss Sullivan, you hain't earned a cent. So don't be afraid to take it—it's your due.' And that's what made Leesy think so much of him—he was so thoughtful of the poor—God bless him! How could anybody have the heart to do it!"

I looked at the officer and found his eyes reading my face. One thought had evidently flashed over both of us; but it was a suspicion which wronged the immaculate memory of Henry

Moreland, and I, for my part, banished it as soon as it entered my mind. It was like him to pay generously the labors of a sickly sewing-girl; it was not like him to take any advantage of her ignorance or gratitude, which might result in her taking such desperate revenge for her wrongs. The thought was an insult to him and to the noble woman who was to have been his wife. I blushed at the intrusive, unwelcome fancy; but the officer, not knowing the deceased as I knew him, and, perhaps, having no such exalted idea of manhood as mine, seemed to feel as if here might be a thread to follow.

"Leesy thought much of him, you think, Mrs. Sullivan," taking a chair unbidden, and putting on a friendly, gossiping air. "Everybody speaks well of him. So she sewed in the family?"

"Six weeks every summer. They was always satisfied with her sewing—she's the quickest and neatest hand with the needle! She'd make them shirts of yours beautiful, if she was to home, sir."

"When did she go to New York to live?"

"Last winter, early. It's nearly a year now. There was something come across her—she appeared homesick like, and strange. When she said she meant to go to the city and get work, I was minded to let her go, for I thought the chance mebbe would do her good. But she's quite ailing and coughs dreadful o'nights. I'm afraid she catched cold in that rain-storm night afore last; she came up all the way from the depot in it. She was wet to the skin when she got here and as white as a sheet. She was so weak-like that when the neighbors came in with the news yesterday, she gave a scream and dropped right down. I didn't wonder she was took aback. I ain't got done trembling yet myself."

I remembered the gentleman who had first spoken to me about the girl said that she had come in on the morning train Saturday; I could not reconcile this with her coming up from the depot at dark; yet I wished to put my question in such a way as not to arouse suspicion of my motive.

"If she came in the six o'clock train she must have been on the same train with Mr. Moreland."

"I believe she was in the seven o'clock cars—yes, she was. 'Twas half-past seven when she got in—the rain was pouring down awful. She didn't see him, for I asked her yesterday."

"In whose shop in New York is she employed?" inquired the officer.

"She's at No 3—Broadway," naming a store somewhere between Wall street and Canal.

"Are you wanting her for any thing?" she asked, suddenly, looking up sharply as if it just occurred to her that our inquiries were rather pointed.

"Oh, no," replied my companion, rising; "I was a bit tired, and thought I'd rest my feet before starting out again. I'll thank you for a glass of water, Mrs. Sullivan. So you won't undertake the shirts?"

"If I thought I could do the button-holes—"

"Perhaps your niece could do them on her next visit, if you wanted the job," I suggested.

"Why, so she could! and would be glad to do something for her old aunt. It's bright you are to put me in mind of it. Shall I come for the work, sir?"

"I'll send it round when I get it ready. I suppose your niece intends to visit you next Saturday?"

"Well, ra'ly, I can't say. It's too expensive her coming every week; but, she'll sure be here afore the whole six is complate. Good-mornin', gintlemen—and they's heard nothin' of the murderer, I'll warrant?"

We responded that nothing had been learned, and descending to the street, it was arranged, as we walked along, that the officer should go to New York and put some detective there on the track of Leesy Sullivan. I informed my companion of the discrepancy between her actual arrival in town and her appearance at her aunt's. Either the woman had purposely deceived us, or her niece had not gone home for a good many hours after landing at Blankville. I went with him to the depot, where we made a few inquiries which convinced us that she had arrived on Saturday morning, and sat an hour or two in the ladies' room, and then gone away up town.

There was sufficient to justify our looking further. I took from my own pocket means to defray the expenses of the officer as well as to interest the New York detective, adding that liberal rewards were about to be offered, and waited until I saw him depart on his errand.

Then, turning to go to the office, my heart so sickened at the idea of business and the ordinary routine of living in the midst of such misery, that my footsteps shrunk away from their familiar paths! I could do nothing, just then, for the aid or comfort of the afflicted. The body was to be taken that afternoon to the city for interment, the next day, in the family inclosure at Greenwood; until the hour for its removal, there was nothing more that friendship could perform in the service of the mourners. My usual prescription for mental ailments was a long and vigorous walk; to-day I felt as if I could breathe only in the wide sunshine, so cramped and chilled were my spirits.

The summer residence of the Morelands lay about a mile beyond the Argyll mansion, out of the village proper, on a hillside, which sloped down to the river. It was surrounded by fine grounds, and commanded one of the loveliest views of the Hudson.

*"A spirit in my feet
Led me, who knows how?"**

in the direction of this now vacant and solitary place—
solitary, I believed, with the exception of the gardener and
his wife, who lived in a cottage back of the gardens, and who
remained the year round, he to attend to out-door matters, and
she to give housekeeper's care to the closed mansion.

The place had never looked more beautiful to me, not even
in the bloom of its June foliage and flowers, than it did as I
approached it on this occasion. The frosts had turned to every
gorgeous color the tops of the trees which stood out here and
there; back of the house, and extending down toward the southern gate, by which I entered, a grove of maples and elms glowed
in the autumn sunshine; the lawn in front sloped down to the
water's edge, which flowed by in a blue and lordly stream, bearing on its broad bosom picturesque white ships. In the garden,
through which I was now walking, many brilliant flowers still
lingered: asters, gold, pink and purple; chrysanthemums; some
dahlias which had been covered from the frost; pansies lurking:
under their broad leaves. It had been the intention of the young
couple to make this their permanent home after their marriage,
going to the city only for a couple of the winter months. The
very next week, I had heard, Eleanor expected to go down to
help Henry in his selection of new furniture.

Here the mansion lay, bathed, in the rich sunshine; the garden
sparkled with flowers as the river with ripples, so full, as it were,

---

* A slight misquotation of lines from the first stanza of Percy Bysshe Shelley's "The
Indian Serenade" (1822), also known as "Lines to an Indian Air" and "Song Written for
an Indian Air": "And a spirit in my feet / Hath led me—who knows how?" Curiously,
the same misquotation—the omission of "Hath"—occurs in an essay, "Maidenvalley,
Spinsterland" by Adams S. Hill, in 1868. These folks may be forgiven, for in the original
manuscript, Shelley wrote, "Has borne me" instead of "Hath led me."

of conscious, joyous *life*, while the master of all lay in a darkened room awaiting his narrow coffin. Never had the uncertainty of human purposes so impressed me as when I looked abroad over that stately residence and thought of the prosperous future which had come to so awful a standstill. I gathered a handful of pansies—they were Eleanor's favorites. As I approached the house by the garden, I came nearly upon the portico which extended across its western front before I perceived that it was occupied. Sitting on its outer edge, with one arm half wound around one of its pillars, and her bonnet in the grass at her feet, I beheld the sewing-girl after whom I had dispatched an officer to New York. She did not perceive me, and I had an opportunity of studying the face of the woman who had fallen under my suspicion, when she was unaware that my eye was upon it, and when her soul looked out of it, unvailed, in the security of solitude. The impression which she made upon me was that of despair. It was written on attitude and expression. It was neither grief nor remorse—it was blank despair. It must have been half an hour that I remained quiet, watching her. In all that time she never stirred hand nor eyelid; her glance was upon the greensward at her feet. When I turn to that page of my memory, I see her, photographed, as it were, upon it—every fold of the dark dress, which was some worsted substance, frayed, but neat; the black shawl, bordered, drawn close about the slender shoulders, which had the slight, habitual stoop of those who ply the needle for a living; the jetty* hair pushed back from her forehead, the marble whiteness and rigidity of the face and mouth.

It was a face made to express passion. And, although the only passion expressed now was that of despair, so intense that it grew like apathy, I could easily see how the rounded chin and

---

* Black, as in jet-black.

full lips could melt into softer moods. The forehead was rather low, but fair, consorting with the oval of the cheek and chin; the brows dark and rather heavy. I remembered the wild black eyes which I had seen the previous day, and could guess at their hidden fires.

This was a girl to attract interest at any time, and I mutely wondered what had entangled the threads of her fate in the glittering web of a higher fortune, which was now suddenly interwoven with the pall of death. All her movements had been such as to confirm my desire to ascertain her connection, if any, with the tragedy. It seemed to me that if I could see her eyes, before she was conscious of observance, I could tell whether there was guilt, or only sorrow, in her heart; therefore I remained quiet, waiting. But I had mistaken my powers, or the eyes overbore them. When she did lift them, as a steamer came puffing around the base of the mountain which ran down into the river at the east, and they suddenly encountered mine, where I stood not ten feet from her, I saw only black, unfathomable depths, pouring out a trouble so intense, that my own gaze dropped beneath their power.

She did not start, upon observing me, which, as I thought, a guilty person, buried in self-accusing reveries, would have done—it seemed only slowly to penetrate her consciousness that a stranger was confronting her; when I raised my eyes, which had sunk beneath the intensity of hers, she was moving rapidly away toward the western gate.

"Miss Sullivan, you have forgotten your bonnet."

With a woman's instinct she put up her hand to smooth her disordered hair, came slowly back and took the bonnet which I extended toward her, without speaking. I hesitated what move to make next. I wished to address her—she was here, in my grasp, and I ought to satisfy myself, as far as possible, about the

suspicions which I had conceived. I might do her an irreparable injury by making my feelings public, if she were innocent of
any aid or instigation of the crime which had been committed,
yet there were circumstances which could hardly pass unchal-
lenged. That unaccountable absence of hers on Saturday, from
three o'clock until an hour after the murder was committed; the
statement of her aunt that she was in the city, and my finding
her in this spot, in connection with the midnight visit to the
window, and the other things which I had observed, were sufficient to justify inquiry. Yet, if I alarmed her prematurely I should
have the less chance of coming upon proofs, and her accomplices, if she had any, would be led to take steps for greater
safety. Anyhow, I would make her speak, and find what there
was in her voice.

"Your aunt told me that you had gone to New York," I said,
stepping along beside her, as she turned away.

"She thought so. Did you come here to see me, sir?" stopping
short in her walk, and looking at me as if she expected me to tell
my business.

This again did not look like the trepidation of guilt.

"No. I came out for a walk. I suppose our thoughts have led
us both in the same direction. This place will have an interest to
many, hereafter."

"Interest! the interest of vulgar curiosity! It will give them
something to talk about. I hate it!" She spoke more to herself
than to me, while a ray of fire darted from those black orbs;
the next instant her face subsided into that passionate stillness
again.

Her speech was not that of her station; I recalled what her
aunt had said about the education she had bestowed on her, and
decided that the girl's mind was one of those which reach out
beyond their circumstances—aspiring—ambitious—and that

this aspiring nature may have led her into her present unhappiness. That she was unhappy, if not sinful, it took but a glance to assure me.

"So do I hate it. I do not like to have the grief of my friends subjected to cold and curious eyes."

"Yet, it is a privilege to have the right to mourn. I tell you the sorrow of that beautiful lady he was to have married is light compared with trouble that some feel. There are those who envy her."

It was not her words, as much as her wild, half-choked voice, which gave effect to them; she spoke, and grew silent, as if conscious that the truth had been wrung from her in the ear of a stranger. We had reached the gate, and she seemed anxious to escape through it; but I held it in my hand, looking hard at her, as I said—"It may have been the hand of envy which dashed the cup of fruition from her lips. Her young life is withered never to bloom again. I can imagine but one wretchedness in this world greater than hers—and that is the wretchedness of the guilty person who has *murder* written on his or her soul."

A spasm contracted her face; she pushed at the gate which I still held.

"Ah, don't," she said; "let me pass."

I opened it and she darted through, fleeing along the road which led out around the backward slope of the hill, like Io pursued by the stinging fly.* Her path was away from the village, so that I hardly expected to see her again that day.

Within two minutes the gardener's wife came up the road to the gate. She had been down to visit the corpse of her young master; her eyes were red with weeping.

---

* Io was a lesser goddess, with whom Zeus fell in love. To protect her from his wife, Hera, he changed Io into a white heifer. Hera plagued her with a gadfly, and as a result, Io wandered the earth.

"How do you do, Mr. Redfield? These be miserable times, ain't they? My very heart is sore in my breast; but I couldn't cry a tear in the room where he was, a-lying there like life, for Miss Eleanor sot by him like a statue. It made me cold all over to see her—I couldn't speak to save me. The father and mother are just broke down, too."

"How is Miss Eleanor, this morning?"

"The Lord knows! She doesn't do anything but sit there, as quiet as can be. It's a bad symptom, to my thinking. 'Still waters run deep.' They're a-dreading the hour when they'll have to remove the body from the house—they're afraid her mind'll go."

"No, no," I answered, inwardly shuddering; "Eleanor's reason is too fine and powerful to be unstrung, even by a blow like this."

"Who was that went out the gate as I came around the bend? Was it that girl, again?"

"Do you mean Leesy Sullivan?"

"Yes, sir. Do you know her? She acts mighty queer, to my thinkin'. She was out here Saturday, sittin' in the summer-house, all alone, 'till the rain began to fall—I guess she got a good soaking going home. I didn't think much about her; it was Saturday, and I thought likely she was taking a holiday, and there's many people like to come here, it's so pleasant. But what's brought her here again to-day is more'n I can guess. Do you know, sir?"

"I do not. I found her sitting on the portico looking at the river. Maybe she comes out for a walk and stops here to rest. She probably feels somewhat at home, she has sewed so much in the family. I don't know her at all, myself; I never spoke to her until just now. Did you get much acquainted with her, when she was in the house?"

"I never spoke to her above a dozen times. I wasn't at the house much, and she was always at work. She seemed fast with her needle, and a girl who minded her own business. I thought she was rather proud, for a seamstress—she was handsome, and I reckon she knew it. She's getting thinner; she had red spots on her cheeks, Saturday, that I didn't like—looked consumptive."

"Did the family treat her with particular kindness?" It was as near as I cared to put into words what I was thinking of.

"You know it's in the whole Moreland race to be generous and kind to those under them. I've known Henry more than once, when the family was going out for a drive, to insist upon Miss Sullivan's taking a seat in the carriage—but never when he was going alone. I heard him tell his mother that the poor girl looked tired, as if she needed a breath of air and a bit of freedom, and the kind-hearted lady would laugh at her son, but do as he said. It was just like him. But I'd stake my everlasting futur' that he never took any advantage of her feelings, if it's that you're thinking of, Mr. Redfield."

"So would I, Mrs. Scott. There is no one can have a higher respect for the character of that noble young gentleman, than I. I would resent an insult to his memory more quickly than if he had been my brother. But, as you say, there is something queer in the actions of Miss Sullivan. I know that I can trust your discretion, Mrs. Scott, for I have heard it well spoken of; do not say any thing to others, not even to your husband, but keep a watch on that person if she should come here any more. Report to me what she does, and what spot she frequents."

"I will do so, sir. But I don't think any harm of her. She may have been unfortunate enough to think too much of the kindness with which he treated her. If so, I pity her—she could hardly help it, poor thing. Henry Moreland was a young gentleman a good many people loved."

She put her handkerchief to her eyes in a fresh burst of tears. Wishing her good-morning, I turned toward the village, hardly caring what I should do next. Mrs. Scott was an American woman, and one to be trusted; I felt that she would be the best detective I could place at that spot.

When I reached the office, on my homeward route, I went in. Mr. Argyll was there alone, his head leaning on his hand, his face anxious and worn, his brow contracted in deep thought. As soon as I came in, he sprung up, closed the outer door, and said to me, in a low voice,

"Richard, another strange thing has occurred."

I stared at him, afraid to ask what.

"I have been robbed of two thousand dollars."*

"When and how?"

"That is what I do not know. Four days ago I drew that amount in bills from the Park Bank. I placed it, in a roll, just as I received it, in my library desk, at home. I locked the desk, and have carried the key in my pocket. The desk has been locked, as usual, every time that I have gone to it. How long the money has been gone, I can not say; I never looked after it, since placing it there, until about an hour ago. I wanted some cash for expenses this afternoon, and going for it, the roll was gone."

"Haven't you mislaid it?"

"No. I have one drawer for my cash, and I placed it there. I remember it plainly enough. It has been stolen"—and he sat down in his chair with a heavy sigh. "That money was for my poor Eleanor. She was to complete her wedding outfit this week, and the two thousand dollars was for refurnishing the place out at the Grove. I don't care for the loss so much—she doesn't need it now—but it's singular—at this time!"

---

* The equivalent of over $300,000 in income in 2020; however, in terms of commodities, it is the equivalent of around $32,000. Samuel H. Williamson, "Purchasing Power Today of a US Dollar Transaction in the Past," MeasuringWorth, 2020, https://www.measuringworth.com.

He looked up at me, vague suspicions which he could not shape floating in his brain.

"Who knew of your having the money?"

"No one, that I am aware of, except my nephew. He drew it for me when he went down to the city last Wednesday."

"Could you identify the money?"

"Not all of it. I only remember that there was one five-hundred-dollar bill in the package, a fresh issue of the Park Bank, of which, possibly, they may have the number. The rest was city money of various denominations and banks.* I can think of but one thing which seems probable. James must have been followed from the city by some professional thief, who saw him obtain the money, and kept an eye upon it, waiting for a suitable opportunity, until it was deposited in the desk. The key is a common one, which could be easily duplicated, and we are so careless in this quiet community that a thief might enter at almost any hour of the night. Perhaps the same villain dogged poor Henry in hopes of another harvest."

"You forget that there was no attempt to rob Henry."

"True—true. Yet the murderer may have been frightened away before he had secured his prize."

"In which case, he would have returned, as the body remained undiscovered all night."

"It may be so. I am dizzy with thinking it over and over."

"Try and not think any more, dear sir," I said, gently. "You are feverish and ill now. I am going, this afternoon, with the friends to the city, and I will put the police on the watch for the money. We will get the number of the large bill, if possible, from the

---

* Until the 1860s, paper currency was issued by privately owned banks, such as the fictitious "Park Bank." The federal government did not issue currency until the Civil War, the first variety being "greenback" (also known as "Demand Notes"), issued in 1861–62.

bank, and I will have investigations made as to the passengers of Wednesday on the train with James. Have you said any thing to him about your loss?"

"I have not seen him since I made the discovery. You may tell him if you see him first; and do what you can, Richard, for I feel as weak as a child."

CHAPTER V.
MR. BURTON, THE DETECTIVE.

When I came out of the office, I encountered James on the steps, for the first time that day. I could not stop to make known the robbery to him, and telling him that his uncle wished to see him a few minutes, I hurried to my boarding-house, where I had barely time to take some lunch in my room, while packing a small bag to be sent to the cars, before hurrying back to Mr. Argyll's to attend the funeral escort to the train. James and I were two of the eight pall-bearers, yet neither of us could summon fortitude to enter the parlor where the body lay; I believe that James had not yet looked upon the corpse. We stood outside, on the steps of the piazza, only taking our share of the burden after the coffin was brought out into the yard. While we stood there, among many others, waiting, I chanced to observe his paleness and restlessness; he tore his black gloves in putting them on; I saw his fingers trembling. As for me, my whole being seemed to pause, as a single, prolonged shriek rang out of the dark-ened mansion and floated off on the sunshine up to the ear of God. They were taking the lover away from his bride. The next moment the coffin appeared; I took my place by its side, and we moved away toward the depot, passing over the very spot where the corpse was found. James was a step in advance of me, and as we came to the place, some strong inward recoil made him pause, then step aside and walk around the ill-starred spot. I noticed it, not only for the momentary confusion into which it threw the line, but because I had never supposed him susceptible to superstitious or imaginative influences.

A private car had been arranged for. James and I occupied one seat; the swift motion of the train was opposed to the idea of death; it had an exhilarating effect upon my companion, whose paleness passed away, and who began to experience a reaction after his depression of feeling. He talked to me incessantly upon trifling subjects which I do not now recall, and in that low, yet sharp voice which is most easily distinguished through the clatter of a moving train. The necessity for attending to him—for making answers to irrelevant questions, when my mind was preoccupied, annoyed me. My thoughts centered about the coffin, and its inmate, taking his last ride under circumstances so different from those under which he had set out, only two days ago, to meet her whom his heart adored; whose hand he never clasped—whose lips he never touched—the fruition of whose hopes was cut off utterly—whose fate, henceforth, was among the mysterious paths of the great eternity.

I could not, for an instant, feel the least lightness of heart. My nature was too sympathetic; the currents of my young blood flowed too warmly, for me to feel otherwise than deeply affected by the catastrophe. My eyes shed inward tears at the sight of the parents, sitting in advance of us, their heads bowed beneath the stroke; and, oh! my heart shed tears of blood at thought of Eleanor, left behind us to the utter darkness of a night which had fallen while it was yet morning.

Musing upon *her*, I wondered that her cousin James could throw off the troubles of others as he did, interesting himself in passing trifles. I have said that I never liked him much; but in this I was an exception to the general rule. He was an almost universal favorite. At least, he seldom failed to please and win those for whom he exerted himself to be agreeable. His voice was soft and well modulated—such a voice as, should one hear it from another apartment, would make him wish to see the speaker; his manner was gracious and flattering. I had often wondered why his evident passion for Eleanor had not secured her interest in return, before she knew Henry Moreland, and had answered myself that it was one of two reasons: either their cousinly intercourse had invested him, to her, with the feelings of a brother or relative, or her fine perceptions, being the superior woman which she was, had unconsciously led her to a true estimate of his qualities. This day I felt less affinity for him than ever before, as I gazed at his dark, thin features, and met the light of eyes brilliant, unsteady and cold. That intense selfishness which I had secretly attributed to him, was now, to my perhaps too acute apprehension, painfully apparent. In my secret heart, as I listened to his light remarks, and perceived the rise of spirits which he hardly endeavored to check, I accused him of gladness that a rival was out of the way, and that the chances were again open for the hand of his beautiful and wealthy cousin. At first he had been shocked, as we all were; but now that he had time to view the occurrence with an eye to the future, I believed that he was already calculating the results with regard to his own hopes and wishes. I turned from him with a feeling of aversion.

After neglecting to reply to him until he was obliged to drop the one-sided conversation, I recollected that I had not yet spoken to him in regard to his uncle's loss; so I said to him quite suddenly,

"Mr. Argyll has been robbed of a sum of money."

An inexplicable expression flashed into his face and passed off; it went as soon as it came.

"So he informed me, just before we started. He says that you will put the police on the track of it—that possibly the five-hundred-dollar bill will be identified. It was taken from his desk, it appears."

"Yes; I wonder what will happen next."

"Ay! I wonder what will."

"Who knows what a narrow escape *you* may have had," said I. "It is well that you came here in broad daylight; else, like poor Henry, you might have fallen a victim to a blow in the dark. Mr. Argyll thinks you must have been followed from the city by some professional burglar."

"He thinks so?" he asked, while the shadow of a smile just showed a second in the mirror of his eyes; it was as if there was a smile in his heart, and a reflection from its invisible self fell athwart his eyes; but he turned them away immediately.

"It's queer," he resumed; "horribly queer; don't you think so? I saw that money in the desk Friday evening. Uncle asked me to hold the lamp a moment, while he found some papers, and I noticed the roll of bills lying in his cash-drawer, just as I had given them to him. It must have been abstracted Saturday or Sunday—it's queer—confoundedly so! There must be some great villain lurking in our midst!"—this last sentence he uttered with an emphasis, looking me through with his black eyes.

There was suspicion in his gaze, and my own fell before it. Innocence itself will blush if obliged to confront the insult of accusation. I had had many wild, and doubtless many wrong and suspicious thoughts about various persons, since the discovery of the murder; and this was turning the tables on me rather suddenly. It never occurred to me that among the dozens upon whom vague and flying suspicions might alight, might be myself.

"There is an awful mystery somewhere," I stammered.

"Humph! yes, there is. My uncle Argyll is just the man to be wronged by some one of his many friends and dependents. He is too confiding, too unsuspecting of others—as I have told him. He has been duped often—but this—this is too bad!"

I looked up again, and sharply, to see what he meant. If he intended covertly to insinuate that *I* was open to imputation as one of the "friends or dependents" who could wrong a benefactor, I wished to understand him. A friend, I knew, Mr. Argyll was to me; a friend to be grateful for; but I was no dependent upon his bounty, as his nephew was, and the hot blood rushed to my face, the fire to my eye, as I answered back the cool gaze of James with a haughty stare.

"There is no love lost between us, Richard," he said, presently, "which is principally your fault; but I am friendly to you; and as a friend, I would suggest that you do not make yourself conspicuous in this affair. If you should put yourself forward at all, being so young, and having, apparently, so small an interest in the matter, you may bring unpleasant remark upon yourself. Let us stand back and allow our elders to do the work. As to that money, whether it has or has not any connection with the—the other affair, time will perhaps show. Let the police do what they can with it—my advice to you is to keep in the background."

"Your course may be prudent, James," was my reply; "I do not ask your approbation of mine. But to one thing I have made up my mind. So long as I live, and the murderer of Henry Moreland is undiscovered, I will never rest. In Eleanor's name, I consecrate myself to this calling. I can face the whole world in her behalf, and fear nothing."

He turned away with a sneer, busying himself with the prospect from the window. During the rest of the ride we said little; his words had given me a curious sensation; I had sustained so many shocks to my feelings within the last forty-eight hours, that this new one of finding myself under the eye of suspicion, mingled in with the perplexing whirl of the whole, until I almost began to doubt my own identity and that of others. A vision of Leesy Sullivan, whose wild footsteps might still be tracking hills and fields, hovered before me—and out of all this distraction, my thoughts settled upon Eleanor. I prayed God earnestly to be with her in this hour; either to strengthen her heart and brain to bear her affliction without falling to ruins beneath the weight, or to take her at once to Himself, where Henry awaited her in the mansions of their eternal home.

The arrival of the train at Thirtieth street recalled me to my present duties. Carriages were in waiting to convey the coffin and its escort to the house of the parents, the funeral being arranged for the following day. I saw the officer who had gone down from Blankville in the morning, waiting in the depot to speak to me; but I did not need to be told that he had not found the sewing-girl at her place of business. I made an appointment to meet him in the evening at the Metropolitan, and took my place in the sad procession to the house of the Morelands.

I was anxious to give notice of the robbery at the bank, and to ascertain if they could identify any of the money, especially the large bill, which, being new, I hoped they would have on record. Banking hours were over, however, for the day, and it was only by intruding the matter upon the notice of Mr. Moreland that I could get any thing accomplished. This I decided to do; when he told me that, by going directly to the bank, he thought I could gain access to the cashier; and if not, he gave me his address, so that I might seek him at his residence. Mr. Moreland also advised me to take with me some competent detective, who should be witness to the statement of the cashier with regard to the money paid to James Argyll, on his uncle's draft, and be employed to put the rest of the force on the lookout for it, or any portion of it which was identifiable. He gave me the name of an officer with whom he had a chance acquaintance, and of whose abilities he had a high opinion; telling me to make free use of his name and influence, if he had any, with him, and the police.

"And please, Mr. Redfield—or James here, if you should be too busy—make out an advertisement for the morning papers, offering a reward of five thousand dollars for the detection and conviction of the—the—murderer."

James was standing by us during the conversation; and I almost withdrew my verdict upon his selfishness, as I marked how he shrunk when the eye of the bereaved father rested upon him, and how vainly he endeavored to appear calm at the affecting spectacle of the gray-haired gentleman forcing his quivering lips to utter the word—"murderer." He trembled much more than myself, as each of us wrung Mr. Moreland's hand, and departed down the steps.

"It unmanned him," he said, stopping a moment on the pavement to wipe the perspiration from his brow, though the day was not at all warm. "I believe," he added, as he walked along, "that if the person who resolves to commit a crime would reflect on all the consequences of that act, it would remain undone for ever. But he does not. He sees an object in the way of his wishes, and he thrusts it aside, reckless of the ruin which will overwhelm surrounding things, until he sees the wreck about him. Then it is too late for remorse—to the devil with it. But I needn't philosophize before you, Richard, who have precociously earned that privilege of wisdom"—with that disagreeable half-laugh of his—"only I was thinking how the guilty party must have felt could he have seen Henry's father as we saw him just now," and again I felt his eye upon me. Certainly, there seemed no prospect of our friendship increasing. I would rather have dispensed with his company, while I put my full energies into the business before me; but it was quite natural that he should expect to accompany me on an errand in which he must have as deep an interest as myself. Coming out of the avenue upon Broadway we took a stage, riding down as far as Grand street, when we got out and walked to the office of the detective-police.

The chief was not in at the moment of our entrance; we were received by a subordinate and questioned as to our visit. The morning papers had heralded the melancholy and mysterious murder through the city; hundreds of thousands of persons had already marveled over the boldness and success, the silence and suddenness with which the deed had been done, leaving not a clue by which to trace the perpetrator. It had been the sensation of the day throughout New York and its environs. The public mind was busy with conjectures as to the *motive* for the crime. And this was to be one of the sharp thorns pressed into the hearts of the distressed friends of the murdered man. Suddenly, into the garish light of day, beneath the pitiless gaze of a million curious eyes, was dragged every word, or act, or circumstance of the life so abruptly closed. It was necessary to the investigation of the affair, that the most secret pages of his history should be read out—and it is not in the nature of a daily paper to neglect such opportunities for turning an honest penny. Here let me say that not one character in ten thousand could have stood this trial by fire as did Henry Moreland's. No wronged hireling, no open enemy, no secret intrigue, no gambling debts—not one blot on the bright record of his amiable, Christian life.

To return to the detective-office. Our errand at once received attention from the person in charge, who sent a messenger after the chief. He also informed us that several of their best men had gone up to Blankville that afternoon to confer with the authorities there. The public welfare demanded, as well as the interest of private individuals, that the guilty should be ferreted out, if possible. The apparent impunity with which the crime had been committed was startling, making every one feel it a personal matter to aid in discouraging any more such practices; besides, the police knew that their efforts would be well rewarded.

While we sat talking with the official, I noticed the only other inmate of the room, who made a peculiar impression upon me for which I could not account.

He was a large man, of middle age, with a florid face and sandy hair. He was quietly dressed in the ordinary manner of the season, and with nothing to mark him from a thousand other men of similar appearance, unless it was the expression of his small, blue-gray eyes, whose glance, when I happened to encounter it, seemed not to be looking at me but into me. However, he turned it away, and occupied himself with looking through the window at the passers-by. He appeared to be a stranger, awaiting, like ourselves, the coming of the chief.

Desiring to secure the services of the particular detective whom Mr. Moreland had recommended, I asked the subordinate in attendance, if he could inform me where Mr. Burton was to be found.

"Burton? I don't know of any one of that name, I think—if I may except my stage experience with Mr. Toodles,"* he added, with a smile, called up by some passing vision of his last visit to the theater.

"Then there is no Mr. Burton belongs to your force?"

"Not that I am acquainted with. He may be one of us, for all that. We don't pretend to know our own brothers here. You can ask Mr. Browne when he comes in."

---

* William Evans Burton (1804–1860) was a well-known English stage actor, best remembered for playing the comic part of Timothy Toodles (Mr. Toodles) in the Broadway play *The Toodles* in the mid-nineteenth century.

All this time the stranger by the window sat motionless, absorbed in looking upon the throng of persons and vehicles in the street beneath; and now I, having nothing else to do, regarded him. I felt a magnetism emanate from him, as from a manufactory of vital forces; I felt, instinctively, that he was possessed of an iron will and indomitable courage; I was speculating, according to my dreamy habit, upon his characteristics, when the chief appeared, and we, that is, James and myself, laid our case before him—at the same time I mentioned that Mr. Moreland had desired me to ask for Mr. Burton to be detailed to aid our investigations.

"Ah! yes," said Mr. Browne, "there are not many outsiders who know that person. He is my right hand, but I don't let the left know what he doeth. Mr. Moreland had his services once, I remember, in tracking some burglars who had entered his banking-house. Poor young Moreland! I've seen him often! Shocking affair, truly. We mustn't rest till we know more about it. I only hope we may be of service to his afflicted father. Burton is just here, fortunately," and he beckoned to the very stranger sitting in the window, who had overheard the inquiries made for him without the slightest demonstration that such a being had any existence as far as he was concerned, and who now slowly arose, and approached us. We four went into an inner room, where we were introduced to each other, and drawing up our chairs in a close circle, we began, in low voices, the discussion of our business.

Mr. Browne was voluble when he heard that a robbery had been committed in Mr. Argyll's house. He had no doubt, he said, that the two crimes were connected, and it would be strange, indeed, if nothing could be discovered relating to either of them. He hoped that the lesser crime would be the means of betraying the greater. He trusted the rogue, whoever he or she might be, had, in this imprudent act, done something to betray himself. He had hopes of the five-hundred-dollar bill.

Mr. Burton said very little, beyond asking two or three questions; but he was a good listener. Much of the time he sat with his eyes fixed upon James, who did a good deal of the talking. I could not, for the life of me, tell whether James was conscious of those blue-gray eyes; if he was, they did not much disturb him; he made his statements in a calm and lucid manner, gazing into Mr. Burton's face with a clear and open look. After a while, the latter began to grow uneasy; powerful as was his physical and mental frame, I saw a trembling of both; he forced himself to remain quiet in his chair—but to me he had the air of a lion, who sees its prey but a little distance off, and who trembles with restraint. The light in his eye narrowed down to one gleam of concentrated fire—a steely, glittering point—he watched the rest of us and said little. If I had been a guilty man I should have shrunk from that observation, through the very walls, or out of a five-story window, if there had been no other way; it struck me that it would have been unbearable to any accusing conscience; but my own mind being burdened with no weightier sins than a few boyish follies—saving the selfishness and earthliness which make a part of all human natures—I felt quite free, breathing easily, while I noticed, with interest, the silent change going on in the detective.

More and more like a lion about to spring, he grew; but whether his prey was near at hand and visible, or far away and visible only to his mental gaze, I could not tell. I fairly jumped, when he at last rose quickly to his feet; I expected to see him bound upon some guilty ghost to us intangible, and shake it to pieces in an honest rage; but whatever was the passion within him, he controlled it, saying only, a little impatiently,

"Enough, gentlemen, we have talked enough! Browne, will

you go with Mr. Argyll to the bank, and see about that money? I do not wish to be known there as belonging to your force. I will walk to his hotel with Mr. Redfield, and you can meet us there at any hour you choose to appoint."

"It will take until tea-time to attend to the bank. Say about eight o'clock, then, we will be at the—"

"Metropolitan,"* said I, and the quartette parted, half going up and half going down town.

On our way to the hotel we fell into an easy conversation on topics entirely removed from the one which absorbed the gravest thoughts of both. Mr. Burton did more talking now than he had done at the office, perhaps with the object of making me express myself freely; though if so, he managed with so much tact that his wish was not apparent. He had but poor success; the calamity of our house lay too heavily on me for me to forget it in an instant; but I was constantly surprised at the character of the man whose acquaintance I was making. He was intelligent, even educated, a gentleman in language and manner—a quite different person, in fact, from what I had expected in a member of the detective-police.

Shut up in the private parlor which I obtained at the Metropolitan, the subject of the murder was again broached and thoroughly discussed. Mr. Burton won my confidence so inevitably that I felt no hesitation in unvailing to him the domestic hearth of Mr. Argyll, whenever the habits or circumstances of the family were consulted in their bearing upon the mystery. And when he said to me, fixing his eye upon me, but speaking gently,

"You, too, loved the young lady,"—I neither blushed nor grew angry. That penetrating eye had read the secret of my

---

* A well-known hotel near Broadway.

heart, which had never been spoken or written, yet I did not feel outraged that he had dared to read it out to me. If he could find any matter against me in that holiest truth of my existence, he was welcome to it.

"Be it so," I said; "that is with myself, and no one else."

"There are others who love her," he continued, "but there is a difference in the quality of love. There is that which sanctifies, and something, called by the same name, which is an excuse for infinite perfidy. In my experience I have found the love of woman and the love of money at the bottom of most mischief—the greed of gain is by far the commonest and strongest; and when the two are combined, there is motive enough for the darkest tragedy. But you spoke of a young woman, of whom you have suspicions."

I told Mr. Burton that in this matter I trusted to his discretion: that I had not brought it to notice before Mr. Browne, because I shrunk from the danger of fixing a ruinous suspicion upon a person who might be perfectly innocent; yet that circumstances were such as to demand investigation, which I was sure he was the person to carry on. I then gave him a careful account of every thing I had seen or learned about the sewing-girl. He agreed with me that she ought to be placed under secret surveillance. I told him that the officer from Blankville would be in after tea, when we could consult together and dispose of the discussion before the arrival of James and Mr. Browne—and I then rung the bell, ordering a light supper in our room.

The Blankville official had nothing to report of Miss Sullivan, except that she had not arrived either at her boarding-house or at the shop where she was employed, and her character stood high at both places. She had been represented to him as a "strictly proper" person, very reserved, in poor health, with a sad appearance, and an excellent workwoman—that no gentlemen were ever known to call to see her, and that she never went out after returning to her boarding-house at the close of work-hours. We then requested him to say nothing about her to his brother officers, and to keep the matter from the newspapers, as we should regret doing an irreparable injury to one who might be guiltless.

It seemed as if the Fates were in favor of the guilty. Mr. Browne, punctually at eight o'clock, reported that there was none of the money paid out to James Argyll at Mr. Argyll's order, which the bank would identify—not even its own bill of five hundred dollars, which was a recent issue. They had paid out such a bill on the draft, but the number was not known to them.

"However," said Mr. Browne, "bills of that denomination are not common, and we shall be on the lookout for them, wherever offered."

"But even should the robber be discovered, there is no proof that it would establish any connection with the murder. It may have been a coincidence," remarked James. "I have often noticed that one calamity is sure to be followed by another. If there is a railroad disaster, a powder-mill explosion, a steamer destroyed by fire, before the horror of the first accident has done thrilling our nerves, we are pretty certain to be startled by another catastrophe."

"I, too," said Mr. Burton, "have remarked the succession of events—echoes, as it were, following the clap of thunder. And I have usually found that, like the echoes, there was a natural cause for them."

James moved uneasily in his chair, arose, pulled aside the curtain, and looked out into the night. I had often noticed that he was somewhat superstitious; perhaps he saw the eyes of Henry Moreland looking down at him from the starry hights; he twitched the curtains together with a shiver, and came back to us.

"It is not impossible," he said, keeping his face in the shadow, for he did not like us to see how the night had affected him, "that some one of the clerks in Mr. Moreland's banking-house—perhaps some trusted and responsible person—was detected by Henry, in making false entries, or some other dishonesty—and that to save himself the disgrace of betrayal and dismissal, he has put the discoverer out of the way. The whole business of the establishment ought to be thoroughly overhauled. It appears that Henry went directly to the cars from the office; so that if any trouble had arisen between him and one of the employees, there would have been no opportunity for his consulting his father, who was not at the place all that afternoon."

"Your suggestion is good," said Mr. Browne, "and must be attended to."

Baffled.

"The whereabouts of every one of the employees, down to the porter, at the time of the murder, are already accounted for. They were all in the city," said Mr. Burton, with precision.

Shortly after, the party separated for the night. An urgent invitation came from Mr. Moreland for James and myself to stop at his house during our stay in the city; but we thought it better not to disturb the quiet of the house of mourning with the business which we wished to press forward, and returned an answer to that effect. It was nearly ten o'clock when James recollected that we had not been to the offices of the daily journals with the advertisements which ought to appear in the morning. It was the work of a few minutes for me to write one out, which we then copied on three or four sheets of paper, and finding an errand-boy below, we dispatched him with two of the copies to as many journals, and ourselves hurried off with the others. I went to one establishment and my companion to another, in order to hasten proceedings, knowing that it was doubtful if we could get them inserted at that late hour. Having succeeded to my satisfaction with my own errand, I thought I would walk over to the next street and meet James, whom, having a little further than I to go, I would probably meet, returning. As I neared the building to which he had gone, and which was brilliantly lighted up for its night-work, I saw James come out on the pavement, look around him an instant, and then start off in a direction opposite to that which would lead back to Broadway and his hotel. He had not observed me, who chanced to be in shadow at the moment; and I, without any particular motive which I could analyze, started after him, thinking to overtake him and offer to join him in a walk. He went, however, at so rapid a pace, that I still remained behind. Our course lay through Nassau and Fulton streets, to the Brooklyn ferry. I quickened my pace almost to a run, as James passed into the ferry-house, for I saw that a boat was about to start; but I had a vexatious delay in finding small change, so that I got through just in time to see the boat move off, James himself having to take a flying leap to reach it after it was under way. At that hour there was a boat only every fifteen minutes; of course I gave up the pursuit; and sitting down at the end of the bridge, I allowed the cool wind from the bay and river to blow against my hot face, while I gazed out on the dark waters, listening to their incessant moaning about the piers, and watching where they glimmered beneath the lights of the opposite shore. The blue and red lamps of the moving vessels, in my present mood, had a weird and ghastly effect; the thousands of masts of the moored shipping stood up naked against the sky, like a forest of blighted, skeleton pines. Sadness, the deepest I had ever felt in my life, fell upon me—sadness too deep for any expression. The shifting water, slipping and sighing about the works of men which fretted it; the un-approachable, glittering sky; the leafless forest, the wind fresh from its ocean solitudes—these partially interpreted it, but not wholly. Their soul, as far as the soul of Nature goes, was in unison with mine; but in humanity lies a still deeper deep, rises a higher hight. I was as much alone as if nearly a million fellow-creatures were not so encircling me. I thought of the many tragedies over which these waters had closed; of the secrets they had hidden; of the many lives sucked under these ruthless bridges; of the dark creatures who haunted these docks at evil hours—but most I thought of a distant chamber, where a girl, who yesterday was as full of love and beauty as a morning rose is full of dew and perfume— whose life ran over with light—whose step was imperial with the happiness of youth—lay, worn and pallid, upon her weary bed, breathing sighs of endless misery. I thought of the funeral procession which to-morrow, at noon, should come by this road and travel these waters, to that garden of repose, whose white tombstones I knew, although I could not see them, gleamed now under the "cold light of stars."*

Thus I sat, wrapped in musings, until a policeman, who, it is likely, had long had his eye upon me, wondering if I were a suspicious character, called out—"Take care of your legs, young man!" and I sprung to my feet, as the return boat came into her slip, drifting—up and bumping sullenly against the end of the bridge where my legs had been dangling.

I waited until, among the not numerous passengers, I perceived James hurrying by, when I slipped my hand into his arm quietly, saying,

"You led me quite a race—what in the world have you been across to Brooklyn for?"

He jumped at my voice and touch; then grew angry, as people are apt to do when they are startled or frightened, after the shock is over.

"What business is that of yours, sir? How dare you follow me? If you have taken upon yourself the office of spy, let me know it."

"I beg your pardon," I answered, withdrawing from his arm, "I walked over to the H—office to meet you, and saw you walk off in this direction. I had no particular object in following you, and perhaps ought not to have done it."

"I spoke too hastily," he said, almost immediately. "Forget it, Richard. You pounced upon me so unexpectedly, you gave me a nervous shock—irritated my combativeness, I suppose. I thought, of course, you had returned to the hotel, and feeling too restless to go back to my little bedroom, there, I determined

---

* From Henry Wadsworth Longfellow's "The Light of Stars" (1838), which he called "the second Psalm of Life."

to try the effect of a ride across the river. The bracing air has toned me up. I believe I can go back and sleep"—offering his arm again, which I took, and we slowly retraced our steps to the Metropolitan.

I will not pain the heart of my reader by forcing him to be one of the mournful procession which followed Henry Moreland to his untimely grave. At two o'clock of Tuesday, all was over. The victim was hidden away from the face of the earth—smiling, as if asleep, dreaming of his Eleanor, he was consigned to that darkness from whence he should never awaken and find her—while the one who had brought him low walked abroad under the sunlight of heaven. To give that guilty creature no peace was the purpose of my heart. James resolved to return to Blankville by the five o'clock train. He looked sick, and said that he felt so—that the last trying scene had "used him up;" and then, his uncle would surely want one of us to assist him at home. To this I assented, intending myself to stay in the city a day or two, until Mr. Burton was prepared to go out to Blankville with me.

After such of the friends from the village as had come down to attend the funeral, had started for home in the afternoon cars, I went to my room to have another interview with the detective. In the mean time, I had heard some of the particulars of Mr. Burton's history, which had greatly increased the interest I already felt in him. He had chosen his present occupation out of a consciousness of his fitness for it. He was in independent circumstances, and accepted no salary for what was with him a labor of love; seldom taking any of the liberal sums pressed upon him by grateful parties who had benefited by his skill, except to cover expenses to which long journeys, or other necessities of the case, might have subjected him. He had been in the "profession" but a few years. Formerly he had been a forwarding-merchant, universally esteemed for integrity, and carrying about him that personal influence which men of strong will and unusual discrimination exercise over those with whom they come in contact. But that he had any extraordinary powers, of the kind which had since been developed, he was as ignorant as others. An accident, which revealed these to him, shaped the future course of his life. One wild and windy night the fire-bells of New York rung a fierce alarm; the flames of a large conflagration lighted the sky; the firemen toiled manfully, as was their wont, but the air was bitter and the pavements sleety, and the wintry wind "played such fantastic tricks before high heaven"*as made the angel of mercy almost despair. Before the fire could be subdued, four large warehouses had been burned to the ground, and in one of them a large quantity of uninsured merchandise for which Mr. Burton was responsible.

The loss, to him, was serious. He barely escaped failure by drawing in his business to the smallest compass, and, by the exercise of great prudence, he managed to save a remnant of his fortune, with which, as soon as he could turn it to advantage, he withdrew from his mercantile career. His mind was bent on a new business, which unfitted him for any other.

The fire was supposed to be purely accidental; the insurance companies, usually cautious enough, had paid over their varying amounts of insurance to those fortunate losers, who

---

* From William Shakespeare's *Measure for Measure* (1603–04), act 2, scene 2:

...*man, proud man,*
Drest in a little brief authority,
Most ignorant of what he's most assured,
His glassy essence, like an angry ape,
Plays such fantastic tricks before high heaven
As make the angels weep; who, with our spleens,
Would all themselves laugh mortal.

were not, like Mr. Burton, unprepared. These losers were men of wealth, and the highest position as business firms—high and mighty potentates, against whom to breathe a breath of slander, was to overwhelm the audacious individual in the ruins of his own presumption. Mr. Burton had an inward conviction that these men were guilty of arson. He knew it. His mind perceived their guilt. But he could make no allegation against them upon such unsubstantial basis as this. He went to work, quietly and singly, to gather up the threads in the cable of his proof; and when he had made it strong enough to hang them twice over—for two lives, that of a porter and a clerk, had been lost in the burning buildings—he threatened them with exposure, unless they made good to him the loss which he had sustained through their villainy. They laughed at him from their stronghold of respectability. He brought the case into court. Alas! for the pure, white statue of Justice which beautifies the desecrated chambers of the law. Banded together, with inexhaustible means of corruption at their command, the guilty were triumphant.

During this experience, Mr. Burton had got an inside view of life, in the marts, on exchange, in the halls of justice, and in the high and low places where men do congregate. It was as if, with the thread in his hand, which he had picked out, he unraveled the whole web of human iniquity. Burning with a sense of his individual wrongs, he could not look calmly on and see others similarly exposed; he grew fascinated with his labor of dragging the dangerous secrets of a community to the light. The more he called into play the peculiar faculties of his mind, which made him so successful a hunter on the paths of the guilty, the more marvelous became their development. He was like an Indian on the trail of his enemy—the bent grass, the broken twig, the evanescent dew—which, to the uninitiated, were "trifles light as air," to him were "proofs strong as Holy Writ."*

In this work he was actuated by no pernicious motives. Upright and humane, with a generous heart which pitied the innocent injured, his conscience would allow him no rest if he permitted crime, which he could see walking where others could not, to flourish unmolested in the sunshine made for better uses. He attached himself to the secret detective-police; only working up such cases as demanded the benefit of his rare powers.

Thus much of Mr. Burton had the chief of police revealed to me, during a brief interview in the morning; and this information, it may be supposed, had not lessened the fascinations which he had for me. The first thing he said, after the greetings of the day, when he came to my room, was,

"I have ascertained that our sewing-girl has one visitor, who is a constant one. There is a middle-aged woman, a nurse, who brings a child, now about a year old, every Sunday to spend half the day with her, when she does not go up to Blankville. On such occasions it is brought in the evening, some time during the week. It passes, so says the landlady, for the child of a cousin of Miss Sullivan's, who was married to a worthless young fellow, who deserted her within three months, and went off to the west; the mother died at its birth, leaving it entirely unprovided for, and Miss Sullivan, to keep it out of the charity-hospital, hired this woman to nurse it with her own baby, for which she pays her twelve shillings a week. She was, according to her story to the landlady, very much attached to her poor cousin, and could not cast off the little one for her sake."

"All of which may be true—"

---

* The first phrase is a direct quote from Iago, in act 2, scene 3, of Shakespeare's *Othello* (1603); the second is a slight misquotation from the same speech.

"Or false—as the case may turn."

"It certainly will not be difficult to ascertain if such a cousin really married and died, as represented. The girl has not returned to her work yet, I suppose?"

"She has not. Her absence gives the thing a bad look. Some connection she undoubtedly has with the case; as for how deeply she was involved in it, we will only know when we find out. Whoever the child's mother may have been, it seems evident, from the tenor of the landlady's story, that Miss Sullivan is much attached to it; it is safe to presume that, sooner or later, she will return to look after it. In her anxiety to reach the nest, she will fly into the trap. I have made arrangements by which I shall be informed if she appears at any of her former haunts, or at the house of the nurse. And now, I believe, I will go up to Blankville with you for a single day. I wish to see the ground of the tragedy, including Mr. Argyll's residence, the lawn, the library from which the money was abstracted, etc. A clear picture of these, carried in my mind, may be of use to me in unexpected ways. If we hear nothing of her in the village, I will return to the city, and await her reappearance here, which will be sure to occur within a month."

"Why within a month?"

"Women risk themselves, always, where a little child demands it. When the nurse finds the baby abandoned by its protector, and the wages unpaid, she will throw the charge upon the authorities. To prevent this, the girl will be back here to see after it. However, I hope we shall not be a month getting at what we want. It will be curious if we don't finish the whole of this melancholy business before that. And, by the way, you and young Argyll had quite a hide-and-seek race the other night!" and when I looked my astonishment at this remark, he only laughed. "It's my profession, you know," was his only explanation.

CHAPTER VI.

TWO LINKS IN THE CHAIN.

We went up to Blankville that evening, arriving late. I confess that I felt a thrill as of cold steel, and peered over my shoulder as we walked up the hill from the depot; but my companion was guilty of no such weakness. He kept as sharp a lookout as the light of a setting moon would permit, but it was only with a view to making himself familiar with the premises. We passed the Argyll mansion on our way to my boarding-place; it was too late to call; the lights were extinguished, except the faint one always left burning in the hall, and in two or three of the chambers. A rush of emotion oppressed me, as I drew near it; I would fain have laid my head against the pillars of the gateway and wept—tears such as a man may shed without reproach, when the woman he loves suffers. A growing anxiety possessed me to hear of Eleanor, no report of her mental or physical condition having reached me since that piercing shriek had announced the parting of her heart-strings when the strain of final separation came. I would have gone to the door a moment, to make inquiries, had I not inferred that a knock at that late hour must startle the family into nervous anticipations. The wan glimmer of the sinking moon struck under the branches of the silent trees, which stood about the dark mass of the stately mansion; not a breath stirred the crisp foliage. I heard a leaf, which loosened itself and rustled downward to the sod.

"It is a fine old place," remarked my companion, pausing because my own steps had come to a standstill.

I could not answer; he drew my arm into his, and we went on. Mr. Burton was growing to me in the shape of a friend, instead of a detective-officer.

That night I gave up my room to him, taking a hall-bedroom adjoining. After breakfast we went forth into the village, making our first call at the office. Mr. Argyll was there, looking thin and care-worn. He said that he was glad to have me back, for he felt unfit for business, and must let the mantle of labor drop upon my shoulders hereafter.

There had been an implied understanding, although it had never been definitely agreed upon, that I was to become a partner in the law with my teacher, when I had been admitted to practice. He had no one associated with him in his large and lucrative business, and he was now getting of an age to feel like retiring from at least the drudgery of the profession. That he designed to offer me the place open for some candidate, I had not doubted, for he had said as much many times. This prospect was an unusually fair one for so young a person as myself; it had urged me to patient study, to eager, ambitious effort. For I rightly deemed that a respect for my habits of mental application and a faith in my as yet undeveloped talents, had decided Mr. Argyll to offer me the contemplated encouragement. This had been another reason for James' dislike of me. He could not look favorably upon one who had, as it were, supplanted him. Instead of seeing that the fault lay in himself, and applying the remedy, he pursued the false course of considering me as a rival and an interloper. He, also, was a student in the office, and that he was a year behind me in his studies, and that, if he ever became a partner, it would be as a third member of the firm, was owing solely to his habitual indolence, which gave him a distaste for the dry details of a lawyer's work. What he would have liked would be to have his examination shirked over, to be admitted on the strength of his uncle's reputation, and then to be employed only in making brilliant oratorical efforts before the judge, jury and audience, after some one else had performed all the hard labor of the case, and placed his weapons ready at his hand.

If Mr. Argyll really intended to take the son of his old friend into the firm, instead of his nephew, it was simply on the prudent principles of business. I was to pass my examination on the first of November; this remark, then, which he made, as I observed how weary and unwell he looked, was not a surprise to me—it came only as a confirmation of my expectations.

At that moment James entered the office. There was a cloud on his brow, called up by his uncle's words; he hardly took time to shake hands with me, before he said,

"How is it, uncle, if you are worried and overworked, that you do not tell *me*? I should have been glad to help you. But it seems I am of no possible account nowadays."

Mr. Argyll smiled at this outbreak, as he would at the vexation of a child. A father could not be kinder to a son than he was to James; but to depend upon him for solid aid or comfort would be to lean upon a broken reed. The cloud upon the young man's face grew thunderous when he perceived Mr. Burton; although, if I had not been looking straight in his eyes, I should not have noticed it, for it passed instantly, and he stepped forward with frank cordiality, extending his hand, and saying,

"We did not know you were to come up. Indeed, we did not expect Richard back so soon. Has any thing transpired?"

"We hope that something will transpire, very soon," answered the detective. "You are very anxious, I see—and no wonder."

"No—no wonder! We are all of us perfectly absorbed—and, as for me, my heart bleeds for my friends, Mr. Burton."

"And your friends' hearts bleed for you."

Mr. Burton had a peculiar voice, searching, though not loud; I was talking with Mr. Argyll, and yet I heard this reply without listening for it; I did not comprehend it, and indeed, I let it in at one ear and out at the other, for I was asking about Eleanor.

"She is better than we hoped for," said the father, wiping the mist from his eyes which gathered at the mention of her name, "but, alas, Richard, that is not saying much. My girl never will be herself again. My pretty Eleanor will never be my sunshine any more. Not that her mind is shaken—that remains only too acutely sensitive. But her heart is broken. I can see that— broken, past mending. She has not left her bed since Henry was carried away; the doctor assures me there is nothing dangerous about her illness—only the natural weakness of the system after intense suffering, the same as if she had endured great physical pain. He says she will rally presently."

"If I could take her burden upon myself, I would ask no greater boon," I said.

My voice must have been very full of the feeling within me, for it made Mr. Argyll give me a wondering look; I think it was the first time he had a suspicion of the hopeless passion I had cherished for his daughter.

"We must all bear our own troubles," he said. "Poor Richard, I fear you have your own, like the rest of us."

When I again noticed what was passing between the other two, James was telling Mr. Burton, with great animation, of some information which had been lodged with the authorities of the village. I became absorbed in it, of course.

A respectable citizen of a town some thirty or forty miles beyond, on the railroad, hearing of the murder, had taken the trouble to come down to Blankville and testify to some things which had fallen under his observation on the night of the murder. He stated that he was a passenger on the Saturday afternoon train from New York; that the seat in front of his own, in the car, was occupied by a young gentleman, who, by the description since given, he knew must be Henry Moreland; that, as there were but few people in that car, he had given the more attention to those near him; that he was particularly attracted by the prepossessing appearance of the young gentleman, with whom he exchanged a few remarks with regard to the storm, and who informed him that he was going no further than Blankville.

"After we had been riding a while," said the witness—I do not give James' words in telling it, but his own, as I afterward read them in the sworn testimony—"I noticed a person who sat on the opposite side of the car, facing us. His forehead was bent on his hand, and he was looking out from under his fingers, at the young man in front of me. It was his sinister expression which compelled me to notice him. His small, glittering, black eyes were fixed upon my neighbor with a look which made me shudder. I smiled at myself for my own sensation—said to myself it was none of my business—that I was nervous—yet, in spite of my attempts to be unconcerned, I was continually compelled to look across at the individual of whose serpent-gaze the young gentleman himself appeared totally unconscious. If he had once met those eyes, I am certain he would have been on his guard—for I assert, without other proof than what afterward transpired, that there was *murder* in them, and that that person was Henry Moreland's murderer. I can not prove it—but my conviction is unalterable. I only wish, now, that I had yielded to my impulse to shake my unknown neighbor, and say to him—'See! there is an enemy! beware of him!' There was nothing but the man's look to justify such a proceeding, and of course I curbed my feelings.

"The man was a common-looking person, dressed in dark clothes; he wore a low-crowned felt hat, slouched down on his forehead; I do not remember about his hair, but his eyes were black, his complexion sallow. I noticed a scar across the back of the hand which he held over his eyes, as if it had sometime been cut across with a knife; also, that he had a large ring, with a red stone in it, on his little finger.

"When the cars stopped at Blankville, this person arose and followed Henry Moreland from the car. I saw him step off the platform behind him, which was the last I saw of either of them."

It may be imagined with what a thrill of fearful interest we listened to this account, and the thousand conjectures to which it gave rise.

"It can not be difficult," I exclaimed, "to find other witnesses to testify of this man."

We were assured by James that every effort had been made to get some trace of him. No person answering to the description was a resident of the village, and no one could be heard of as having been seen in the vicinity. Not a solitary lounger about the depot, or the hotel close at hand, could recall that he had seen such a stranger leave the cars; no such person had stopped at the hotel; even the conductor of the train could not be certain of such a passenger, though he had a dim recollection of a rough fellow in the car with Mr. Moreland—he had not observed where he left the train—thought his ticket was for Albany.

"But we do not despair of some evidence, yet," said Mr. Argyll.

"The New York police, not being able to do any thing further here, have gone home," continued James. "If such a villain lurks in New York, he will be found. That scar on the hand is a good point for identifying him—don't you think so, sir?" to Mr. Burton.

"Well—yes! unless it was put on for the purpose. It may have been done in red ocher, and washed off afterward. If the fellow was a practiced hand, as the skill and precision of the blow would imply, he will be up to all such tricks. If he had a real scar, he would have worn gloves on such an errand."

"You think so?" and James drew a long breath, probably of discouragement at this new statement of the case.

"I would like to go down to the depot, and along the docks for an hour," continued Mr. Burton, "if there's nothing else to be done immediately."

James politely insisted upon accompanying us.

"What the deuce did you bring another of those detectives up here for?" he asked me, *sotto voce*, at the first opportunity. "We've had a surfeit of them—they're regular bores! and this Burroughs or Burton, or whatever his name is, is the most disagreeable of them all. A conceited fellow—one of the kind I dislike, naturally."

"You mistake his character. He is intelligent and a gentleman."

"I wish you joy of his society," was the sneering reply.

Nevertheless, James favored us with his company during our morning's tour. One sole fact the detective ascertained in the course of his two hours' work. A fisherman had lost a small-boat during the storm of Saturday night. He had left it, fastened to its accustomed moorings, and, in the morning, found that the chain, which was old and rusty, had parted one of its links, probably by the extreme violence with which the wind had dashed the boat about. Mr. Burton had asked to see the remnant of the chain. It was still attached to the post around which it had been locked. An examination of the broken link showed that it was partly rusted away; but there were also marks upon it, as if a knife or chisel might have been used.

"I see my boy, Billy, a-tinkerin' with it," said the fisherman. "Like as not he's been a-usin' of it to whittle on. That boy breaks more knives'n his neck's wuth. He's goin' on nine, now, and he's had six jack-knives in as many months."

Mr. Burton stood, holding the chain in his hand, and looking up and down the river. His face glowed with a light which shone through from some inward fire. I, who had begun to watch his varying expressions with keen interest, saw that he was again becoming excited; but not in the same way as on that first evening of our meeting, when he grew so leonine.

He looked at the water and the sky, the fair shores and the dull dock, as if these mute witnesses were telling to him a tale which he read like a printed book. A few moments he stood thus in silence, his countenance illuminated by that wonderful intelligence. Then, saying that his researches were through with in this part of the village, we returned, almost in silence, to the office; for when this man was pondering the enigmas whose solution he was so certain to announce, sooner or later, he grew absorbed and taciturn.

Mr. Argyll made us go home with him to dinner. I knew that I should not see Eleanor; yet, even to be under the same roof with her, made me tremble. Mary, who was constantly in attendance upon her sister, would not appear at the table. She came down, for a moment, to greet me, and to thank me for my poor efforts. The dear child had changed some, like the rest of us. She could not look like any thing but the rosebud which she was—a fresh and pure young creature of sixteen summers—a rosebud drenched in dew—a little pale, with a quiver in her smile, and bright tears beading her eye-lashes, ready, at any moment, to drop. It was touching to see one naturally so joyous, subdued by the shadow which had fallen over the house. Neither of us could say much; our lips trembled when we spoke *her* name; so, after a moment's holding my hand, while the tears began to flow fast, Mary unclasped my fingers, and went upstairs. I saw Mr. Burton hide those blue-gray eyes of his in his handkerchief; my respect for him deepened as I felt that those eyes, sharp and penetrating as they were, were not too cold to warm with a sudden mist at the vision he had beheld.

"Ah!" murmured I to myself, "if he could see Eleanor!"

When dinner was over, Mr. Argyll went up to see his children, giving me permission to show the house and grounds to the detective. James went on the portico to smoke a cigar. Mr. Burton sat a short time in the library, taking an impression of it on his mind, examined the lock of the desk, and noticed the arrangement of the one window, which was a large bay-window opening to the floor and projecting over the flower-garden which lay behind the house and bordered the lawn to the right. It was about three feet to the ground, and although quite accessible, as a mode of entrance, to any one compelled to that resource, the window was not ordinarily used as a mode of ingress or egress. I had sometimes chased Mary, when she was not so old as now, and sent her flying through the open casement into the mignonette and violets beneath, and I after; but since we had both grown more sedate, such pranks were rare.

We then went out upon the lawn. I took my companion to the tree beneath which I had stood, when that dark figure had approached, and passed me, to crouch beneath the window from which the death-candles shone. From this spot, the bay-window was not visible, that being at the back of the house and this on the side. Mr. Burton looked carefully about him, walking all over the lawn, going up under the parlor windows, and thence pursuing his way into the garden and around to the bay-window. It was quite natural to search closely in this precinct for some mark or footsteps, some crushed flowers, or broken branches, or scratches upon the wall, left by the thief, if he or she had made his or her entrance at this spot. Going over the ground thus, inch by inch, I observed a bit of white lawn,* soiled and weather-beaten, lying under a rose-bush a few feet from the window. I picked it up. It was a woman's handkerchief, of fine lawn, embroidered along the edge with a delicate running vine, and a spray of flowers at the corner.

"One of the young ladies has dropped it, some time ago," I said, "or it has blown across from the kitchen grass-plot, where the linen is put out to dry."

Then I examined the discolored article more closely, and, involved in the graceful twinings of the spray of flowers, I saw worked the initials—"L. S."

"Leesy Sullivan," said my companion, taking it from my hand.

"It seems too dainty an article for her ownership," I said, at last, for, at first, I had been quite stupefied.

"A woman's vanity will compass many things beyond her means. This thing she has embroidered with her own needle—you remember, she is a proficient in the art."

"Yes, I remember. She may have lost it Sunday-night, during that visit which I observed; and the wind has blown it over into this spot."

"You forget that there has been no rain since that night. This handkerchief has been beaten into the grass and earth by a violent rain. A thorn upon this bush has pulled it from her pocket as she passed, and the rain has set its mark upon it, to be used as a testimony against her."

---

* Fine linen, resembling cambric.

"The evidence seems to conflict. She can not be a man and woman both."

"Why not?" was the quiet reply. "There may be a principal and an accomplice. A woman is a safer accomplice for a man than one of his own sex—and *vice versa*."

The face which I had seen, in its despair, the face of Leesy Sullivan, rose in my memory, full of passion, marked in every soft yet impressive lineament with slumbering power—"such a nature," I thought, "can be maddened into crime, but it will not consort with villainy."

Mr. Burton put the handkerchief in the inside pocket of his coat, and we returned into the house. He inquired the names of the servants, none of whose initials corresponded with those we had found, nor could I recall any lady visitors of the family to whom the handkerchief might belong by virtue of its inscription. There was not the shadow of a doubt but that it had been the property of the sewing-girl. Some errand, secret and unlawful, had brought her to these grounds, and under this window. We now considered it proper to show the handkerchief to Mr. Argyll, and relate to him our grounds of suspicion against the girl. Mary and James were admitted to the council. The former said that she remembered Miss Sullivan; that she had been employed in the family, for a few days at a time, on several different occasions, but none of them recent. "We liked her sewing very much, and wanted to engage her for the next six weeks," she added, with a sigh, "but on inquiring for her, learned that she was now employed in New York."

"She must, then, have been perfectly familiar with the arrangement of the house, and with the habits of the family; as for instance, at what hour you dined. She might enter while the family were at table, since, had she been surprised by the entrance of a servant, or other person, she could affect to have called on an errand, and to be waiting for the young ladies," remarked Mr. Burton.

The servants were then summoned, one at a time, and questioned as to whether they had observed any suspicious persons whatever about the house or grounds within a week. They were, of course, in a national state of high excitement, and immediately upon a question being put to them, answered every other imaginary case in the world but that, blessed themselves, called on the Virgin Mary, gave an account of all the beggars as called at the kitchen last year and the year afore, cried abundantly, and gave no coherent information.

"Ah, sure!" said Norah, the cook, "there was the blackin'-and-bluin' man* come around last Wednesday, and I tuk a bottle of the blue for the clothes. It's a poor mimiry I have, sure, since I came across the say. Afore that I could recollect beyond any thing, and the praste used to praise my rading. I think it was the tossin' an' rollin' ov the ship upsot my brain. It was Saturday, it wur, and oh, Lordy, it is setting me all of a trimble a-thinkin' of that day, and I see a little yeller dog a-stickin' his nose into the kitching door, which was open about half, and says I, there's vagabonds around sure, now, I knew by the dog, and I wint and looked out, and sure as me name's Norah, there was an old lame man wid a stick a-pretinding to look for rags an' bones in the alley to the stable, which I niver allows such about, as it's against the master's orthers, and I druv him off immajetly—and that, I think, was Saturday two weeks now, but I won't be sure; and I don't mind nobody else but the chany-woman,† wid her basket, which I don't think it could have been her as done any thin' bad, for she's been round rig'ler, for a good while, and is a

---

* A laborer who did cleaning and polishing. "Bluing" was also used to bleach clothing.

---

† A "China-woman," surely, who commonly took up the trade of laundry.

dacent-spoken body that I've had some dalin's wid myself. I sowld her my old plaid gown for the match-box of ebony that sits on the kitching-mantel now, and oh dear! but my heart's dead broke, sure! Margaret and I daren't set in the kitching of nights no more, unless Jim's there, an' I've woke up scr'amins; two nights now—och hone! and if I'd seed any thing, I'd a told it long afore, which I wish I had, seein' you've axed me, sir. It don't do no good a-cooking delicacies which nobody eats no longer—I wish I had never come to Amyriky, to see poor Miss Eleanor so tuk down!" and having relieved herself of the sympathy which she had been aching to express, without the opportunity, she threw her apron over her head, and sobbed after the manner of her people.

Margaret's testimony was no more to the point than Norah's. Mr. Burton let each one go on after her own heart, putting up with the tedious circumlocution, in the hope of some kernel of wheat in the bushel of chaff.

After a deluge of tears and interjections, Maggie did finally come out with a statement which arrested the attention of her listeners.

"I've never seen none gawking about as didn't belong here— not a living sowl. The howly Virgin prevint that iver I should see what Jim did—it wasn't a human being at all, but a wraith, and he seen it that very night. He niver told us of it, till the Tuesday night, as we sot talking about the funeral, and it frightened us so, we niver slept a wink till morning. Poor Jim's worried with it, too; he pretinds he isn't afraid of the livin' nor dead, but it's no shame to the best to stand in awe of the sperits, and I see he's backward about going about the place, alone, after dark, and no wonder! Sure, he saw a ghost!"

"What was it like?"

"Sure, you'd best call him, and let him describe it for

hisself—it'll make your blood run cold to think of sich things in a Christian family."

Jim was summoned. His story, weeded out, was this: On Saturday evening, after tea, his mistress, Miss Eleanor, had asked him to go to the post-office for the evening mail. It was very dark and rainy. He lighted the lantern. As he went out the back gate, he stopped a minute and lifted his lantern to take a look about the premises, to see if there was any thing left out which ought to be taken in from the storm. As he waved the light about, he saw something in the flower-garden, about six feet from the bay-window. It had the appearance of a woman; its face was white, its hair hung down on its shoulders; it stood quite still in the rain, just as if the water was not coming down by bucketfuls. It had very large, bright eyes, which shone when the candle threw the light on them, as if they had been made of fire. He was so frightened that he let his lantern fall, which did not happen to extinguish the candle, but when he lifted it up again, the wraith had vanished. He felt very queer about it, at the time; and next day, when the bad news came, he knew it was a warning. They often had such in the old country.

We did not undeceive Jim as to the character of the phantom. With the assurance that it probably would not come again, since its mission had been accomplished, and a caution not to make the girls in the kitchen too nervous about it, we dismissed him.

CHAPTER VII.
ELEANOR.

One week, another—a third—a fourth, passed by. Our village was as if it had never been shaken by a fierce agitation. Already the tragedy was as if it had not been, except to the household whose fairest flower it had blighted. People no longer looked over their shoulders as they walked; the story now only served to enliven the history of the little place, when it was told to a stranger.

Every thing that human energy could accomplish had been done to track the murder to its origin; yet not one step had been gained since we sat, that Wednesday afternoon, in the parlor, holding a council over the handkerchief. Young and healthful as I was, I felt my spirits breaking down under my constant, unavailing exertions. The time for my examination came, which could not be unsuccessful, I had so long been thoroughly prepared, but I had lost my keen interest in this era of my life, while my ambition grew torpid. To excel in my profession had become, for the time, quite the secondary object of my life; my brain grew feverish with the harassment of restless projects—the recoil of thwarted ideas. There was not one in the family group (always excepting that unseen and cloistered sufferer) who betrayed the wear-and-tear of our trouble so much as I. James remarked once that I was improved by losing some of my boyish ruddiness—I was "toning down," he said. On another occasion, with that Mephistophiles* smile of his, he observed that it must be that I was after the handsome rewards—the sum-total would make a comfortable setting-out for a person just starting in the world.

I do not think he wished to quarrel with me; he was always doubly pleasant after any such waspish sting; he was naturally satirical, and he could not always curb his inclination to be so at my expense.

In the mean time an impression grew upon me that he was watching me—with what intent I had not yet decided.

In all this time I had not seen Eleanor. She had recovered from her illness, so as to be about her room, but had not yet joined the family at meals. I went frequently to the house; it had been a second home to me ever since I left the haunts of my boyhood and the old red-brick mansion, with the Grecian portico, whose massive pillars were almost reflected in the waters of Seneca lake, so close to the shore did it stand—and where my mother still resided, amidst the friends who had known her in the days of her happiness—that is, of my father's life.

With the same freedom as of old, I went and came to and from Mr. Argyll's. I was not apprehensive of intruding upon Eleanor, because she never left her apartments; while Mary, gay young creature, troubled and grieved as she was, could not stay always in the shadow. At her age, the budding blooms of womanhood require sunshine. She was lonely, and when she left her sister to the solitude which Eleanor preferred, she wanted company, she said. James was gloomy, and would not try to amuse her—not

---

* Usually spelled "Mephistopheles," this is the demon or devil with whom Faust dealt in Johann Wolfgang von Goethe's play *Faust* (1808, 1832). In Christopher Marlowe's *The Tragical History of Doctor Faustus* (1604), the devil is Lucifer.

that she wanted to be amused, but every thing was so sad, and she felt so timid, it was a relief to have any one to talk to, or even to look at. I felt very sorry for her. It became a part of my duty to bring her books, and sometimes to read them aloud, through the lengthening evenings; at others to while away the time with a game of chess. The piano was abandoned out of respect for the mourner in the chamber above. Carols would rise to Mary's lips, as they rise from a lark at sunrise, but she always broke them off, drowning them in sighs. Her elastic spirit constantly asserted itself, while the tender sympathy of a most warm, affectionate nature as constantly depressed it. She could not speak of Eleanor without tears; and for this my heart blessed her. She did not know of the choking in my own throat which often prevented me from speaking, when I ought, perhaps, to be uttering words of help or comfort.

James was always hovering about like a restless spirit. It had been one of his indolent habits to spend a great deal of time with the young ladies; and now he was forever in the house; but so uneasy, so irritable—as Mary said—he was not an agreeable companion. He would pick up a book in the library; in five minutes he would throw it down, and walk twice or thrice up and down the hall, out upon the piazza, back into the parlor, and stand looking out of the windows—then to the library and take up another book. He had the air of one always listening—always waiting. He had, too, a kind of haunted look, if my reader can imagine what that is. I guessed that he was listening and waiting for Eleanor—whom, like myself, he had not seen since the Sunday so memorable; but the other look I did not seek to explain.

There had been a light fall of snow. It seemed as if winter had come in November. But in a few hours this aspect vanished; the snow melted like a dream; the zenith was a deep, molten blue, transfused with the pale sunshine, which is only seen in Indian-summer; a tender mist circled the horizon with a zone of purple. I could not stay in the office that afternoon, so infinitely sad, so infinitely lovely. I put aside the law-papers which I had been arranging for a case in which I was first to appear before a jury and make my maiden argument. The air, soft as that of summer and scented with the indescribable perfume of perishing leaves, came to me through the open window, with a message calling me abroad; I took up my hat, stepped out upon the pavement, and wandering along the avenue in the direction of the house, went in upon the lawn. I had thought to go out into the open country for a long walk; but my heart drew me and held me here. The language of all beauty, and of infinity itself, is love. The divine melancholy of music, the deep tranquillity of summer noons, the softened splendor of autumn days, haunting one with ineffable joy and sadness—what is the name of all this varying demonstration of beauty, but love?

I walked beneath the trees, slowly, my feet nestling among the thickly-strewn leaves, and pressing a faint aroma from the moist earth. To and fro for a long time I rambled, thinking no tangible thoughts, but my soul silently filling, all the time, like a fountain fed by secret springs. To the back of the lawn, extending around and behind the flower-garden, was a little ascent, covered by a grove of elms and maples, in the midst of which was a summer-house which had been a favorite resort of Eleanor's. Hither I finally bent my steps, and seating myself, looked musingly upon the lovely prospect around and beneath me. The rustic temple opened toward the river, which was visible from here, rolling in its blue splendor across the exquisite landscape. There is a fascination in water which will keep the eyes fixed upon it through hours of reverie; I sat there, mindful of the near mountains, the purple mist, the white ships, the

busy village, but gazing only at the blue ripples forever slipping away from the point of my observation. My spirit exhaled
like the mist and ascended in aspiration. My grief aspired, and
arose in passionate prayers to the white throne of the eternal
justice—it arose in tears, etherealized and drawn up by the
rays from the one great source and sun—the spirit of Love. I
prayed and wept for *her*. No thought of myself mingled with
these emotions.

Suddenly a slight chill fell upon me. I started to perceive
that the sun had set. A band of orange belted the west. As the
sun dropped behind the hills the moon came up in the east. It
seemed as if her silver light frosted what it touched; the air grew
sharp; a thin, white cloud spread itself over the river. I had sat
there long enough, and I was forcing myself to a consciousness
of the fact, when I saw one coming through the flower-garden
and approaching the summer-house.

My blood paused in my veins when I saw that it was Eleanor.
The sunset yet lingered, and the cold moonlight shone full on
her face. I remembered how I had seen her, that last time but
one, glowing and flushing in triumphant beauty, attired with the
most skilled coquetry of a young, beloved woman, who is glad
of her charms because another prizes them.

Now she came along the lonesome path, between the withered flower-beds, clothed in deepest black, walking with a feeble
step, one small white hand holding the sable shawl across her
chest, a long crape vail thrown over her head, from which her
face looked out, white and still.

A pang like that of death transfixed me, as I gazed at her. Not
one rose left in the garden of her young life! The ruin through
which she walked was not so complete—but this garden would
resurrect itself in the months of another spring—while for her
there was no spring on this side of the grave.

Eleanor.

Slowly she threaded her way, with bent gaze, through the garden, out upon the hillside, and up to the little rustic temple in which she had spent so many happy hours with him. When she had reached the grassy platform in front of it, she raised her eyes and swept a glance around upon the familiar scene. There were no tears in her blue eyes, and her lips did not quiver. It was not until she had encircled the horizon with that quiet, beamless look, that she perceived me. I rose to my feet, my expression only doing reverence to her sorrow, for I had no words.

She held out her hand, and as I took it, she said with gentleness—as if her sweetness must excuse the absence of her former smiles,

"Are you well, Richard? You look thin. Be careful of yourself—is it not too chilly for you to be sitting here at this hour?"

I pressed her hand, and turned away, vainly endeavoring to command my voice. *I* had changed!—but it was like Eleanor to put herself aside and remember others.

"Nay, do not go," she said, as she saw that I was leaving her out of fear of intruding upon her visit, "I shall remain here but a few moments, and I will lean upon your arm back to the house. I am not strong, and the walk up the hill has tired me. I wanted to see you, Richard. I thought some of coming down-stairs a little while this evening. I want to thank you."

The words were just whispered, and she turned immediately and looked away at the river. I understood her well. She wanted to thank me for the spirit which had prompted me in my earnest, though unsuccessful efforts. And coming down to the family group a little while in the evening, that was for Mary's sake, and her poor father's. Her own light had expired, but she did not wish to darken the hearthstone any more than was unavoidable. She sunk down upon the seat I had vacated, remaining motionless, looking upon the river and the sky. After a time, with a long, tremulous sigh, she arose to go. A gleam from the west fell upon a single violet which, protected from the frost by the projecting roof, smiled up at us, near the door of the summer-house. With a wild kind of passion breaking through her quiet, Eleanor stooped, gathered it, pressed it to

her lips, and burst into tears—it was her favorite flower*—
Henry's favorite.

It was agony to see her cry, yet better, perhaps, than such
marble repose. She was too weak to bear this sudden shock
alone; she leaned upon my shoulder, every sob which shook her
frame echoed by me. Yes! I am not ashamed to confess it! When
manhood is fresh and unsullied, its tears are not wrung out in
those single drops of mortal anguish which the rock gives forth
when time and the foot of the world have hardened it. I could still
remember when I had kissed my mother, and wept my boyish
troubles well upon her breast. I should have been harder than the
nether millstone, had I not wept tears with Eleanor then.

I mastered myself in order to assist her to regain compo-
sure, for I was alarmed lest the violence of her emotion should
break down the remnant of her frail strength. She, too, struggled
against the storm, soon growing outwardly calm, and with the
violet pressed to her bosom with one hand, with the other she
clung to my arm, and we returned to the house, where they were
already looking for Eleanor.

Under the full light of the hall-lamp we encountered James.
It was his first meeting with his cousin as well as mine. He gave
her a quick, penetrating look, held out his hand, his lips moved
as if striving to form a greeting. It was evident that the change
was greater than he expected; he dropped his hand, before her
fingers had touched it, and rushing past us through the open
door, he closed it behind him, remaining out until long after tea.

When he came in, Eleanor had retired to her chamber, and
Mary brought him the cup of tea which she had kept hot for
him.

---

* On page 36, the narrator identifies Eleanor's favorite flowers as pansies. Technically,
violets and pansies are species of the same genus *Viola*, but perhaps the narrator did not
know Eleanor as well as he thought!

"You are a good girl, Mary," he said, drinking it hastily, as if to get rid of it. "I hope nobody will ever make you look like *that!* I thought broken hearts were easily mended—that girls usually had theirs broken three or four times, and patched them up again—but I have changed my mind."

That gloomy look, which Mary declared she dreaded, clouded his face again. His countenance was most variable; nothing could excel it in glitter and brilliant color when he was in his pleasing mood, but when sullen or sad, it was sallow and lusterless. Thus it looked that evening. But I must close this chapter now and here—it is consecrated to that meeting with the object of my sorrow and adoration, and I will not prolong it with the details of other events.

CHAPTER VIII.
THE HAUNTED GRAVE.

When I returned to my boarding-house that same evening, I found a telegram awaiting me from Mr. Burton, asking me to come down to the city in the morning. I went down by the earliest train, and, soon after ringing the bell at the door of his private residence in Twenty-third street, a servant ushered me into the library, where I found the master of the house so absorbed in thought, as he sat before the grate with his eyes bent upon the glowing coals, that he did not observe my entrance until I spoke his name. Springing to his feet, he shook me heartily by the hand; we had already become warm personal friends.

"You are early," he said, "but so much the better. We will have the more time for business."

"Have you heard any thing?" was my first question.

"Well, no. Don't hope that I have called you here to satisfy you with any positive discoveries. The work goes on slowly. I was never so baffled but once before; and then, as now, there was a woman in the case. A cunning woman will elude the very Prince of Lies, himself, to say nothing of honest men like us. She has been after the child."

"She has?"

"Yes. And has taken it away with her. And now I know no more of her whereabouts than I did before. There! You must certainly feel like trusting your case to some sharper person to work up"—he looked mortified as he said it.

Before I go further I must explain to my reader just how far the investigation into the acts and hiding-place of Leesy Sullivan had proceeded. Of course we had called upon her aunt in Blankville, and approached the question of the child with all due caution. She had answered us frankly enough, at first—that Leesy had a cousin who lived in New York, whom she was much attached to, and who was dead, poor thing! But the moment we intruded the infant into the conversation, she flew into a rage, asked if "we'd come there to insult a respectable widdy, as wasn't responsible for what others did?" and wouldn't be coaxed or threatened into any further speech on the subject, fairly driving us out of the room and (I regret to add) down the stairs with the broomstick. As we could not summon her into court and compel her to answer, at that time, we were compelled to "let her alone." One thing, however, became apparent at the interview—that there was shame or blame, or at least a family quarrel, connected with the child.

After that, in New York, Mr. Burton ascertained that there had been a cousin, who had died, but whether she had been married, and left a babe, or not, was still a matter of some doubt.

He had spent over a week searching for Leesy Sullivan, in the vicinity of Blankville, at every intermediate station between that and New York, and throughout the city itself, assisted by scores of detectives, who all of them had her photograph,* taken from a likeness which Mr. Burton had found in her deserted room

---

* Photography, primarily in the form of daguerreotypes, was still far from common at this time, and almost exclusively shot in a studio with the subjects immobilized—even the slightest movement would blur the image.

at her boarding-place. This picture must have been taken more than a year previous, as it looked younger and happier; the face was soft and round, the eyes melting with warmth and light, and the rich, dark hair dressed with evident care. Still, Leesy bore resemblance enough to her former self, to make her photograph an efficient aid. Yet not one trace of her had been chanced upon since I, myself, had seen her fly away at the mention of the word which I had purposely uttered, and disappear over the wooded hill. We had nearly made up our minds that she had committed suicide; we had searched the shore for miles in the vicinity of Moreland villa, and had fired guns over the water; but if she had hidden herself in those cold depths, she had done it most effectually.

The gardener's wife, at the villa, had kept vigilant watch, as I had requested, but she had never any thing to report—the sewing-girl came no more to haunt the piazza or the summer-house. Finally, Mr. Burton had given over active measures, relying simply upon the presence of the child in New York, to bring back the protectress into his nets, if indeed she was still upon earth. He said rightly, that if she were concealed and had any knowledge of the efforts made to discover her, the surest means of hastening her reappearance would be to apparently relinquish all pursuit. He had a person hired to watch the premises of the nurse constantly; a person who took a room next to hers in the tenement-house where she resided, apparently employed in knitting children's fancy woolen garments, but really for the purpose of giving immediate notification should the guardian of the infant appear upon the scene. In the mean time he was kept informed of the sentiments of the nurse, who had avowed her intention of throwing the babe upon the authorities, if its board was not paid at the end of the month. "Hard enough," she avowed it was, "to get the praties* for the mouths of her own chilther; and the little girl was growing large now. The milk wouldn't do at all, at all, but she must have her praties and her bit bread wid the rest."

In answer to these complaints, the wool-knitter had professed such an interest in the innocent little thing, that, sooner than allow it to go to the alms-house, or to the orphan asylum, or any other such place, she would take it to her own room, and share her portion with it, when the nurse's month was up, until it was certain that the aunt was not coming to see after it, she said.

With this understanding between them, the two women got along finely together; little Norah, just toddling about, was a pretty child, and her aunt had not spared stitches in making up her clothes, which were of good material, and ornamented with lavish tucks and embroidery. She was often, for half a day at a time, in the room with the new tenant, when her nurse was out upon errands, or at work; and the former sometimes took her out in her arms for a breath of air upon the better streets. Mr. Burton had seen little Norah several times; he thought she resembled Miss Sullivan, though not strikingly. She had the same eyes, dark and bright.

Two days before Mr. Burton telegraphed for me to come down to New York, Mrs. Barber, the knitting detective, was playing with the child in her own room. It was growing toward night, and the nurse was out getting her Saturday afternoon supplies at Washington Market; she did not expect her back for at least an hour. Little Norah was in fine spirits, being delighted with a blue-and-white hood which her friend had manufactured for her curly head. As they frolicked together, the door opened, a young woman came in, caught the child to her breast, kissed

---

* Potatoes.

it, and cried. "An-nee—an-nee," lisped the baby—and Mrs. Barber, slipping out, with the excuse that she would go for the nurse, who was at a neighbor's, jumped into a car, and rode up to Twenty-third street. In half an hour Mr. Burton was at the tenement-house; the nurse had not yet returned from market, and the bird had flown, carrying the baby with her. He was sufficiently annoyed at this *dénouement*. In the arrangements made, the fact of the nurse being away had not been contemplated; there was no one to keep on the track of the fugitive while the officer was notified. One of the children said that the lady had left some money for mother; there was, lying on the table, a sum which more than covered the arrears due, and a note of thanks. But the baby, with its little cloak and its new blue hood, had vanished. Word was dispatched to the various offices, and the night spent in looking for the two; but there is no place like a great city for eluding pursuit; and up to the hour of my arrival at Mr. Burton's he had learned nothing.

All this had fretted the detective; I could see it, although he did not say as much. He who had brought hundreds of accomplished rogues to justice did not like to be foiled by a woman. Talking on the subject with me, as we sat before the fire in his library, with closed doors, he said the most terrible antagonist he had yet encountered had been a woman—that her will was a match for his own, yet he had broken with ease the spirits of the boldest men.

"However," he added, "Miss Sullivan is not a woman of that stamp. If *she* has committed a crime, she has done it in a moment of passion, and remorse will kill her, though the vengeance of the law should never overtake her. But she is subtle and elusive. It is not reason that makes her cunning, but feeling. With man it would be reason; and as I could follow the course of his argument, whichever path it took, I should soon overtake it. But a woman, working from a passion, either of hate or love, will sometimes come to such novel conclusions as to defy the sharpest guesses of the intellect. I should like, above all things, a quiet conversation with that girl. And I will have it, some day."

The determination with which he avowed himself, showed that he had no idea of giving up the case. A few other of his observations I will repeat:

He said that the blow which killed Henry Moreland was given by a professional murderer, a man, without conscience or remorse, probably a hireling. A woman may have tempted, persuaded, or paid him to do the deed; if so, the guilt rested upon her in its awful weight; but no woman's hand, quivering with passion, had driven that steady and relentless blow. It was not given by the hand of jealousy—it was too coldly calculated, too firmly executed—no passion, no thrill of feeling about it.

"Then you think," said I, "that Leesy Sullivan robbed the family whose happiness she was about to destroy, to pay some villain to commit the murder?"

"It looks like it," he answered, his eye dropping evasively.

I felt that I was not fully in the detective's confidence; there was something working powerfully in his mind, to which he gave me no clue; but I had so much faith in him that I was not offended by his reticence. Anxious as I was, eager, curious—if it suits to call such a devouring fire of longing as I felt, curiosity—he must have known that I perceived his reservations; if so, he had his own way of conducting matters, from which he could not diverge for my passing benefit. Twelve o'clock came, as we sat talking before the fire, which gave a genial air to the room, though almost unnecessary, the "squaw winter" of the previous morning being followed by another balmy and sunlit day. Mr. Burton rung for lunch to be brought in where we were; and while we sipped the strong coffee, and helped ourselves to the contents of the tray, the servant being dismissed, my host made a proposition which had evidently been on his mind all the morning.

I was already so familiar with his personal surroundings, as to know that he was a widower, with two children; the eldest, a boy of fifteen, away at school; the second, a girl of eleven, of delicate health, and educated at home, so far as she studied at all, by a day-governess. I had never seen this daughter—Lenore, he called her—but I could guess, without particular shrewdness, that his heart was wrapped up in her. He could not mention her name without a glow coming into his face; her frail health appeared to be the anxiety of his life. I could hear her, now, taking a singing-lesson in a distant apartment, and as her pure voice rose clear and high, mounting and mounting with airy steps the difficult scale, I listened delightedly, making a picture in my mind of the graceful little creature such a voice should belong to.

Her father was listening, too, with a smile in his eye, half forgetful of his coffee. Presently he said, in a low voice, speaking at first with some reluctance,

"I sent for you to-day, more particularly to make you the confidential witness of an experiment than any thing else. You hear my Lenore singing now—has she not a sweet voice? I have told you how delicate her health is. I discovered, by chance, some two or three years since, that she had peculiar attributes. She is an excellent clairvoyant. When I first discovered it, I made use of her rare faculty to assist me in my more important labors; but I soon discovered that it told fearfully upon her health. It seemed to drain the slender stream of vitality nearly dry. Our physician told me that I must desist, entirely, all experiments of the kind with her. He was peremptory about it, but he had only need to caution me. I would sooner drop a year out of my shortening future than to take one grain from that increasing strength which I watch from day to day with deep solicitude. She is my only girl, Mr. Redfield, and the image of her departed mother. You must not wonder if I am foolish about my Lenore. For eighteen months I have not exercised my power over her to place her in the trance state, or whatever it is, in which, with the clue in her hand, she will unwind the path to more perplexed labyrinths than those of the fair one's bower. And I tell you, solemnly, that if, by so doing, she could point out pots of gold, or the secrets of diamond mines, I would not risk her slightest welfare, by again exhausting her recruiting energies. Nevertheless, so deeply am I interested in the tragedy to which you have called my attention—so certain am I that I am on the eve of the solution of the mystery—and such an act of justice and righteousness do I deem it that it should be exposed in its naked truth before those who have suffered from the crime—that I have resolved to place Lenore once more in the clairvoyant state, for the purpose of ascertaining the hiding-place of Leesy Sullivan, and I have sent for you to witness the result."

This announcement took away the remnant of my appetite. Mr. Burton rung to have the tray removed, and to bid the servant tell Miss Lenore, as soon as she had lunched, to come to the library. We had but a few minutes to wait. Presently we heard a light step; her father cried, "Come in!" in answer to her knock, and a lovely child entered, greeting me with a mingled air of grace and timidity—a vision of sweetness and beauty more perfect than I could have anticipated. Her golden hair waved about her slender throat, in glistening tendrils. Seldom do we see such hair, except upon the heads of infants—soft, lustrous, fine, floating at will, and curled at the end in little shining rings. Her eyes were a celestial blue—celestial, not only because of the pure heavenliness of their color, but because you could not look into them without thinking of angels. Her complexion was the most exquisite possible, fair, with a flush as of sunset-light on the cheeks—too transparent for perfect health, showing the wandering of the delicate veins in the temples. Her blue dress, with its fluttering sash, and the little jacket of white cashmere which shielded her neck and arms, were all dainty, and in keeping with the wearer. She did not have the serene air of a seraph, though she looked like one; nor the listless manner of an invalid. She gave her father a most winning, childish smile, looking full of joy to think he was at home, and had sent for her. She was so every way charming that I held out my arms to kiss her, and she, with the instinct of children, who perceive who their real lovers are, gave me a willing yet shy embrace. Mr. Burton looked pleased as he saw how satisfactory was the impression made by his Lenore.

Placing her in a chair before him, he put a photograph of Miss Sullivan in her hand.

"Father wants to put his little girl to sleep again," he said, gently.

An expression of unwillingness just crossed her face; but she smiled, instantly, looking up at him with the faith of affection which would have placed her life in his keeping, and said, "Yes, papa," in assent.

He made a few passes over her; when I saw their effect, I did not wonder that he shrunk from the experiment—my surprise was rather that he could be induced to make it, under any circumstances. The lovely face became distorted as with pain; the little hands twitched—so did the lips and eyelids. I turned away, not having fortitude to witness any thing so jarring to my sensibilities. When I looked again, her countenance had recovered its tranquillity; the eyes were fast closed, but she appeared to ponder upon the picture which she held.

"Do you see the person now?"

"Yes, papa."

"In what kind of a place is she?"

"She is in a small room; it has two windows. There is no carpet on the floor. There is a bed and a table, a stove and some chairs. It is in the upper story of a large brick house, I do not know in what place."

"What is she doing?"

"She is sitting near the back window; it looks out on the roofs of other houses; she is holding a pretty little child on her lap."

"She must be in the city," remarked Mr. Burton, aside; "the large house and the congregated roofs would imply it. Can you not tell me the name of the street?"

"No, I can not see it. I was never in this place before. I can see water, as I look out of the window. It appears like the bay; and I see plenty of ships, but there is some green land across the water, besides distant houses."

"It must be somewhere in the suburbs, or in Brooklyn. Are there no signs on the shops, which you can read, as you look out?"

"No, papa."

"Well, go down the stairs, and out upon the street, and tell me the number of the house."

"It is No.—," she said, after a few moments' silence.

"Go along until you come to a corner, and read me the name of the street."

"Court street," she answered, presently.

"It is in Brooklyn," exclaimed the detective, triumphantly. "There is nothing now to prevent us going straight to the spot. Lenore, go back now, to the house; tell us on which floor is this room, and how situated."

Again there was silence while she retraced her steps.

"It is on the fourth floor, the first door to the left, as you reach the landing."

Lenore began to look weary and exhausted; the sweat broke out on her brow, and she panted as if fatigued with climbing flights of stairs. Her father, with a regretful air, wiped her forehead, kissing it tenderly as he did so. A few more of those cabalistic touches, followed by the same painful contortions of those beautiful features, and Lenore was herself again. But she was pale and languid; she drooped against her father's breast, as he held her in his arms, the color faded from her cheeks, too listless to smile in answer to his caresses. Placing her on the sofa, he took from a nook in his secretary a bottle of old port, poured out a tiny glassful, and gave to her. The wine revived her almost instantly; the smiles and bloom came back, though she still seemed exceedingly weary.

"She will be like a person exhausted by a long journey, or great labor, for several days," said Mr. Burton, as I watched the child. "It cost me a pang to make such a demand upon her; I hope it will be the last time—at least until she is older and stronger than now."

"I should think the application of electricity would restore some of the vitality which has been taken from her," I suggested.*

"I shall try it this evening," was his reply; "in the mean time, if we intend to benefit by the sacrifice of my little Lenore, let us lose no time. Something may occur to send the fugitive flying again. And now, my dear little girl, you must lie down a while this afternoon, and be careful of yourself. You shall dine with us to-night, if you are not too tired, and we shall bring you some flowers—a bouquet from old John's conservatory, sure."

---

* Electricity, usually in the form of electrical belts, was widely touted throughout the second half of the nineteenth century as a virtual panacea for a wide variety of ills, including impotence, sterility, pain relief, and almost any imaginable complaint. Devices to provide electrical stimulation were widely sold, and quack practitioners who sold these remedies abounded.

Committing his darling to the housekeeper's charge, with many instructions and warnings, and a lingering look which betrayed his anxiety, Mr. Burton was soon ready, and we departed, taking a stage for Fulton Ferry a little after one o'clock.

About an hour and a quarter brought us to the brick house on Court street, far out toward the suburbs, which had the number indicated upon it. No one questioned our coming, it being a tenement-house, and we ascended a long succession of stairs, until we came to the fourth floor, and stood before the door on the left-hand side. I trembled a little with excitement. My companion, laying his hand firmly on the knob, was arrested by finding the door locked. At this he knocked; but there was no answer to his summons. Amid the assortment of keys which he carried with him, he found one to fit the lock; in a moment the door stood open, and we entered to meet—blank solitude!

The room had evidently been deserted but a short time, and by some one expecting to return. There was a fire covered down in the stove, and three or four potatoes in the oven to be baked for the humble supper. There was no trunk, no chest, no clothing in the room, only the scant furniture which Lenore had described, a few dishes in the cupboard, and some cooking utensils, which had been rented, probably, with the room. On the table were two things confirmatory of the occupants—a bowl, containing the remains of a child's dinner of bread-and-milk, and a piece of embroidery—a half-finished collar.

At Mr. Burton's request I went down to the shop on the first floor, and inquired in what direction the young woman with the child had gone, and how long she had been out.

"She went, maybe, half an hour ago; she took the little girl out for a walk, I think. She told me she'd be back before supper, when she stopped to pay for a bit of coal, and to have it carried up."

I returned with this information.

"I'm sorry, now, that we inquired," said the detective; "that fellow will be sure to see her first, and tell her that she has had callers; that will frighten her at once. I must go below, and keep my watch from there."

"If you do not care for a second person to watch with you, I believe I will go on to Greenwood. We are so near it, now, and I would like to visit poor Henry's grave."

"I do not need you at all now; only, do not be absent too long. When I meet this Leesy Sullivan, whom I have not yet seen, you remember, I want a long talk with her. The last object I have is to frighten her; I shall seek to soothe her instead. If I can once meet her face to face, and voice to voice, I believe I can tame the antelope, or the lioness, whichever she turns out to be. I do not think I shall have to coerce her— not even if she is guilty. If she is guilty she will give herself up. I may even take her home to dinner with us," he added, with a smile. "Don't shudder, Mr. Redfield; we often dine in company with murderers—sometimes when we have only our friends and neighbors with us. I assure you I have often had that honor!"

His grim humor was melancholy to me—but who could wonder that a man of Mr. Burton's peculiar experience should be touched with cynicism? Besides, I felt that there was more in the inner meaning of his words than appeared upon their outer surface. I left him, sitting in a sheltered corner of the shop below, in a position where he could command the street and the entrance-hall without being himself observed, and making himself friendly with the busy little man behind the counter, of whom he had already purchased a pint of chestnuts. It would be as well that I should be out of the way. Miss Sullivan knew me, and might take alarm at some distant glimpse of me, while Mr.

Burton's person must be unknown to her, unless she had been the better detective of the two, and marked him when he was ignorant of her vicinity.

Stepping into a passing car, in a few minutes I had gone from the city of the living to the city of the dead. Beautiful and silent city! There the costly and gleaming portals, raised at the entrance of those mansions, tell us the name and age of the inhabitants, but the inhabitants themselves we never behold. Knock as loud and long as we may at those marble doors, cry, entreat, implore, they hold themselves invisible. Never more are they "at home" to us. We, who once were never kept waiting, must go from the threshold now, without a word of welcome. City of the dead—to which that city of the living must soon remove—who is there that can walk thy silent streets without a prescience of the time when he, too, will take up his abode in thee for ever? Strange city of solitude! where thousands whose homes are ranged side by side, know not one the other, and give no greeting to the pale new-comers.

With meditations like these, only far too solemn for words, I wandered through the lovely place, where, still, summer seemed to linger, as if loth to quit the graves she beautified. With Eleanor and Henry in my heart, I turned in the direction of the family burial-plot, wishing that Eleanor were with me on that glorious day, that she might first behold his grave under such gentle auspices of light, foliage and flowers—for I knew that she contemplated a pilgrimage to this spot, as soon as her strength would warrant the attempt.

I approached the spot by a winding path; the soft plash of a fountain sounded through a little thicket of evergreens, and I saw the gleam of the wide basin into which it fell; a solitary bird poured forth a mournful flood of lamentation from some high branch not far away. It required but little aid of fancy to hear in that "melodious madness"* the cry of some broken heart, haunting, in the form of this bird, the place of the loved one's sleep.

There were other wanderers than myself in the cemetery; a funeral train was coming through the gate as I passed in, and I met another within a few steps; but in the secluded path where I now walked I was alone. "With the slow steps of one who meditates sad things, I approached Henry's grave. Gliding away by another devious path, I saw a female figure.

"It is some other mourner, whom I have disturbed from her vigil by some of these tombs," I thought—"or, perchance, one who was passing further on before reaching the goal of her grief,"—and with this I dismissed her from my mind, having had, at the best, only an indistinct glimpse of the woman, and the momentary flutter of her garments as she passed beyond a group of tall shrubs and was lost to view.

The next moment I knelt by the sod which covered that young and noble form. Do not think me extravagant in my emotions. I was not so—only overpowered, always, by intense sympathy with the sufferers by that calamity. I had so mused upon Eleanor's sorrow that I had, as it were, made it mine. I bowed my head, breathing a prayer for her, then leaning against the trunk of a tree whose leaves no longer afforded shade to the carefully-cultivated family inclosure, my eyes fell upon the grave. There were beautiful flowers fading upon it, which some friendly hand had laid there within a week or two. Ten or fifteen minutes I may have passed in reverie; then, as I arose to depart, I took up a fading bud or two and a sprig of myrtle, placing them in my vest-pocket to give Eleanor on my return. As I stooped to gather them, I perceived the imprint of a child's foot, here and

---

* Percy Bysshe Shelley's 1820 poem "To a Skylark" uses the phrase "harmonious madness," occasionally reprinted as "melodious madness." As we have seen earlier, the narrator was fond of Shelley's poetry.

there, all about the grave—a tiny imprint, in the fresh mold, as of some toddling babe whose little feet had hardly learned to steady themselves.

There were one or two marks of a woman's slender shoe; but it was the infant feet which impressed me. It flashed upon me what female figure it was which I had seen flitting away as I approached; now that I recalled it, I even recognized the tall, slender form, with the slight stoop of the shoulders, of which I had obtained but a half-glance. I hastily pursued the path she had taken; but my haste was behind hers by at least a quarter of an hour.

I realized that I would only lose time by looking for her in those winding avenues, every one of which might be taking me from instead of toward the fugitives; so I turned back to the gate and questioned the keeper if he had seen a tall young woman with a little child pass out in the last half-hour. He had seen several children and women go out in that time; and as I could not tell how this particular one was dressed, I could not arouse his recollection to any certainty on the point.

"She was probably carrying the child," I said; "she had a consumptive look, and was sad-looking, though her face was doubtless hidden in her vail."

"It's quite likely," he responded; "mostly the women that do come here look sad, and many of them keep their vails down. However, it's my impression there hasn't no child of that age been past here, lately. I noticed one going in about two o'clock, and if it's *that* one, she hasn't come out yet."

So while Mr. Burton sat in the shop in Court street keeping watch, I sat at the gates of Greenwood; but no Leesy Sullivan came forth; and when the gates were closed for the night, I was obliged to go away disappointed.

The girl began to grow some elusive phantom in my mind. I

could almost doubt that there was any such creature, with black, wild eyes and hectic cheeks, whom I was pursuing; whom I chanced upon in strange places, at unexpected times, but could never find when I sought her—who seemed to blend herself in this unwarrantable way with the tragedy which wrung some other hearts. What had she to do with Henry's grave? A feeling of dislike, of mortal aversion, grew upon me—I could not pity her any more—this dark spirit who, having perchance wrought this irremediable woe, could not now sink into the depths where she belonged, but must haunt and hover on the edges of my trouble, fretting me to follow her, only to mock and elude.

Before leaving the cemetery I offered two policemen a hundred dollars if they should succeed in detaining the woman and child whose description I gave them, until word could be sent to the office of the detective-police; and I left them, with another on guard at the gates, perambulating the grounds, peering into vaults and ghostly places in search of her. When I got out at the house on Court street, I found my friend quite tired of eating chestnuts and talking to the little man behind the counter.

"Well," said he, "the potatoes will be roasted to death before their owner returns. We have been led another wild-goose chase."

"I have seen her," I answered.

"What?"

"And lost her. I believe she is a little snaky, she has such a slippery way with her."

"Tut! tut! so has a frightened deer! But how did it happen?"

I told him, and he was quite downcast at the unlucky fortune which had sent me to the cemetery at that particular time. It was evident that she had seen me, and was afraid to return to this new retreat, for fear she was again tracked.

"However," said he, "I'm confident we'll have her now before long. I *must* go home to-night to see my Lenore; I promised her, and she will make herself sick sitting up."

"Go; and let me remain here. I will stay until it is perfectly apparent that she does not expect to return."

"It will spoil the dinner. But, now that we have sacrificed so much, a few hours more of inconvenience—"

"Will be willingly endured. I will get some bread and cheese and a glass of beer of your friend, the penny-grocer, and remain at my post."

"You need not stay later than twelve; which will bring you home about two, at the slow rate of midnight travel. I shall sit up for you. *Au revoir.*"

I changed my mind about supping at the grocer's as the twilight deepened into night. The dim light of the hall and staircase, part of them in total darkness, enabled me to steal up to the deserted room unperceived by any one of the other inmates of the great building.

Here I put fresh coal on the fire, and by the faint glow which soon came from the open front of the stove, I found a chair, and placing it so that it would be in the shadow upon the opening of the door, I seated myself to await the return of the occupants. The odor of roasting potatoes, given forth at the increased heat, admonished me that I had partaken of but a light lunch since an early and hasty breakfast; drawing forth one from the oven, I made a frugal meal upon it, and then ordered my soul to patience. I sat long in the twilight of the room; I could hear the bells of the city chiming the passing hours; the grocer and variety-storekeepers closing the shutters of their shops; the shuffling feet of men coming home, to such homes as they had in the dreary building, until nearly all the noises of the street and house died away.

Gazing on the fire, I wondered where that strange woman

was keeping that little child through those unwholesome hours. Did she carry it in her arms while she hovered, like a ghost, amid the awful quiet of drooping willows and gleaming tombstones? Did she rock it to sleep on her breast, in the fearful shadow of some vault, with a row of coffins for company? Or was she again fleeing over deserted fields, crouching in lonely places, fatigued, distressed, panting under the weight of the innocent babe who slumbered on a guilty bosom, but driven still, on, on, by the lash of a dreadful secret? I made wild pictures in the sinking embers, as I mused; were I an artist I would reproduce them in all their lurid light and somber shadow; but I am not. The close air of the place, increased in drowsiness by the gas from the open doors of the stove, the deep silence, and my own fatigue, after the varying journeys and excitements of the day, at last overcame me; I remember hearing the town clock strike eleven, and after that I must have slumbered.

As I slept, I continued my waking dreams; I thought myself still gazing in the smoldering fire; that the sewing-girl came in without noise, sat down before it, and silently wept over the child who lay in her arms; that Lenore came out of the golden embers, with wings tipped with ineffable brightness, looking like an angel, and seemed to comfort the mourner, and finally took her by the hand, and passing me, so that I felt the motion of the air swept by her wings and garments, led her out through the door, which closed with a slight noise.

At the noise made by the closing door, I awoke. As I gathered my confused senses about me, I was not long in coming to the conclusion that I had, indeed, heard a sound and felt the air from an open door—some one had been in the room. I looked at my watch by a match which I struck, for the fire had now entirely expired. It was one o'clock. Vexed beyond words that I had slumbered, I rushed out into the empty passages, where, standing silent, I listened for any footstep. There was not the echo of a sound abroad. The halls were wrapped in darkness. Quietly and swiftly I felt my way down to the street; not a soul to be seen in any direction. Yet I felt positive that Leesy Sullivan, creeping from her shelter, had returned to her room at that midnight hour, had found me there, *sleeping,* and had fled.

Soon a car, which now ran only at intervals of half an hour, came along, and I gave up my watch for the night, mortified at the result.

It was three o'clock when I reached Mr. Burton's door. He opened it before I could ring the bell.

"No success? I was afraid of it. You see I have kept up for you; and now, since the night is so far spent, if you are not too worn out, I wish you would come with me to a house not very far from here. I want to show you how some of the fast young men of New York spend the hours in which they ought to be in bed."

"I am wide awake, and full of curiosity; but how did you find your little daughter?"

"Drooping a little, but persisting that she was not ill nor tired, and delighted with the flowers."

"Then you did not forget the bouquet?"

"No, I never like to disappoint Lenore."

Locking the door behind us, we again descended to the deserted street.

CHAPTER IX.

THE SPIDER AND THE FLY.

"Come," said my cicerone,* "we are already very late."

A rapid walk of a few minutes brought us to the entrance of a handsome house, having the appearance of a private residence, and standing on a fashionable street.

"Why," said I, inclined to draw back, as he ascended the steps, "you surely would not think of disturbing the people here at this hour of the night? There is not a light to be seen, even in the chambers."

Mr. Burton's low laugh made me blush at my own "greenness." His ring at the bell was followed by a knock, which I was quick-witted enough, in spite of my verdancy, to perceive had something significant about it. The door immediately swung a little open, my friend said a few words which had the effect to unclose the mysterious portals still wider, and we entered a modest hall, which a single gas-burner, half-turned off, dimly illuminated. The man-servant who admitted us was sable as ebony, muscular, much above the medium size, dressed in a plain livery, and with manners as polished as his own

---

* An obsolete word for a guide.

shining skin—an African leopard, barring the spots, smooth and powerful.

"Is Bagley still here?" asked my companion.

"Yes, sir. In de library, jus' where you lef' him."

"Very well. You need not disturb him. I've brought my young friend in to introduce him to the house, in view of further acquaintance."

The ebony man smiled respectfully, bowing for us to pass into the parlor. I thought I saw in that quiet smile a lurking ray of satisfaction—a gloating, as it were, over my prospective intimacy at this respectable house. He had probably been usher to the maelstrom long enough to know that those whose feet were once caught in the slow, delightful waltz of the circling waters never withdrew them, after the circle grew narrow and swift, and the rush of the whirlpool sounded up from the bottomless pit.

We entered a suit* of rooms in no manner differing from the parlors of a private house. They were richly furnished and well lighted, close inner blinds, hidden by heavy silk curtains, shutting in the light from the observation of the street. There were three rooms in this suit; the two first were now deserted, though the odor of wine, and scented hair and handkerchiefs, showed that they had been recently occupied. In these two the chandeliers were partially obscured, but the third room was still brilliantly illuminated. We walked toward it. Magnificent curtains of amber silk depended from the arch which separated it from the parlors. Only one of these curtains was now drawn back, the others trailing on the carpet, and closing the apartment from our observation. Mr. Burton placed me in the shadow of the curtains, where I could see—myself unseen. The room was

---

* An obsolete spelling for the word "suite."

furnished as a library, two of its walls being covered with books; I particularly noticed a marble bust of Shakspeare[*], very fine. A severe, yet liberal, taste marked the choice and arrangement of every thing. A painting of Tasso reading his poems to the Princess,[†] hung between the two back windows.

It was a well-arranged library, certainly; yet the four occupants were engrossed in a study more fascinating than that of any of the books by which they were surrounded. If Mephistophiles could have stepped from his binding of blue and gold, and made the acquaintance of the company, he would have been quite charmed. Two couples sat at two tables playing cards. All the other visitors to the establishment had gone away, some of them to theft or suicide, perhaps, save those four, who still lingered, wrapped up in the dread enchantment of the hour. The two at the table I first glanced at, were both strangers to me; at the second, I could not see the face of one of the players, whose back was toward me; but the face of the other was directly in front of me, and under the full light of the chandelier. This person was James Argyll. My astonishment was profound. That I had never fraternized with him, I considered partly my own fault—there are persons so naturally antagonistic as to make real friendship between them impossible—and I had often blamed myself for our mutual coldness. But, with all my dislike of some of his qualities—as, for instance, his

---

[*] The playwright's name is spelled many ways in various nineteenth-century literature, including Shakespear, Shaksper, and Shakspere. According to the 1910 edition of the *Encyclopædia Britannica*, in the Council Book of the Stratford corporation, the last name of William Shakespeare's father, John, appeared 166 times and was spelled 16 different ways! Scholars also point out (not unanimously) that the poet-playwright signed his name "Shakspere."

[†] Torquato Tasso (1544–1595) was an Italian poet, remembered for his love poems written to various women. Which princess is depicted in the painting is unknown, but it is likely Princess Leonore, the heroine of Goethe's play *Torquato Tasso* (1794) and the sister of the Duke of Ferrara.

indolent acceptance of his uncle's bounty, which, in the eyes of a person of my disposition, took away half his manliness—with all my unfriendly aversion to him, I had never suspected him of absolutely bad habits.

I had to look twice to assure myself of his identity. And having looked, I could not take away my eyes from the strange attraction of a countenance transformed by the excitement of the gaming-table. His dark complexion had blanched to a sallow paleness; cheeks and lips were of the same color; his nose seemed to have sharpened, and was drawn in about the face with a pinched look; his eyebrows were very slightly contracted, but fixed, as if cut in marble, while underneath them the lids were drawn together, so that only a line of the eye was visible—a narrow line, letting out a single steady ray from the lurid world within. The lids appeared as if the eyeballs had shrunken in the intensity of their gaze.

Silently the cards were dealt and played. It was evidently the closing game, upon which much depended—*how* much, for James, I could only guess by the increasing pallor and absorption of his countenance.

"I wish I could see his opponent's face," I whispered to my companion.

"You would see nothing but the face of the devil coolly amusing himself. Bagley never gets excited. He has ruined a dozen young men already."

The last card was thrown down; the two players arose simultaneously.

"Well, Bagley," said James, with a desperate laugh, "you will have to wait for the money until I—"

"Marry the young lady," said the other; "that is the agreement, I believe; but don't consent to a long engagement."

"I shall find some means to pay these last two debts before

that happy consummation, I hope. You shall hear from me within a month."

"We will make a little memorandum of them," said his opponent; and as they went together to a writing-desk, Mr. Burton drew me away.

I could hardly breathe when we got into the street, I was so suffocated with rage at hearing the reference made by those two men, under that unholy roof, to the woman so revered and sacred in my thoughts. I was certain that Miss Argyll was the young lady whose fortune was to pay these "debts of honor," contracted in advance upon such security. If his strong hand had not silently withheld me, I do not know but I should have made a scene, which would have been as unwise as useless. I was thankful, afterward, that I was prevented, though I chafed under the restraint at the time. Neither of us spoke until we were in the house of my host, where a fire in the library awaited us. Before this we seated ourselves, neither of us feeling sleepy after our night's adventures.

"How did you know that Argyll was at that house? I had no idea that he intended coming to the city to-day," I said.

"He had no intention until he learned of your sudden departure. He came down in the next train, to see what *you* were about. He is uneasy about you, Mr. Redfield, didn't you know it? As he could ascertain nothing satisfactory about your doings, or mine, he had nothing better on his hands, this evening, than to look up his friend Bagley."

"How do you know all this?"

The detective half smiled, his piercing eyes fixed reflectively on the fire.

"I should be poorly able to support my pretensions, if I could not keep the circle of my acquaintance under my observation. I was informed of his arrival in town, upon my return from

Brooklyn, and have known of his whereabouts since. I could tell you what he had for supper, if it would interest you."

The uneasy feeling which I had several times experienced in Mr. Burton's society, came over me again. I spoke a little quickly.

"I wonder if you have your secret agents—spirits of the air, or electricity, they might almost seem to be—hovering always on *my* steps."

He laughed, but not unpleasantly, looking me through with those steel-blue rays:

"Would it trouble you to fancy yourself under surveillance?"

"I never liked fetters, of any kind. I yield my choice of will and action to nobody. However, if any one finds satisfaction in playing the part of my shadow, I don't know that I shall suffer any restraint upon that account."

"I don't think it would disturb you seriously," he said.

"No one likes to be watched, Mr. Burton."

"We are all watched by the pure and penetrating eye of the All-seeing One, and if we are not fearful before Him, whom need we shrink from?"

I looked up to see whether it was the secret-police-agent who was preaching to me, or whether my host, in his power of varying the outer manifestations of his character, had not dropped the mystic star for the robe of the minister; he was gazing into the fire with a sad, absorbed expression, as if he saw before him a long procession of mortal crimes, walking in the night of earth, but, in reality, under the full brightness of infinite day. I had seen him before in these solemn, almost prophetic moods, brought on him by the revelation of some new sin, which seemed always in him to awaken regret, rather than the exultation of a detective bent on the successful results of his mission. So soft, so gentle he appeared then, I inwardly wondered that he had the sternness to inflict disgrace and exposure upon the "respectable" guilty—which class of criminals he was almost exclusively employed with—but I had only to reflect upon the admirable equipoise of his character, to realize that with him justice was what he loved best. For those who prowled about society in the garb of lambs and shepherd-dogs, seeking whom they might devour, and laying, perhaps, the proofs of guilt at the doors of the innocent, he had no mercy of the "let us alone" type. A little time we were silent; the dropping of an ember from the grate startled us.

"Why do you think that James watches me? What does he watch me for?"

I asked this, going back to the surprise I had felt when he made the remark.

"You will know soon enough."

It was useless for me to press the question, since he did not wish to be explicit.

"I did not know," I continued, "I never dreamed, that James had bad associates in the city. I know that his uncle and cousins do not suspect it. It pains me more than I can express. What shall I do? I have no influence over him. He dislikes me, and would take the most brotherly remonstrance as an insult."

"I do not wish you, at present, to hint your discovery to him. As for your not suspecting his habits, those habits themselves are recent. I doubt if he had ever ventured a dollar on cards three months ago. He had some gay, even dissolute companions in the city, of whom the worst and most dangerous was Bagley. But he had not joined them in their worst excesses—he was only idle and fond of pleasure—a moth fluttering around the flames. Now he has scorched his wings. He has not spent more than three or four nights as he spent this; and the only money he has lost has been to the person you saw him with to-night. Bagley is one of the vampires who fatten on the characters and purses of young men like James Argyll."

"Then ought we not to make some earnest effort to save him before it is too late? Oh, Mr. Burton, you who are wise and experienced—tell me what to do."

"Why do you feel so much interest in him? You do not like him."

"I could not see the merest stranger go down toward destruction without stretching forth my hand. There is no great friendship between us, it is true; but James is nearly connected with the happiness and reputation of the family I honor most on earth. For its sake, I would make the utmost endeavor."

"For the interests of justice, then, it is well that I am not related to the Argylls by the personal ties which affect you. I will tell you one thing—James does not gamble so much from weakness of will to resist temptation, as he does to forget, for a time, under the influence of the fascinating excitement, an anxiety which he carries about with him."

"You're a close observer, Mr. Burton. James has, indeed, been deeply troubled lately. I have noticed the change in him—in his appetite, complexion, manners, in a thousand trifles—a change which grows upon him daily. He is gnawed upon by secret doubts—now raised by hopes, now depressed by fears, until he is fitful and uncertain as a light carried in an autumn wind. But I can tell you that he is all wrong in indulging this vain hope, which creates the doubt. I know what it is, and how utterly without foundation. It is weakness, wickedness in him to allow a passion which ought only to ennoble him and teach him self-control, to chase him to such ruin as I saw to-night."

"That is *your* way of viewing the matter, Mr. Redfield. We all see things according to the color of the spectacles we happen to wear. Then you think it is a growing certainty that Miss Argyll, even under her present relief from past vows, will never favor his suit, nor that of any man, which is driving her cousin to these reckless habits?"

I was half offended with him for mentioning her name in that manner; but I knew that mine was an extreme, if not a morbid sensitiveness, where she was concerned, and I swallowed my resentment, answering,

"I fear it is."

"That may explain his disquiet to you—so be it."

Still Mr. Burton was keeping something back from me—always keeping something back. I did not feel at all sleepy. I was full of eager thought. I reviewed, with a lightning glance, all that he had ever said—all James had recently done or said—and, I swear, had it not been for the almost affectionate kindness of his general manner to me, and my belief in his candor, which would not allow him to play the part of a friend while acting the part of an enemy, I should have felt that Mr. Burton suspected *me* of that appalling crime which I was so busily seeking to fix upon the head of a frail, frightened woman! Again the idea, and not for the first time, crept through my veins, chilling me from head to foot, I looked him full in the eyes. If he *had* such a thought, I would pluck it out from behind that curtain of deception, and make him acknowledge it. If he had such a thought, James had introduced it to his mind. I knew that James had had some interviews with him, of which I was only cognizant by casual observations dropped by my host. How many more conclaves they may have held, was left to my imagination to conjecture. What was this man before me playing this double part for?—a friend to each, but never to both together. The reader may smile, and answer that it is the very calling and existence of a detective to play a double part; and that I ought not to be chagrined to find him exercising his fine talents upon me. Perhaps James also had reason to fancy himself this man's confidant and friend, who was playing us, one against the other, for purposes of his own. It was the thought that Mr. Burton, before whom more than any

other person in this world, except my mother, I had been wiled
to lay open my soul, could suspect me of any hidden part in that
dark tragedy, which chilled me to the marrow.

But no!—it was impossible! I saw it now in the frank and
smiling eyes which met my searching and lengthy gaze.

"There!" he cried, gayly, "there is a ray of actual sunrise. The
fire is out; the room is chilly—the morning has come upon us.
We have sat out the night, Richard! Let me show you to your
room; we will not breakfast until nine o'clock, and you can catch
a couple of hours' repose in the mean time." He took up a lamp,
and we ascended the stairs. "Here is your chamber. Now, remember, I bid you sleep, and let that clock in your brain run down. It
is bad for the young to think too deeply. Good——morning."

He passed on, as I closed the door of my chamber. His tone
had been that of an elder friend, speaking to a young man whom
he loved; I had wronged him by that unpleasant idea which had
shivered through me.

Closed shutters and thick curtains kept out the broadening
light of dawn; yet I found it difficult to compose myself to sleep.
That haunting shadow which had flitted from Henry's grave as
I approached it yesterday—the dream which I had in the little
chamber, awakening to the reality of the sewing-girl's escape—I
could not banish these any more than I could the discovery
made in that house of sin, where the bloated spider of Play
weaves his glittering net, and sits on the watch for the gay and
brilliant victims who flutter into its meshes.

One feeling I had, connected with that discovery, which
I had not betrayed to Mr. Burton—which I would not fairly
acknowledge to my own soul—which I quarreled with—drove
out—but which persisted in returning to me now, banishing
slumber from my eyelids. When I had stood behind those silken
curtains, and beheld James Argyll losing money in play, I had

experienced a sensation of relief—I might say of absolute gladness—a sensation entirely apart from my sorrow at finding him
in such society, with such habits. Why? Ah, do not ask me; I
can not tell you yet. Do not wrong me by saying that it was triumph over the fall of my rival in Mr. Argyll's affections, in business, possibly, and in the regards of those two noble girls whose
opinions we both prized so highly. Only do not accuse me of
this most apparent reason for my gladness, and I will abide my
time in your judgment. But no! I will confess this much to-night
myself.

If this stealthy and flying creature whom we two men were
hunting from one hiding-place to another, whose wild face had
been seen pressing toward the library window on that night of
nights, and whose handkerchief the very thorns of the roses had
conspired to steal from her, and hold as a witness against her—
if this doubtful, eluding creature, flitting darkly in the shadows
of this tragedy, had not abstracted that money from Mr. Argyll's
desk, I had dared to guess who might have taken it. Simply and
solely—not because I did not like him—but because, to go
back to the Friday before that fatal Saturday, I had been late in
the parlors. The girls were singing and playing at the piano; I
left turning the music for them to go for a volume in the library
which I desired to carry off with me to read in my room that
night; I opened the door suddenly, and startled James, who was
leaning over that desk.

"Have you seen my opera-glass?" said he. "I left it on the desk
here."

I answered him that I had not seen it, got my book, and
returned to the music, thinking no more of that trifling
occurrence—which I never more should have recalled had it
not been for a peculiar expression in James' face, which I was
afterward forced to remember against my will. Yet so little did

I wish to wrong him, even in my secret thoughts, that when the investigations were taking place, I was convinced, with all the others, that, the unlawful visitor of the garden had, in some manner, possessed herself of the money. It only came back to me as I watched James this night, in the gambling saloon, that, if he ever had been tempted to rob from his uncle more than the unfailing generosity of that good gentleman allowed him, I was glad that it was *play* which had tempted him to the wrongful act. This was the shadowy nature of my pleasure. Who has complete mastery of his thoughts? Who does not sometimes find them evil, unwarrantable, uncomfortable, and to be ashamed of?

From the perplexity of all these things I sunk into a slight slumber, from which I was almost immediately aroused by the tinkling of the breakfast-bell. I arose, dressed, and, upon descending to the library, was met by a servant, who ushered me at once into a cheerful apartment, where my host sat by the window, reading the morning paper, and where the table only waited my appearance to be graced by a well-ordered meal.

"Lenore usually presides over the tea-urn," said Mr. Burton, as we sat down. "We have a little affair which answers for two, and which is adapted to the strength of her little hands. It seems pleasantest so; and we both like it—but she has not arisen this morning."

"I hope she is not more unwell than usual," I said, with real solicitude.

"To tell you the truth, she was not at all benefited by what occurred yesterday. She is nervous and exhausted; I have been up to see her. I know that when the doctor comes to-day, he will guess what I have been about, and blame me. I mean it shall be the last time in which I experiment upon her."

"I shall regret it, if she is really injured by it, despite my intense desire to learn what she revealed. Perhaps it was from our selfishness in making use of this exquisite instrument for purposes so earthly that we are punished by the fruitlessness of the results."

Mr. Burton laughed.

"Perhaps. Punishment, however, seldom appears fitly meted out, this side the Stygian river. My Lenore will be better this afternoon; and I have strong hopes that, with the light now before us, we shall secure our prize. If that woman escapes me now, I shall set her down as a lunatic—only an insane person could have the consummate cunning to thwart me so long."

"There never was one less insane," I said. "The impression which she made upon me was that of one in whom the emotions and intellect were both powerful. Her will and cunning are well-nigh a match for yours. You will have to look sharp."

"It is easier to pursue than to evade pursuit. She has much the most difficult strategy to conceive and execute. I tell you, Mr. Redfield, I'm bound to see that woman. I shall be so piqued at my failure, as to go into a decline, if I'm disappointed." He seemed two-thirds in earnest, through his jocular assertion.

We did not linger long over the breakfast, being anxious to get back to Brooklyn. After we had withdrawn from the table, he gave me the paper to look over, while he ran up a moment to say something to his daughter. While he was absent, the door-bell rung, and the servant showed a gentleman into the room where I was.

"Well, really," were the first words I heard, "has Mr. Burton taken you for an apprentice, and do you lodge with your employer?"

It was James—as usual, when addressing me, with the gay smile covering the sneer. He did not even extend his hand, but stood looking at me a moment, with a sort of defiant menace, which ended with an uneasy glance about the place. If he had been conscious of my secret visit to his haunts, he would have worn something such an expression; I construed it that his restless conscience made him suspicious of his friends.

"I came down, unexpectedly, yesterday morning, at his request. We got some trace of Leesy Sullivan; and I shall stay until we do something about it."

"Indeed!"—he seemed relieved, putting off his ugly look and condescending to be gentlemanly again. "Have you found out where the wretched creature has hidden herself? Upon my word, I think if Eleanor knew the case in all its bearings, it might be useful in keeping her from quite killing herself of grief."

It was now my turn to be angry; I turned upon him with a flushed face:

"For God's sake, don't slander the dead, even by imputation, however slight. Whoever put Henry where he lies now, and for what purpose, this much I believe—that no injustice nor sin of his own brought that high heart low. And the villain, I say the villain, who could breathe such a whisper in Eleanor's ear would be base enough to—to—"

"Speak out," smiled James, holding me with his softly glittering gaze.

"I will say no more," I ended, abruptly, as I heard Mr. Burton's steps approaching. It was evident to me that there was to be no peace between us two.

I watched my host while he greeted the new arrival; I wished to satisfy myself if there was a difference in his manner of treating us which would justify my belief that Mr. Burton was not playing a part with me. He was courteous, affable, every thing that was desirable or to be expected in a gentleman receiving a friendly acquaintance—that was all; again I assured myself that it was only toward me that he displayed real liking and affection. But this he did not now display. His face had on its mask—that conventional smile and polish, that air of polite interest, than which nothing is more impenetrable. It was because, in our intercourse alone together, Mr. Burton laid this mask aside, that I flattered myself I was his friend and confidant.

"Richard got the start of me," observed James, after the compliments of the day were over; "I had not the least idea that he was in town. I came down yesterday to buy myself an overcoat— important business, wasn't it?—and stayed over to the opera, last night being the opening of the new season. Did either of you attend? I did not see you, if there. He tells me that he left in the early morning train, before the one I took. Have you any information of importance, Mr. Burton?"

"We have seen Miss Sullivan."

"Is it possible? And have you really made up your mind that the poor thing is guilty? If so, I hope you will not fail to have her arrested. I should like, very much indeed, to have the affair sifted to the dregs."

"Yes, I suppose so. It is quite natural that you should take an interest in having it sifted, as you say. I assure you that if I have reason enough to warrant an indictment, I shall have one gotten out. In the mean time we must be cautious—the interests involved are too serious to be played with."

"Certainly, they are, indeed. And unless that young woman is really the dreadful being we believe her, we ought not to ruin her by open accusation. Still, I must say she acts extremely like a guilty person."

"She does, Mr. Argyll; I see but one explanation of her conduct—she is herself *particeps criminis*,* or she knows who is."

"Quite likely. Indeed, we can not well think otherwise. Did you say you had actually seen the girl, Mr. Burton?"

---

* An accomplice or partner in crime.

"We saw her yesterday—that is, Mr. Redfield did."

"May I inquire the result? or am I not supposed to be sufficiently interested in the case to have any right to ask questions?
If so, I beg you, don't trouble yourselves. There are doubtless
others who have deeper and different reasons from mine, for
being conspicuous in the matter." As James said this, he looked
directly at me. "You know, Mr. Burton, I have intimated as much
before; and, if I am sometimes imprudent in my speech, you
must know how hard it is for me to control myself always."

I was conscious that I grew pale, as Mr. Burton glanced
swiftly at me, I felt so certain that James meant something personal, yet so uncertain how to accuse him of it, or to compel him
to explain himself, when he would probably deny there was any
thing to explain.

"I don't think there's any one has a deeper interest in the
matter than you, Mr. Argyll," said Mr. Burton, with a kind of
smooth distinctness of tone which might seem to be impressive,
or mean nothing, as the listener chose to understand it. "About
seeing the girl, Redfield has not half so much to tell as I wish he
had. In fact, he let her slip through his fingers."

A dry laugh was James' comment upon this avowal. Mr.
Burton saw that we were inwardly chafing, ready, as it were, to
spring upon each other; he took up his hat and gloves.

"Come, gentlemen, we have business on hand of too much
importance to permit of ceremony. Mr. Argyll, I must excuse
myself. But if you'll join us, we shall be glad of your aid and
company. We are going over to Brooklyn, to seek for another
glimpse of Leesy Sullivan."

James slightly started as Brooklyn was mentioned. He had
no reason to suppose that any thing but courtesy prompted
the invitation he received; yet he did not hesitate to accept it.
Whether from mere curiosity, or jealousy at being kept out

of the detective's full confidence, or a desire to pry into my
actions and motives, or a praiseworthy interest—whatever it
was prompted him, he kept with us all day, expressing regret as
deep as our own when another night came without any results.
Being belated, we took our supper in a saloon, as we had done
our dinner. I could not but notice that Mr. Burton did not invite
James to the house to spend the night, nor converse with him at
all about his daughter or his personal affairs.

The next morning James returned home; but I remained in
the city several days, all this time the guest of Mr. Burton, and
becoming more attached to him and his beautiful child. After
the first day, Lenore recovered pretty rapidly from the ill effects
of the trance; I was, as the ladies say, "perfectly charmed" with
her. A gayer, more airy little sprite never existed than she, when
her health permitted her natural spirit to display itself. Her grace
and playfulness were befitting her age—childish in an eminent
degree, yet poetized, as it were, by an ethereal spirituality, which
was all her own. To hear her sing would be to wonder how such
a depth and hight and breadth, such an infinity of melody, could
be poured from so young and slender a throat—as I had often
wondered, when gazing at the swelling breast of some little triumphant bird, where was hidden the mechanism for all that
marvelous power of music.

It is said that children know who are their true friends. I do not think that "flitting, fairy"* Lenore doubted for an instant that I was hers. We acknowledged a mutual attraction, which it seemed to give her father pleasure to observe. She was, to both of us, a delight and a rest, to which we looked forward after the vexations and disappointments of the day—vexations and disappointments which increased upon us; for every night we had the dissatisfaction of finding some slender thread of probability, which we had industriously unraveled and followed, either abruptly broken off, leaving us standing, perplexed and foolish, or else leading to persons and purposes most irrelevant. I should dislike to say how many pale, dark-eyed young women, with pretty babies, made our unexpected acquaintance during the following week—an acquaintance as brief as it was unsolicited on their part.

---

* The first stanza of Alfred, Lord Tennyson's charming poem "Lilian" (from *Fairy Lilian and Other Poems*, 1888) is:

> *Airy, fairy Lilian,*
> *Flitting, fairy Lilian,*
> *When I ask her if she love me,*
> *Claps her tiny hands above me,*
> *Laughing all she can;*
> *She'll not tell me if she love me,*
> *Cruel little Lilian.*

CHAPTER X.
THE ANNIVERSARY.

I have said that I expected Mr. Argyll to offer me a partnership, now that I was prepared to begin my legal career. In this I was not presumptuous, inasmuch as he had frequently and plainly hinted his intention. Such an arrangement would be a desirable one for me; I appreciated its many advantages; at the same time, I expected, by taking all the hard work upon myself, and by the constant devotion of such talent as I had to the interests of the firm, to repay, as far as possible, my obligations to the senior member.

When I returned from New York, I appeared in court with a case which had chanced to be intrusted to me, perhaps from the inability of my client to employ an older and more expensive lawyer. I did well with it, and was complimented by several of Mr. Argyll's fraternity upon my success in handling the case. Much to my surprise and mortification, Mr. Argyll's congratulations were in constrained and studied terms. He had appeared to be more formal, less open in his manner of treating me, ever since my last visit to the city. At first I thought it my fancy, or caused by some temporary ill-health, or mental trouble, under which he might be laboring. Day by day the impression deepened upon me that his feelings toward me were not what they had been. The plainest proof I had of this was, that no offer of partnership was made. I was placed in a disagreeable situation for one of my proud temperament. My studies completed to the point where admission to practice had been granted, I had nothing to do but continue in his office, reading, reading away—not but that my time was most usefully employed thus, and not that I was in any great hurry to go into business, though my income was narrow enough, and I knew that my mother had pinched her domestic arrangements to afford me that—but I began to feel like an intruder. My ostensible use of his books, office, and instructions was at an end; I began to feel like a hanger-on. Yet I could not go away, or offer to associate myself with others, hastily. I felt that he ought either to put in execution his implied promise, or to inform me that he had changed his plans, and I was free to try elsewhere.

Can any invalid tell me why he feels a prescience of the storm in his aching bones and tingling nerves while the sun still shines in a cloudless sky, and not one hint on the outward face of nature tells of a change in the weather? Neither can I explain the subtle influences which affected me, depressing me so deeply, and making me sensible of a change in that atmosphere of home which had brooded for me over the Argyll mansion. I had felt this first in the more business air of the office; gradually, it seemed to me to be creeping over the household. Mary, that sweet child of impulse, too young to assume much dignity, and too truthful to disguise her innocent face in falsehood, who had clung to me in this affliction as a sister clings to an elder brother, awakening all my tenderest instincts of protection and indulgence—this fair girl, doubly dear to me as the sister of that other woman whom I adored, began to put on an air of reserve toward me. She was kind and gentle, but she no longer ran to me with all those pretty demands and complaints, those trifling confidences, so sweet because an evidence of trust and affection; sometimes I caught her eyes fixed upon me in a sad, wondering way, which puzzled and disconcerted me; when I caught her glance, she would turn quickly, and blush.

I could not help believing, although I had no proof of it, that James was covertly working to produce an impression against me in the family. His manner toward me had never been so friendly; when we were alone together he grew quite confidential, sometimes descending to small flatteries, and almost entirely neglecting the use of those little nettles of satire with which he once delighted in stinging me whenever any one whom I esteemed was present. I could not pick a quarrel with him, had I desired it. Yet I could not rid myself of the consciousness that he was undermining my footing in the house of those friends I loved best. In what manner, it was difficult for me to conjecture. If he slandered my habits or associations, nothing could be easier than for Mr. Argyll to quietly ascertain, by inquiries unknown to myself, the truth of his statements; justice to me would require that he should take that trouble before he cast off, as unworthy his further kindness, the son of his dead friend. I could think of but one matter which he could use to my prejudice; and in that my conscience accused me loudly enough. I said to myself that he had told them of my love for Eleanor. He had torn that delicate and sacred secret from my heart, where it lay under the pitying light of God's eye alone—discovered it through hate and jealousy, which are next to love in the keenness of their perceptions—and exposed it to those from whom I had most shrinkingly hidden it. Even then, why should they blame me, or treat me coldly, for what I could not help, and for which I alone must suffer? Certainly not for my presumption, since I had not presumed. One dreadful idea preyed upon me. It was, that, in order to rid himself of me for ever to drive me out from the friendship of those whom he wanted to himself, for his own selfish aims, James was representing to them not only that I loved Eleanor, but that I was looking forward to the future with hopes which mocked her present desolation.

I can not describe the pain and humiliation this idea gave me. If I could have discovered it, or in any way denied it, I should not have felt so hurt and helpless. As it was, I felt that my honor was being stabbed in the dark, without a chance to defend itself— some secret enemy was wounding it, as some base assassin had planted that deadly wound in the heart of Henry Moreland.

In the mean time, the Christmas holidays were approaching. It was a season of gloom and mourning, mocked by the merry preparations of happier people. On the twenty-third day of December came Eleanor's nineteenth birthday. It was to have been her wedding-day. A glorious winter morning dawned; the sun shone in a sapphire sky; it seemed as if every plant in the conservatory put forth double bloom—the japonicas, the white roses, were incomparable. I could not help but linger about the house. Eleanor kept herself in her room. If every word which refers to her were written in tears, it could not express the feelings with which we all were moved with the thought of her bereavement. We moved about like people in dreams, silent and abstracted. The old housekeeper, when I met her on the stairs, was wiping her eyes with the corner of her apron. Mr. Argyll, unquiet and pale, wandered from room to room. The office remained closed; the front blinds of the house were shut—it was like the day of the funeral.

I went into the conservatory; there was sunshine there, and sweetness—a bright luxuriance of beauty. It was more solemn to me than the darkened parlors. I plucked a white rose, holding it idly in my fingers. It was half-past eleven—at twelve the ceremony should have been performed. Mary came in while I stood there wrapped in emotion more than thought. Her eyes were swollen with weeping, her hands trembled, and when she spoke, her lips quivered:

"She has taken out all the wedding apparel, for the first time since that day. She is dressing herself. She has put on the robe and vail; and now she has sent me down to make the bouquet. She wants some white flowers for her bosom. She stands before the mirror, putting on every thing as carefully as if poor Henry—were—down-stairs. Oh, Richard," she cried, breaking down utterly in a burst of tears, and throwing herself into my arms, "it would break your heart to see her! It almost kills me, but I must get the flowers. It is best to indulge her."

"Yes, it is best," I answered, soothing her as best I could, when my own voice and hands were so shaken. "I will help you. Don't keep her waiting."

I took the scissors from her, cutting the fairest buds, the most perfect flowers, arranging them with care and skill.

"I will tell you what she said," continued Mary, as I hastily made up the bouquet; "she says that to-day they will be married, the same as if Henry were on earth instead of in heaven; that their vows shall be consummated at the hour appointed, and that thereafter she shall hold herself his wife just as surely as if he had come in the body to fulfill his part of the contract. She has her prayer-book open at the marriage ceremony. She looks so sweet and calm, as beautiful as if she, too, were an angel with dear Henry—only so very white, so very solemn—oh, dear, I cannot bear it!" and again I had to compose her, wiping away her tears, before I sent her up with the bouquet. As she went out into the breakfast, or family-room, which opened into the conservatory, I saw James by the door, and I knew, by the expression of his face, that he had heard what passed between us. Through a kind of alarm and vexation there was a flash of disdain, as if he wanted to say, what he dared not:

"What a fool the girl is to cling to that dust and ashes! Married, indeed! She shall be the wife of some one besides a ghost, or I lose my guess."

"What a crotchety idea!" he said, as he caught my eye. "I never thought Eleanor would be so whimsical. She ought to have some one to exert a healthy influence over her, or she will injure herself—she surely will."

"You ought to attempt to teach her a more practical view of life's misfortunes. I'm afraid, however, you'll find her a stupid pupil."

His eye flashed into mine a triumphant gleam.

"'Perseverance conquers all obstacles,' the wise ones say; and I'm a persevering man, you know, Richard."

He took up his cap and lounged out into the garden. I felt a sinking at my heart as he thus openly avowed his hopes and expectations; I could not entirely banish the heavy foreboding, even by recalling the image of the stricken girl, at that moment binding herself, in awful and mysterious companionship, with the spirit that waited for her across the portals of Time. I watched James pacing back and forth, with disquiet steps, through the frozen walks of the garden; presently he lit a cigar, and went out on the lawn, and from thence into the streets. His was one of those minds which do not like their own company when they are uneasy. How he managed to while away the day I do not know; to me it was long and oppressive; Mary remained up-stairs with her sister; Mr. Argyll sat in the library with a book, which he held open but did not read. As the sun declined, I felt that a brisk walk in the cold air would be the best medicine for my drooping spirits—it was my usual remedy.

If I remember aright, I had not been in the direction of

Moreland villa since that singular meeting I had there with the person who had since played so conspicuous a part in our thoughts, if not in our eyes—except twice, when I had gone with Mr. Burton through the vicinity, in hopes of tracing her from the point of her disappearance—but to-day, I mechanically chose that road, led thither by the chain of association. Snow glistened on the hilltops, the shores of the river were skirted with ice, though its central current still rolled bluely between those crystal walls. It was sunset when I began my walk; before I reached the villa, the pink flush was fading from the snowy summits; one large star, preternaturally bright, hung over the turrets of the lonely house, shining through the flush of twilight; gray shadows stretched over the barren hillsides, and a cold steel-blue tinged the ice in the river. How desolate the place looked, stripped of its summer garments! I leaned over the gate, while the night approached, making a picture of how the villa would have appeared at this hour, had that which had happened not happened. It would have been a blaze of light, full of flowers and feasting, and alive with happy human creatures. It had been the intention of the young couple to go immediately to their new home, after the wedding-breakfast, and to begin their housekeeping with a reception of their friends that same evening. Instead of warmth and light, gay laughter and music, rolling carriages and prancing horses, feasting, congratulations, love, beauty and happiness, there was silence and desertion, oh, how appalling! I could not bear the contrast between what was and what should have been.

Before returning to the village I thought I would call upon the gardener's wife, Mrs. Scott, and inquire if she had any tidings of Miss Sullivan; though I knew very well that if she had, she would have let me hear them without waiting for a visit from me. I had grown chilly, leaning so long over the gate, after my rapid walk, and the glow through the window of the little cottage standing at the back of the kitchen-garden, looked inviting. I made my way around to the gate at the back of the premises, and was soon knocking at the door. I had heard Mrs. Scott singing her baby to sleep as I approached the house; but after I knocked there was silence, yet no one answered the summons.

I knocked thrice, the last time rather imperatively, for I was chilly, and did not like waiting so long, when I knew I must be heard. At this the door was opened a little way, very cautiously, the mistress peering out suspiciously.

"Laws! Mr. Redfield, is it you?"—throwing the door wide open. "I beg your pardon for keeping you waiting. If I'd had any idea it was *you*, I shouldn't a' been skeered. But husband's gone to the village, and I was alone with the children, and when you knocked so sudden, my heart came right up in my mouth. I didn't like to see who 'twas. Do come in. How cold 'tis out to-night. You look real blue. Take a chair by the stove and warm yourself. I'm real ashamed I kept you standing so long. How is all the family, sir?"

"About as usual, Mrs. Scott. So you are cowardly when you are alone evenings, are you? I've mistaken your character, then; I've given you credit for being one of the strong-minded women."

"Wal, the truth is," she said apologetically, "I never did used to be afraid of any thing, dead or alive. But, since young Mr. Henry was took away so sudden, I've been nervous and frightened like. I've never got over the shock. I'll holler right out, sometimes, in broad daylight, if any thing startles me, if it's only a door slamming. Husband laughs at me and scolds me, but I can't help it."

"Nobody's going to hurt *you*, because another had evil happen to him."

"I know that as well as anybody. It's not because I've reason to be afeard, that I am—it's the shock, you see. There, there, Johnny, be still, will you? I used to go all over the place the darkest night that ever was—but now, really, I'm ashamed to tell you, I dasn't put my face out after dark."

"I should think it would be unpleasant, such a chronic state of fear," and I half smiled through my own melancholy, at the woman's anxious face.

"Onpleasant! I reckon it is mighty onpleasant. But there's good reason for it."

"You just acknowledged that there was no reason—that it was fancy, Mrs. Scott."

"You're goin' to trip me over my own words, Mr. Redfield. It *was* fancy, at first, just nervousness; but lately—lately, as I said, there's been things—"

"What things?"

"I know you'll laugh at me, sir; and you won't half believe me, neither—so I guess I'd better not make a fool of myself before you. But if you, or any other livin' person, had seen what I seen, and heard what I heard, then you'd know what I know—that's all!"

She spoke with such evident earnestness, and I had hitherto felt so much respect for the sturdy strength and integrity of her New England character, that my curiosity was somewhat aroused. I thought best to let her quiet herself, however, before leading her to converse about the subject most on her mind, as I saw that she still trembled from the fright I had given her by my sudden knock at the door.

"How's the place getting on since the winter weather set in? I suppose your husband had the plants housed long ago. Has he been making any changes with the grounds? I suppose not, since the family has so completely deserted the villa. I came out tonight to take a look at it. This is the twenty-third of December, do you remember?"

"I've been thinkin' of it all day, Mr. Redfield."

"It's terrible to see the house standing there in silence and darkness, to-night. There seemed to me something ghostly about it—I could not endure it. Have you been through the rooms lately?"

This last question I asked without any other object than to keep up the conversation; she had started and looked curiously at me, when I casually used the figurative expression of "ghostly," and now she shook her head.

"I've *not* been through the house lately," she said. "I ought to go, I know—it wants airin', and there's bedclothes and things in the closet wants lookin' after."

"Then why do you not attend to it?"

"That's it," she answered, looking me uneasily in the face.

"What?"

"Well, sir, to tell you the truth, it's my opinion, and I know, laugh as you may—"

"I haven't laughed, Mrs. Scott."

She arose, looked at her boy, now fast asleep in his cradle, went to the window, drew the little white curtain across the lower half, resumed her chair, glanced about the room, and was opening her lips to speak, when a slight rattling sound against the panes of glass, made her clasp her hands together and utter a cry.

"What on earth was that?"

I did indeed now laugh at her pale face, answering, in some vexation,

"It was the snow breaking from the eaves, and slipping down against the window."

"Oh!" drawing a long breath. "You are provoked at me, Mr. Redfield. If you knew all, you wouldn't be."

"Well, tell me all, at once, then, and let me judge."

Again she gave a cautious look about, as if invisible guests might hear and not relish her revelation, drew her chair a little nearer mine, and said, impressively,

"*The house is haunted!*"

"Is that all?" I asked, feeling quite relieved, for her manner had startled me in spite of myself.

"It's enough!" was the significant response. "To tell you flatly, sir, John's about concluded to write to Mr. Moreland, and give up the situation."

"Your husband! is he so foolish, too? There are no such things as haunted houses, Mrs. Scott; and to give up a permanent and excellent home like this, upon any such idle fancy, seems to me very unwise."

"Goodness knows I've liked the place," she cried, bursting into tears, "and that we don't know what to turn to when we leave this. But I'm worn out with it—I can't stand it no longer! You see how unsettled I am now."

Unsettled enough, certainly, from the usually composed and self-reliant woman in whose judgment I had placed considerable confidence.

"You haven't told me any thing to prove your assertion. I don't believe in ghosts, I warn you; but I'd like to hear your reasons for thinking the villa has got one."

"I always made fun of ghosts, myself, and so did John, until this happened. He won't own up now, 'cept that he's ready to leave the place, and won't go in with me in broad daylight, to 'tend to the rooms. So I know he's just as scairt as I am. And you know John's no coward with any thing he can see or handle, and it's no disgrace to a body to be shy of onearthly things. I'm a bold woman myself, but I ain't ready to face a spook."

"What makes you think the house is haunted?"

"Plenty of things."

"Please mention a few. I'm a lawyer, you know, and demand the proofs."

"I've seen a curious light hovering over the roof of the house of nights."

"Did your husband see it also?"

"Yes, he did see it, night before last. He wouldn't believe till he see it. I've seen it seven or eight times myself."

"What was it like?"

"Oh, Lordy, I'm sure I can't tell exactly what it was like, when I never saw any thing of the kind before; I suppose it's like them dead-lights that's been seen over graves. It's more like a bright shadow than an actual light—you can see through it like air. It wanders about the roof, then stops over one particular place. It would make your flesh creep to see it, sir!"

"I would like, above all things, to try it. Do you suppose, if we went out now, we should have the opportunity?"

"It's too early; leastways, I've never seen it so early in the evenin'. The first time, my baby was sick, and I got up in the night to get him some drops, and as I looked out the window, there was the thing shinin'."

"Is that all that makes you think the house haunted?"

"No, sir; we've heard things—curious sounds—even in the daytime."

"What were the sounds like?"

"I couldn't rightly explain 'em to you, sir. They were not human sounds."

"Try and give me some idea of them."

"They'd rise and fall, rise and fall—not like singing, nor crying, nor talking—a kind of wailing music, only not like it, either—that is, not like any thing I ever heard. It seems to come mostly from the family-room, back o' the library. John and me followed it up one evenin'. We went close up on the porch, and put our ears to the shutters. We heard it plain. We was so frightened, we've been glad not to go near the house again. I don't feel as if I ever could."

"I think I know what it was," I said, half inclined to laugh. "The doors or sashes have been left open in such a way as to make a draught. It is the wind, singing through the crevices of the deserted mansion. I, myself, have heard the wind make most unearthly music under such circumstances."

"'Twa'n't wind at all," said the gardener's wife, in an offended tone.

"Perhaps persons have obtained access to the house that have no business there. They may deface the furniture, or carry off articles of value. You really ought to look to it, Mrs. Scott; it's part of your duty."

"There's nobody got in—I'm certain of that. We've examined every door and window. There's not the least sign of any human being about the premises. I tell you, Mr. Redfield, it's spirits; and no wonder, considering how poor Henry was took away."

She said this solemnly, relapsing into moody silence.

I felt quite convinced that the imaginations of the pair, already awed and excited by the murder, had converted some trifling atmospheric or other phenomena, or some combination of circumstances, easily explained when the key to them was found, into the mystery of a haunted house. I was sorry, for two reasons: first, that they thought of leaving, when I knew that their departure would give trouble to Mr. Moreland, who had left the entire charge of the place to them for years, and at a time when he was too bowed with heavier cares to be vexed with these small matters; second, that the couple would be sure to spread the report through the village, causing gossip and conjecture, and exciting a prurient interest which would throng the vicinity with idle wonder-seekers. So I said,

"I wish your husband was at home to-night. I must see him. It will not do for him to trouble Mr. Moreland at this time, by throwing up his situation. You would both of you be sorry and ashamed at such a movement, before many weeks, I'm convinced. What do you say to my coming out here to-morrow, and to our going through the house together? If there is any thing in it which ought not to be, we will turn it out. I will stay until you have aired the house and looked at the clothing; then you can lock it up, and leave it for a few weeks without the necessity of going through it."

"Well, Mr. Redfield, if you're willin' to do it, I ought to be ashamed to hang behind. I'll do it, of course, and be thankful to you; for my conscience hain't been easy, lettin' them things go so. I'm right glad you happened out."

"And tell your husband, please, not to say any thing about this matter to others. It will make it unpleasant for the friends."

"I did tell him not to. He ain't said nothin' yet, I'm sure. It's the last thing we'd be willin' to do, make any more trouble for them that has too much, now, and that has always been kind to us. Must you go, sir?"

"Yes; I'll say good-night, Mrs. Scott. You may expect me in the morning, a little before noon. By the way, have you seen or heard any thing of Miss Sullivan?"

"Not the least thing. She's kept clear of here since that day you found her here. So she's run away, entirely, has she? Well, well, well—I never! I declare, I turn these things over in my brain, some days, till my head gets dizzy."

"So does mine, and my heart sick. Good-night, ma'am."

"Good-night, and good luck to you, this dark night."

She waited to see me through the gate, which led by a little lane past the kitchen-garden, and thence by a private road along down into the main one. As I passed the gate into the lawn, on my way out, I paused perhaps half an hour, in the hope of hearing or seeing the marvels of which the woman had spoken. There was no mystic light, blue or yellow, playing lambently over the roof; no sound, sinking and rising, came wildly on the starlit air; all was profound silence and darkness and coldness like that of the grave.

My half-contemptuous pity of the state of mind into which the gardener's wife had worked herself, gave place to deeper emotions; I turned away, almost running along the smooth, hard-frozen road whose course was clearly discernible in the winter starlight. I met the gardener going home, but did not stop to speak with him—went directly to my lodgings. The fire was out in my room, and I crept into bed, forgetting that I had gone without my tea.

True to my promise, I went the next day to the villa. Mrs. Scott brought the keys, I unlocked the doors, and together we entered the long-vacant place. There is always something impressive, one might say, "ghostly," about a deserted building. When you enter into it, you feel the influence of those who were last within it, as if some portion of them lingered in the old local-ity. I confess that I felt an almost superstitious awe and dread, as I stepped over the threshold which I had last crossed with *him*. How joyful, how full of young and princely life, he had then been, his face lit up, as a man's face lights up when he attends upon the woman he loves and expects soon to make his own! He was leading Eleanor to a carriage; they had been talking about the improvements they were going to make in the house. How every look and tone came back to me! With a silent shudder, I stepped into the hall, which had that moldy smell of confined air belong-ing to a closed dwelling. I hastened to throw open the shutters. When I unclosed a door, I flung it wide, stepping quickly in, and raising the windows, so as to have the sunlight before looking much about. I had to do it all, for my companion kept close to me, never stirring from my elbow. I went into every room on every floor, from the kitchen to the garret. Into the latter I only glanced, as Mrs. Scott said there was nothing up there which she wanted, or which required attention. It was a loft, rough-floored, of comfortable hight, with a window at the gable end. The roof ran up sharply in the center, the villa being built in the Gothic style. There was such a collection of rubbish in it as is usual to such places—broken-down furniture, worn out trunks, a pile of mattresses in a corner, over which a blanket had been thrown to keep them from the dust, some clothing depending from a line, and three or four barrels. Mrs. Scott was standing at the foot of the ladder, which led up into the attic out of a small room, or closet, used for storing purposes. I saw she was uneasy at having me even that far from her, and after a brief survey of the garret, I assured her there were no ghosts there, and descended.

"Help yourself to some of them apples," said the woman, pointing to some boxes and barrels in the room where we now stood. "They're winter pippins. John's going to send them into the city, to the family, in a week or two. We've permission to keep 'em here, because it's dry and cool, and the closet being in the middle of the house, it don't freeze. It's a good place for fruit. Hark! What was that?"

"It was a cat," said I, as I put a couple of the apples in my overcoat pocket. "It sounded like a cat—in the garret. If we shut it up there, it'll starve."

I went up the ladder again, looking carefully about the attic, and calling coaxingly to the animal, but no cat showed itself, and I came down, saying it must have been in one of the lower rooms, and had probably run in since we opened the doors.

"It sartingly sounded overhead," persisted my companion, looking nervous, and keeping closer to me than ever.

I had heard the noise, but would not have undertaken to say whether it came from above or below.

"If that is the material she makes ghosts of, I'm not surprised that she has a full supply," I thought.

In going out, the woman was careful to close the door, and I could see her stealing covert glances into every corner, as we passed on, as if she expected, momently, to be confronted by some unwelcome apparition, there in the broad light of day. There were no traces of any intruders having made free with the house. The clothes and china closets were undisturbed, and the bureaus the same.

"This was Harry's room; he liked it because it had the best view of the river," said Mrs. Scott, as we paused before a chamber on the second floor.

We both hesitated; her apron was at her eyes, and my own throat swelled suddenly: reverently I opened the door, and stepped within, followed by the housekeeper. As I raised the window, and flung back the shutter, she gave a scream. I was really startled. Turning quickly, I saw her with her hands thrown up, an expression of terror upon her face.

"I told you the house was haunted," she murmured, retreating backward toward the door.

"What do you see?" I asked, glancing about for the cause of her alarm.

"This room," she gasped—"it was his—and he comes here still. I know it!"

"What makes you think so? Has it been disturbed? If it has, rest assured it has been by the living, not the dead."

"I wish I thought so," she said, solemnly. "It can not be. No other part of the house is in the least disturbed. No one has had admission to it—it is impossible; not a crack, not a cranny, by which any thing but a spirit could have got in. Harry's been here, Mr. Redfield; you can't convince me different."

"And if he has," I said, calmly, for I saw that she was much agitated, "are you any more afraid of him now than you were when he was in the body? You loved him then; think you he will harm you now? Rather you ought to be glad, since you believe in ghosts, that it is a good spirit which haunts these premises— the innocent spirit of the murdered, not the guilty one of the murderer."

"I know it," she said. "I'm not afraid—I don't think I could be really afraid of Henry's ghost, even if I should see it; but it's so—awful, isn't it?"

"Not to me, at all. If such things were permitted, I should like to meet this spiritual visitant, and ask him the one question—if, indeed, he could answer it. I should like to have him point out the guilty. If his hand could reach out from the spiritual world, and stretch a blasting finger toward his murderer, that would be awful to the accursed one, but it would be welcome to me. But what makes you think Henry his been here?"

She pointed to the bed; there was a pressure upon it, as if some light shape had lain there—just the faintest indentation of a head on one of the pillows; from thence she pointed to a little writing-table, between the windows, on which a book lay open, and where there were some papers and engravings; then to a pair of slippers standing on the carpet at the head of the bed. The room was a delightful one, furnished with blue and white—Henry's favorite colors. Two or three exquisite little pictures hung on the walls, and not the slightest toy occupied a niche in any place but spoke of the taste and refinement which had chosen it. From the two windows, the view of the river flowing amidst the hills, and the lovely country spreading far away, was such as would satisfy the eye of a poet, turned from the page before him on the little writing-table, to rest upon the fairer page of nature.

"I came into this room the day of the funeral," said the housekeeper, with a trembling voice, "and I sot all to rights, as if the master was coming back the next day. But little I thought he would really come! I spread that bed as smooth as paper; I put on fresh slips on the pillows, and sot 'em up without a dent or wrinkle in 'em; I put his slippers with their toes to the wall, and now they're standin' as he always left 'em when he took 'em off. Them papers has been stirred, and he's been readin' in that book. *She* gave him that, and it was a favorite with him; I've often seen him with it in his hand. You may shake your head, Mr. Redfield, but *I know* Henry's been back here in his room."

"If any thing in this room has been disturbed, rest assured there's been some living intruder here. A spirit would have had no need of slippers, and would have made no impression on your smooth bed."

"You can talk your big words, for you are an edicated man, Mr. Redfield, but you can't convince me against my own persuasion. It's been no human being has mussed that spread—why, it's hardly wrinkled—you can just see it's been laid on, and that's all. Besides, how did they get in? Can you tell me that? Through the keyhole, mebbe, and went out the same way!"

Her voice was growing sharp and a little sarcastic. I saw that it was in vain to try to disabuse her mind of its impression while she was in her present excited state. And, indeed, I had no worthy argument to offer. To all appearance the rest of the house had been undisturbed; there was not a broken fastening, a displaced bar of any kind, and nothing missing. It would seem as if nothing weightier than a shadow had stirred the pillow, and moved about the room. As long as I could not tell what it *was*, I could not positively assert what it was *not*.

I sat by the open window, while she smoothed the pillow,

and placed every article with an exactness which would inevitably betray the slightest disturbance.

"You shall see for yourself, sir, the next time you come here," she muttered.

As I waited, I lifted a little volume, which lay, with others, on the table before me. It was Mrs. Browning's, and it opened at a page where a book-mark had been left—once I had seen Eleanor embroidering that very mark, I was sure. The first lines which caught my eye were these:

> *"It trembled on the grass*
> *With a low, shadowy laughter;*
> *The sounding river, which rolled forever,*
> *Stood dumb and stagnant after."*

Just then a cloud swept over the noonday sun; a chill struck through the open window; the wind which blew in, fluttering the page, could not have been more dreary had it blown across a churchyard. Shivering, I continued to read:

> *"It trembled on the grass*
> *With a low, shadowy laughter;*
> *And the wind did toll, as a passing soul*
> *Were sped by church-bell after;*
> *And shadows 'stead of light,*
> *Fell from the stars above,*
> *In flakes of darkness on her face*
> *Still bright with trusting love.*
> *Margret! Margret!*
>
> *He loved but only thee!*
> *That love is transient, too;*

*The wild hawk's bill doth dabble still
In the mouth that vowed thee true.
Will he open his dull eyes,
When tears fall on his brow?
Behold the death-worm in his heart
Is a nearer thing than thou,
Margret! Margret!"**

I know not if the housekeeper spoke to me. The clouds thickened about the sun; a dampness came in from the air. I held the book, staring at it, like one in a trance, and pondering the strange coincidence. Evidently, Henry had read these verses when he last opened the book—perhaps the lovers had read them together, with a soft sigh for the fate of Margret, and a smile in each other's faces to think how safe *their* happiness was—how far removed from this doleful "Romaunt."† Now would he "open his dull eyes," for Eleanor's tears? I seemed to hear the low laugh of the mocking fiend; a more than wintry sereness settled upon the landscape:

"It trembled on the floor!"

Yes! I was fast getting into the mood for believing any thing which Mrs. Scott might assert about the occupant of this chamber. Emotions which I had never before experienced chilled my heart; shapes began to gather in every obscure corner; when the rising wind suddenly blew a door shut, in the hall beneath, I started to my feet.

"We're goin' to have a stormy Christmas," said my companion.

---

* From "The Romaunt of Margret," *The Seraphim and Other Poems* (1838), by Elizabeth Barrett Browning.

---

† A romance or romantic tale or poem.

"It'll suit our feelin's better'n a sunny one, I'm sure. Hark! there's my Johnny cryin', I do believe! I should think his father could keep him quiet a bit, till I get the house shut up again."

"It was that cat, I thought."

"Never mind. I'm through now, if you please, sir. Take a look at this room, and fix it on your mind, if you will; and the next time you're out here, we'll open it together."

We reclosed and barred the shutters throughout the house, carefully fastened the doors, once more leaving it to its desolation. We had seen no ghosts; I do not suppose the woman expected to *see* any, but I felt certain that her fears were in no manner dispelled.

"You see the place is all right," I said, when I handed her the keys. "There is nothing in the world to make you uneasy. I would as soon sleep alone in the villa as in my own room. I will do it, soon, if you are not satisfied. All I ask of you is not to write to Mr. Moreland until I have seen you again. I shall come out before many days, to see how you get along."

"We shall wait until you come again, sir, before we say any thing. I feel better, now things are 'tended to. There's Johnny crying again! Well, Mr. Redfield, good-by. It'll snow by the time you get home."

I had a wild walk back to the village—full of lonely magnificence and gloom, which suited my temper. Gray mists hung over the river and swept about the bases of the hills; gray clouds whirled around their summits; gray snow came down in blinding drifts; a savage wind seemed to be blowing the universe about my ears.

CHAPTER XI.
THE LITTLE GUEST AND
THE APPARITION.

I went to Mr. Argyll's to the Christmas dinner. I was surprised to meet Eleanor in the family group; for, though she now frequently joined the home circle, I thought that on this holiday her own loss would press upon her with overwhelming weight. Instead of this, I saw a light in her countenance which it had never before worn; her face, totally devoid of smiles or color, yet shone with a serene and solemn luster, the most touching, the most saddening, and yet elevating, of any expression I had ever seen upon human features. My intense sympathy with her taught me how to translate this new phase of her mind; I felt that, in those mystic vows which she had taken upon herself with a spirit, she had derived a comfort; that she joyed in the consciousness that she was now and from henceforth evermore the bride of him who waited for her in the mansions of the heavenly country. This life was transient—to be meekly borne a little while alone—then she would go to him who awaited her in the only true and abiding home. I, and I only, looked upon her as the wife of Henry Moreland, as sacredly as if he were her living partner. I only was fitted, by the power of my own passion and suffering, to appreciate her position, and the feelings with which she now returned to her friends, to play such a part in life as duty still pointed out. I can not explain with what an emotion of reverence I took and pressed the little, attenuated hand, which she placed in mine.

There had been, as yet, no change in Eleanor's demeanor toward me. Whether I imagined it in the rest of the family, or whether they had changed, this much was still certain, and gave me the deepest pleasure I could now know: Eleanor was the same to me as she had ever been—the benignant, gentle sister, who loved and trusted me as a dear brother—more dear than ever since I had given such proofs of my devotion to her cause— since she could not but see how my very heart was wrung with the pain which tore her own. As long as she continued to treat me thus, as long as I could give her one smallest atom of pleasure in any way, I felt that I could bear any thing from the others. Not that there was any thing to bear—nothing—nothing, except that indefinable air which a sensitive spirit feels more keenly than any open slight. The new year was now approaching; it would be the most natural time for entering into new business relations; I felt that if Mr. Argyll intended to offer me the partnership, he would do it then. If he did not—I must look out for myself—I must go away.

The Christmas dinner was the sumptuous feast which it always had been, the old housekeeper having taken it into her own hands. She, to judge by her provision, felt that such kind of painstaking would be a relief to the general gloom. No guests were invited, of course. It was touching to see how the servants persisted in placing every imaginable delicacy before Miss Eleanor, which she could not, by any possibility, even taste. A cup of coffee, with a piece of bread, made up her slender Christmas feast. Yet it was a joy to her father to have her at the table at all. Mary's affectionate glances continually sought her face; parent and sister both felt relieved and comforted by its tranquil expression.

James, too, was cheerful; he would have been brilliant had an opportunity offered. I, who read him tolerably well, knew that it was the sight of Eleanor's tranquillity which had inspired him—and that he did not understand that saintly resignation as I did.

In the course of the conversation around the table, which I did my best to make cheerful, I happened to speak of Lenore Burton. It was not the first time I had mentioned her, always with such enthusiasm as to excite the interest of the ladies. Mary asked me many questions about her, finally turning to her sister, and saying,

"You were always so fond of children, Eleanor. May I not send for this beautiful little girl to spend a few days with us?"

"Certainly, Mary, if you think you would like her company."

"Do you think her father would trust her to us a little while, Richard?"

"He can be persuaded, without doubt."

After we had left the table, Mary came to me, with much animation, to whisper her ideas about the proposed visit; she thought the sight of an agreeable, lovely child about the house might interest Eleanor more than any thing else possibly could, and would, at least, delight her father, who was drooping under the silence and mourning in his home. I quite agreed with her in her opinions, deciding to write that evening a pressing plea to Mr. Burton, promising the most careful attention to his frail little household blossom which a trusty housekeeper and loving friends could extend. I would come down to the city for her, and attend her dutifully on her little journey, if his consent was given, and Miss Lenore herself approved the action.

The next day I had an answer. Mr. Burton wrote that Lenore

was delighted with the invitation, and that he accepted it the more willingly, as he was called unexpectedly to Boston, where he should be absent a week or ten days, and that he had not liked leaving his daughter so lonely during the holidays. He added that he was obliged to leave that morning; but I might come for Lenore at any time; I would find her ready; and that, upon his return from Boston, he would come up to Blankville after her; closing his note with polite thanks for our friendly interest in his little girl, etc. Thus every thing was satisfactory. The third day after Christmas I went down, in the morning, to New York, returning in the afternoon with my little treasure, who was brimful of happiness, enjoying the ride with the zest of childhood, and confiding herself to my guardianship with a joyful content, which awakened my tenderest care in response. This artless faith of the child in the providence of the grown-up man it is which brings out the least selfish part of his character, bowing his haughty, hardened nature to minister to the humblest of its confiding wants.

The sisters both came into the hall to receive their little visitor. They took her into the parlors, bright with chandelier and firelight, unhooding and uncloaking her before the grate. I was anxious to witness the impression she made, for I had been so lavish of my praises, as to run the risk of creating a disappointment.

It was impossible to be disappointed in Lenore. She made conquest of the whole family in the half-hour before tea. It was not her exquisite beauty alone, but her sweet expression, her modest self-possession amid her stranger-friends, enhancing its effect. Mr. Argyll brightened as I had not lately seen him; every other minute Mary would repeat the welcome of her little guest with another kiss, declaring, in her pretty, willful way, that Mr. Richard was not going to monopolize Miss Lenore because he was the oldest acquaintance—Lenore having chosen her seat by my side, with her hand nestled in mine.

James was not in the house; he did not come home until some time after we had taken our tea—drank his alone in the dining-room—and joined our circle quite late in the evening. As he came in we were sitting about the fire. Lenore had gone, of her own inclination, to Miss Argyll's side, where she sat on a low stool, with her head against the lady's lap. She made a gay picture as she sat there, framed around with the black of Eleanor's garments. Her traveling-dress was of crimson merino, and her cheeks—what with the ride in the cold air, and the glow of the present fire, were almost as red as her dress; while her golden curls streamed in shining strands over the sable habiliments against which she rested. She was replying archly to some teasing remark of Mr. Argyll's, and I was thinking what a brightness she would give to the dull house, when James came forward, holding out his hand, with one of his pleasantest smiles, saying,

"This is the little lady, is it, whom we have been so anxiously waiting to see? Can I be introduced, cousin Mary, or does not the Queen of Fairies allow herself to make the acquaintance of ordinary mortals?"

You have noticed, reader, how some little cloud, floating in the west at sunset, will be flashed through with rosy light, and how, instantly, while you gaze, it will turn gray, losing every particle of radiance. So the child changed when he approached and spoke to her. Her cheeks faded to a gray whiteness; her eyes were riveted on his, but she could not smile; she seemed to struggle with some inward repugnance and her sense of what courtesy demanded; finally she laid her little cold hand in his, without a word, suffered him to kiss her, and, clinging close to Eleanor, remained pale and quiet—her gayety and bloom were alike gone. Mr. Argyll could not rally her—she shrunk like a sensitive plant.

"If that pallid, stupid little creature is the marvelous child Richard promised us, I must say, he has shown his usual good taste," commented James in an aside to Mary. He was not flattered by the reception he had met.

"Something is the matter with her, James. She is wearied with her journey. I am afraid we are keeping her up too late. She was gay enough a little while since."

"Are you tired? Would you wish to go to bed?" whispered Miss Argyll.

"If you please," she replied, with an air of relief.

"You are not getting homesick so soon?" asked Mr. Argyll.

"I am not; I like it here very much," answered Lenore, candidly. "Something is the matter with me now, sir, and you must please excuse me. My head began to ache just now—so I suppose I had better go to bed."

She bade us good-night with a smile so restrained that I felt afraid she was not going to enjoy her visit. Eleanor herself took her away to the maid who was to attend upon her, and did not return to us until her little guest was in bed.

"Come, Mary, let's drop the baby question, and play chess," said James, impatiently, as we discussed the visitor; "I'm tired of the subject."

"Wait until to-morrow, and you will become interested too," she responded.

"I like hearty little bread-and-butter girls," said he, "but not such die-away misses as that. She looks to me as if she read Coleridge already.* Children should be children, to please me."

The repulsion was mutual. I, only, had noticed the strange

---

* Samuel Taylor Coleridge (1772–1834), a leading Romantic poet, was probably at this time best remembered for his "Rime of the Ancient Mariner," a long, gloomy, and somewhat gory poem first published in 1798. The poem made a great impression on the teenage Mary Godwin (later Mary Shelley) when she heard it recited by Coleridge in her father's house.

effect wrought upon my pet by a sight of James, and knowing, as I did, the peculiarities of her temperament, it had astonished me, and aroused my curiosity. By the ill-humor with which he received any allusion to Lenore, I believed that James himself was conscious that the pure eyes of the child looked straight into the darker chambers of his heart, and was frightened by what she saw there. A young man who was gambling away his uncle's property upon the credit of a daughter's hand which he had not yet won, could not have a very easy conscience; and it was not a pleasant thing to be reminded of his delinquencies by the clear eyes of an innocent child. As he became absorbed in his game of chess, I sat studying his countenance, and thinking of many things. I wondered if his uncle and cousins were not aware of the change which was coming over him; that reckless, dissipated look which writes certain wrinkles in a young man's face, overwritten in his by outer smiles, which could not hide the truth from a discerning eye. I asked myself if I could justify my course in keeping silence about what I had seen; it was my plainest duty to inform Mr. Argyll, not only on his account, but on James' also. Such a knowledge, coming to his uncle, though it would be terribly mortifying to his nephew, might be the means of breaking his new fetters of habit before they were riveted upon him. Such, I felt, was my duty. At the same time, I shrunk from it, as a person situated as I was naturally would shrink; I was liable to have my motives misconstrued; to have it hinted that self-interest was prompting me to place James in a bad light. No, I couldn't do it! For the hundredth time I came to this conclusion, against the higher voice of the absolute right. I was glad to strengthen myself in my weak course by remembering that Mr. Burton had requested my silence, and that I was not at liberty to betray his confidence. Looking at him, thinking these things, with my thoughts more in my eyes than they ought to have been had I been on my guard, James suddenly looked up and encountered my gaze. He pushed the board aside with an angry motion, which overthrew half the men and entirely disconcerted the game.

"Well, how do you like my looks, Richard?"

"Well, how do you like my looks, Richard?" the defiant eyes glittering with a will which overpowered my own, smiling a deadly smile which threatened me.

"How peevish you are, James! I believe you threw up the game because you saw I was checkmating you," cried his cousin.

"That's it, my dear child; I never would allow myself to be checkmated!"

"Then you shouldn't play!"

"Oh, sometimes I allow women to win the game; but when I play with men, I never give up. The man who attempts the chances with me must prepare for defeat."

"How generous you are to the witless sex," said Mary, sarcastically. "I am much obliged to you, that you sometimes allow us to win. Just pick up that castle you have sent tumbling in ruins, if you please, sir—and don't ask me to play chess for at least a fortnight."

I perceived a threat in his words of which the girl was quite innocent; he was throwing down the gauntlet to *me*; again and again his air, his words, were such that I could put no other construction upon them. He was determined to misunderstand me—to look upon me as a person seeking to injure him. I was in his way—I must get out of it. This was the manner he put on to me. I felt that night, more than ever, the conviction that my connection with the Argylls was about to be broken. If James felt thus toward me, I should be unwilling to take a position which he regarded as belonging, of right, to himself. Worse than all, I felt that his treacherous nature was working secretly against me, and that his efforts had already told upon those whose love and respect was most precious to me.

Shortly after, I took my leave; he was so engrossed, with his back toward me, looking over some old engravings, that he did not turn to say good-night. My room at my boarding-house had a particularly cheerless air that evening; I felt lonely and embittered. My heart ached for sympathy. I resolved that, if a partnership was not offered on New Year's, I would propose a visit to my mother, for whose love and encouragement I longed. The event of going away, too, would give Mr. Argyll the opportunity of declaring himself in one way or another.

Lenore's visit was a decided success—in the way, too, which I had hoped for. Her fine and spiritual nature was drawn toward Eleanor in a manner which made the latter love her, and grow to feel a consolation in the touch of the little hand, the unsought kiss, and the silent sympathy which brought the child to sit hours by her side, saying nothing, but looking with wonder and reverence at a sorrow too deep for her young heart to fathom. Lenore frolicked with Mr. Argyll, chatted and sung with Mary; but she was always ready to leave either for her quiet corner by Miss Argyll. Mary pretended jealousy, though we were all glad to see the interest Eleanor took in the child. One of our greatest pleasures was in Lenore's singing. I have mentioned the purity and great compass of her voice. To hear her sing some of Handel's music, of a Sabbath twilight, was almost to obtain a glimpse into the heaven toward which her voice soared. I saw Eleanor quietly weeping while she sung, and I knew the music was loosening the tense strain upon her heart-chords.

I was interested in watching two things—first, the attachment between Miss Argyll and Lenore; secondly, the persistent effort of James to overcome his first aversion, and his ultimate success. By the second day he had mastered his chagrin at the evident dislike of the child, who could hardly compel herself to be polite to him, and who grew constrained and pale whenever he was near her. James Argyll was not the man to allow a child to slight him with impunity. His indolence was a repugnance to business and study; it was no weakness of the will, for when he

set his resolves upon an object, he usually accomplished it. I saw
that he had resolved to conquer Lenore. He paid court to her
as if she were a "lady of the land," instead of a little girl; on New
Year's he overwhelmed her with splendid presents; he took her
out sleigh-riding with him, in a fancy cutter,* which he declared
was only just large enough for those two, with chimes of silver
bells and a spirited horse. I ought not to have felt grieved that
Lenore, also, like the rest of the world, proved faithless to me.
But I did. I was more hurt by her growing indifference to me and
her increasing fascination for James than the subject warranted.
I should have known that rides and dolls, flowers and flatteries,
and a dainty little ring for her forefinger, would win any little
maiden of eleven; but I had estimated Lenore's character higher.
I had noticed her attractions and repulsions, the former always
toward noble and true persons—the latter toward the unworthy.
Now, however, my little bird was charmed by the serpent's eye;
she was under the influence of James' will, and I resigned her.

—

About ten days after my visit to Mrs. Scott, I kept my promise
to her, by returning to inquire about the present condition of
Moreland villa. I saw, as soon as I entered the cottage, that her
mind was preyed on by the same convictions which had troubled her on the former occasion.

"If there ain't at least one ghost in that house, then there never
was such a thing, and there never will be—now! You've seen for
yourself there ain't a human being in it—*and there is something!*
I've seen it and heard it, and you can't convince a person against
them two senses, I reckon."

---

* A lightweight, open horse-drawn sleigh, usually for two.

"I don't want to convince you, Mrs. Scott; I only want to convince myself what this thing is which you have seen and heard. Have you had any new revelations?"

"I've seen the death-light once since, standing over the house; we saw it, too, shinin' out of that room—John and I saw that together. We was so set on findin' out whether it was spirits or not, we mustered up courage to go through the house ag'in the next day, and as sure as you're settin' there, *something* had been back and laid down on that bed ag'in—something: light, that scarcely made a dent—you needn't tell me 'twas any human mortal, which it wasn't. We've heard children cryin', too, which is an evil omen, the dream-book says; an' to clap the climax, Mr. Redfield, there's no use keepin' it back—*we've seen the ghost!*"

I was now as interested as the woman could desire; she had stopped, mysteriously, after making this grave declaration, and sat looking me in the eyes. I returned her gaze with one of silent inquiry, leaning a little forward in my chair. Mrs. Scott smoothed her apron absently, with her large hands, still looking into my eyes, as if she saw the ghost in their distending pupils. I made up my mind that I was going to hear either something of ridiculous shadowyness magnified into an apparition, or something which would give some tangible clue to the mystery, if there was a mystery, of Moreland villa.

"You have been fortunate," said I. "What was it like, pray?"

"You've noticed there was a little balcony under the windows of Henry's room?"

"I know there is such a balcony."

"It was there we saw it. You know how bright the nights have been lately, with the full moon and the snow. John and I walked out, night before last, to the front of the villa, to see what we could see—and there it was! It was as light as day, and we both had a good look at it. I don't know how long it might have stayed if I hadn't screamed. John clapped his hand over my mouth to stop me, but he was too late; it sort of riz right up and disappeared."

"But what was it like—man, woman, or child?"

"It was like a ghost, I tell you," replied the housekeeper, stoutly. "I s'pose sperits are dressed purty much alike in the next world, whether they're men or women. We read in the Bible of the white robes—and I've never heard of a spook that was dressed in any other way. It may have been Henry in his shroud, for all I know—that's what I believe it was—there now!"

"Henry was never dressed in a shroud," I answered, gravely; "he was buried in a black-broadcloth suit. So you see that you were not correct there."

"Oh, well, Mr. Redfield, we can't understand these things—it isn't given to us. I can tell you what John and I saw, and you can make up your own mind. There was a shape, on the balcony, standing straight up, white all over. A long white garment hung from its head to its feet; its face was turned up to the moon, and its arms were raised as if it prayed. Its eyes was wide open, and its face as pale as a corpse's. John and I will both make our affy-davit to it, in court, if it's necessary."

"Where did it go to when it disappeared?"

"It seemed to me to turn into the air; but that I wouldn't be so sure about. John thought it went right through the side of the house."

"Was the window open behind it?"

"Wal, really now, I wouldn't swear that it was, or wasn't. The fact is, I was so scaart the minit I saw it, I like to have dropped. John was for staying 'to see if it wouldn't come ag'in,' but I wouldn't let him, so we both cut and run."

"I am sorry you didn't use your eyes to better advantage."

"When you see a thing like that, I reckon you'll run, too. It ain't at all likely the window was open, or we would have noticed it. It was all shut up the next mornin', the same as ever."

"That was yesterday. I suppose you have not been in the villa since?"

"Lord! no, sir. I wouldn't go now for a hundred dollars."

"Have you noticed any thing else peculiar?"

"Yes, sir. There's been footsteps around the house in the snow."

"Indeed?" I said, eagerly; "that is more like something. Can I see them now?"

"No, sir; the sun's melted 'em all off. But if you think they're the tracks of persons comin' about the house for any purpose, just tell me, will you, sir, how they happened to be just about the porch, and soon, and not a track to it, nor away from it, in no direction?"

"Indeed, I can not explain it, until I've rooted out the mystery from the beginning."

"Nor it can't be explained," cried the housekeeper, triumphantly.

It worried her to think I was so skeptical when she had given such absolute proofs; the idea of the haunted villa was making her really sick, yet she would not give up her cherished belief in its being haunted. I think she would have been disappointed if any one had come forward and sworn himself the ghost.

I sat a little while pondering her statements. There had been nothing, on the former occasion, to convince me that any intruder, human or spiritual, had been in the villa—except the shadowy imprint of a form on Henry's bed, and for the proof that it had not been made before the house was cleaned up, I had nothing but her word. As for the death-light and the wailing sounds, I conceived that, in that lonesome, solitary place, two persons of the class to which these belonged, with their excited imaginations reacting upon each other, might easily persuade themselves of such marvels. Even in this last statement, that both of them had clearly and distinctly seen a white form on the balcony of the room, I did not find much to disturb me. There is nothing better for producing all kinds of shapes and phantoms to a frightened or superstitious eye, than a bright, moonlight night. It is far better than the deepest darkness. The earth is full of weird shadows; the most familiar objects take on an unnatural appearance in the gleaming rays, enhanced in their strange effect by the black, fantastic shadows which stretch away from them. Add to this, a garment of snow spread over every thing. The landscape on which we have rested our gaze, every day, for years, under these circumstances will be as novel to us, as if it were a bit of scenery transplanted from some strange and far country. A vivid fancy, predisposed to the work, can make an excellent ghost out of a rose-bush or a fence-post—a fearful apparition out of the shadow of a cornice heaped with snow. In the present case, not only were the man and his wife in that feverish state in which the eye makes visions for itself, but they were quite ready to link such phantoms with Henry's room, which they had previously decreed to be the favorite abode of the ghost. A review of the whole case led me rather to be vexed with them, than satisfied there was any reason for the mental "stew" into which they had heated themselves. The only tangible things of the whole medley were—the footprints. If there were actually traces of feet walking about the premises, that was enough to satisfy me—not of a ghost, but of a person, engaged in prying about the villa for some unlawful purpose. I made up my mind to watch for this person, and entrap him. It occurred to me, at once, that one of those dare-devil spirits, to be found in every community, was purposely getting up scenic effects on the premises, for the amusement of spreading the report that the villa was haunted, and exciting the gossip and credulity of the village. I was indignant at the heartlessness of the plan, and resolved, should I catch the perpetrator, to inflict such summary chastisement, as would cure him of his taste for practical joking. The assertion of the woman that the tracks began and ended nowhere—that no one had approached the house, because there were no footsteps coming in from any direction—did not receive entire credit from me. Were that actually the case, then, it was positive evidence that the person was secreted in the dwelling—an idea foolish and incredible on the face of it, for many reasons.

However, I was in earnest, now, about the matter; I would ascertain the truth or explode the falsehood, and make an end of it; before painful reports should reach the ears of friends, or every idle ragamuffin in the country make that hallowed place, consecrated by the ties and memories of the one now gone, the focus of his vulgar curiosity.

"Where is your husband?"

"He's sortin' pertaters, or tyin' up seeds, in the loft."

"Please call him down, and give me the keys of the house."

The gardener came, following very reluctantly, at my bidding, while I again entered the villa, and went over every room, stationing him in the hall, so that no one could possibly escape during my visit to the lower and upper floors. I searched from cellar to garret, while Mrs. Scott, with her pale-blue eyes wide open, and affecting a bustling bravery which her looks belied, accompanied me. Once, at a sudden noise, she seized the skirts of my overcoat, but resigned them when I told her it was caused by John's shutting the front hall-door.

"Dear! dear! there's rats in the villa, at last!" she exclaimed, removing the cover of a flour-barrel which stood in the store-room. "They've been in this flour! I'm sorry, for they're an awful pest. They'll make trouble if I don't watch 'em clost. I believe I'll pizen 'em. Mrs. Moreland told me to take this flour home and use it up; but we haven't needed it yet, and I've left it here, and now they've made pretty work with it."

"If there are rats here, I shan't be surprised at all kinds of noises," I remarked. "Rats are equal to almost any thing. They will tramp like an army of men, or stalk like a solitary burglar. They will throw down plates and cups—like this one, broken on the floor here, since we came here last; muss pillows and drag books out of place. You really will have to keep a sharp lookout."

"They won't cry like a child, nor moan like a sick person, nor stand on balconies dressed in shrouds!" observed the housekeeper.

"I think they would do the first two," and I smiled, "but as to the latter, I'm not prepared to assert."

"I reckon not. I only wish you'd seen it, Mr. Redfield."

"I shall stay to-night in the hope of that pleasure, Mrs. Scott."

"I'm right glad to hear you say so, sir. It's not pleasant to be placed in the situation I am—to know what I know, and not to have my word taken."

It was true; it could not be pleasant for her to have her earnest statements received with so much skepticism; I did not wonder that she felt hurt, almost offended; at the same time I felt as if I, in my turn, should be intensely aggravated if I found out there was nothing in all this flurry.

This second search resulted in nothing, like the first. It was nearly dark when we returned to the cottage, where Mrs. Scott allowed me to dandle her fat, good-natured baby, Johnny, while she prepared tea in a style befitting the important occasion of "company."

"If you're in earnest about sittin' up to watch, I'll make coffee, instid of tea, if it's agreeable to you, Mr. Redfield. It's better to keep one awake."

I assented to this assertion, being of a similar opinion myself. She set her husband to grinding the delectable berry in a hand-mill, and soon an excellent supper, with cold ham and hot biscuits, was placed upon the table. The night promised to be clear and cold; the moon would not rise until about eleven; I fortified myself against the hardships of my adventure by two cups of strong coffee, with a substantial meal; passed an hour or two chatting with the couple and singing Johnny to sleep; then, about eight o'clock, I buttoned my overcoat close, tied my muffler about my neck, and went forth to begin picket-duty.

"I'll leave the coffee-pot on the stove, and a good fire," was the parting promise of the good woman, who seemed to think I had rather a solemn time before me.

"Thank you, Mrs. Scott; if I make no discoveries by one or two o'clock, I shall come in to warm myself, and give up the hope for this occasion. You know midnight is the witching-hour—it will be useless to stay much later."

"The Lord be with you," she said, earnestly.

Armed with a stout walking-stick, with which I intended to inflict punishment upon any intruder of earthly mold, I walked out on the lawn, taking such a survey as I could in the dim light; like the rain in the children's riddle, I went "round and round the house," and finally took station on the front porch, where I walked softly back and forth, listening for sounds within and without. I heard and saw nothing. The long hours slipped slowly away. Just before moonrise the darkness seemed to deepen, as it does before dawn. My intention was to take up some position on the lawn, where, unseen myself, I could command the approaches to the villa, and also have a view of Henry's room, with the balcony. It was time now to secrete myself, before the approaching moon should reveal me to the person or persons who might themselves be on the watch. Accordingly, I selected a seat on the little rustic bench, completely encircled with bushy evergreens, which not only concealed my person, but afforded me considerable protection from the cold. I can not, to this day, breathe the pungent odor of the spicy trees, without recalling the experiences of that night. A silence, like that which Dr. Kane speaks of as one of the most impressive features of the long Arctic night,* brooded around; over against the hills came gradually stealing the silvery luster of the rising moon, while the valleys yet lay in profoundest gloom; the dimly glimmering stretches of snow broadened into whiter fields; the picturesque villa, with its turrets and porches and pointed roof, stood black and quiet before me. I could hear a dog barking afar off, as it were some dream-dog barking in some dream-world. I had almost forgotten the cause of my being there, at that strange hour, in that lone spot, gazing at that dark mass of building, empty of life and warmth as was *her* heart of joy or hope; the intense cold, the odor of the pines and hemlock, the trance of thought into which I had fallen, were benumbing me.

Suddenly I saw a shapeless and shadowy brightness hovering amid those dark turrets. It was the death-light of which Mrs. Scott had told me. A warm thrill ran through my fingers and toes, arousing me to the keenest consciousness. I watched it flutter and move—stand still—flutter again—and disappear. It lasted perhaps three minutes. In that time I had made up my mind as to the mysterious appearance—it was the light of a lamp or candle being carried about in a person's hand. That was what it most resembled; but who carried it, and how was the reflection thrown *there*, over the roof? There was certainly a mystery about this which, had I been at all superstitious, or even nervous, would have unfitted me for any further cool

---

* Elisha Kent Kane, M.D., published his memoirs of two Arctic expeditions (1853–55) to search for the lost explorer Sir John Franklin, the second of which Kane commanded.

investigation. I resolved that if I could not master the marvel then, I would do it by the light of day. I watched intently, hoping it would reappear, and give me some glimpse of its origin. While I waited, a ray of light pierced through the shutters of Henry's room. I will acknowledge that for one single instant the hand of the dead seemed laid on my heart; it turned cold, and refused to beat. The next, I smiled grimly at myself. I had never been a moral or physical coward. The solution of the mystery was now in my grasp, and I had no idea of letting it slip. I was confident that some person was playing the mischief in the deserted house; but if I had really expected to confront the inhabitants of another world, I should not have hesitated. The key of the main entrance was in my pocket; I walked swiftly to the house, unlocked the door as softly as possible, and grasping my stick firmly in my hand, sprung up the stairs. It was quite dark in the house, although it was now light out of doors; in my haste, I hit my foot against a chair at the bottom of the stairs, and overthrew it. I was provoked, for I wished to come upon these midnight prowlers unawares. Knowing just where the room was situated, I went directly toward it; it was very dark in the upper passage, all the blinds being closed; I groped for the handle of the door—something rustled, something stirred the air—I flung the door open. There was no light in it. All was dark and silent. Before I could fling the shutter open, letting in a peaceful flood of silver moonlight, my hope of detecting the intruder was almost at an end. I was certain that something had passed me in the obscurity of the hall; I had been conscious of that subtle magnetism which emanates from a human form, perceived in the blackest night. It might be the magnetism of soul instead of body, and a disembodied spirit might have sent the same electric current through me. At all events, I had now nothing for my labor. I did not think that another journey over the house would result in any discovery, since the warning had been given; I had no lamp or lantern with me; I reluctantly, after lingering and listening some time in vain, closed the room and the house, and returned to the cottage, where I drank the coffee which awaited me, laid down on a buffalo-robe before the stove, and slept away my vexation.

I was not very communicative as to my adventures when eagerly questioned by my entertainers the following morning. They were satisfied, by my very reticence, that I had seen something to puzzle me, and were both alarmed and triumphant. In answer to their inquiries, which they were too respectful to press, I assured them that I had reason to think, with them, that the villa required attention. I had not been able to satisfy myself who was disturbing the premises; but that I should not rest until I knew. I should return that night and sleep in the villa; I wished to enter it very quietly, probably before dark, so as not to alarm the inmate or inmates; and I was confident that I should thus be able to pounce upon the ghost. Mrs. Scott regarded me with admiring awe.

"She wouldn't go for to sleep in that house alone for all the riches of Solomon," and wouldn't I, at least, provide myself with pistols?

When I went into Mr. Argyll's office that morning, he greeted me with marked coldness. At last I could not conceal from myself that, not only had his manner changed, but that he wished me to feel that it had. He gave me, as I entered, a searching, suspicious glance, saying, "Good-morning, Richard," in the most formal tone. Nothing further. I took up a book, hiding my pain and embarrassment in an attempt to read; but my mind was not on the legal difficulties expounded therein: I was wondering at the causes of the situation in which I found myself. A hanger-on! yes, an unwelcome hanger-on in an office where I no longer had any conceded rights—in a home where I was no longer trusted.

"Has Mr. Argyll placed a spy on my actions? Does he know already that I was out the entire night? and does he judge me before he has an explanation?" I asked myself, indignantly. "If he thinks I am forming bad habits, doing wrong in any respect, why does he not remonstrate with me—give me a chance to defend myself?"

I had intended to take his advice in the matter of the haunted house; but now I sat, angry and silent, feeling, oh, so wounded and forlorn. I did not stay long in the office; going to my room, I wrote a long letter to my mother, telling her I should come soon to pay her the visit which should have been sooner made had I not been engrossed with the duty to which I had vowed myself.

Yes! I had pledged my own heart to devote myself to the discovery of Henry Moreland's murderer; and if Eleanor herself had put her foot on that heart, and crushed it yet more, I do not know that I should have held my vow absolved.

I should not have gone to the mansion that day, had not a message been sent, late in the afternoon, that Mr. Burton had arrived, and expected me to meet him at tea. I went; and had the pleasure of seeing little Lenore enthroned by the side of James, who attended upon her as if she were a princess, and of being treated with bare civility by all save Mr. Burton. Miss Argyll was ill, and did not come down.

I saw the observant eye of Mr. Burton watching the intimacy between his daughter and her new friend; whether he was pleased or not, I could not decide; the eye which read the secret thoughts of other men did not always betray its own impressions. I was certain, too, that he observed the change in the demeanor of the family toward me, and my own constrained manner.

CHAPTER XII.
THE NIGHT IN MORELAND VILLA.

Mr. Burton's arrival prevented my fulfilling the intention of sleeping at Moreland villa that night; I immediately resolved to defer my explorations until he could keep me company. The next day he came to my room, and we had, as usual when we met, a long talk over things past, present and to come. I did not introduce the subject of the mystery at the villa until we had discussed many other matters. My companion was preoccupied with important business of his own — the same which had taken him to Boston; but his interest was pledged, almost as earnestly as mine, to unmask the criminal of the Blankville tragedy, and any reference to that sad subject was sure to secure his attention. Baffled we acknowledged ourselves, as we talked together that morning, but not discouraged. Mr. Burton told me that he was on the track of two five-hundred-dollar bills of the Park Bank, which had left the city the week after the murder, taking widely-different flights; there had one come back from St. Louis, whose course his agents were tracing. As for the sewing-girl, she had the power of vanishing utterly, like a light extinguished, leaving no trace behind, and her pursuers literally in the dark. This comparison of the detective reminded me of the curious light which had led me, like a Jack-o'-lantern, into a quagmire of uncertainty; I was about to begin my account of it, when he gave me one of those peculiar piercing looks of his, saying,

"You have not yet entered into the contemplated partnership?"

"No, Mr. Burton; and I hardly think now that I shall."

There was some bitterness in my tone; he evinced no surprise, asking, simply,

"Why?"

"I think James has been chosen to fill the place."

"But, he has not been admitted to the bar."

"He is studying a little recently; probably in order to pass an examination."

"The wind is changing," said Mr. Burton, speaking like the old gentleman in Bleak House." "I see how the land lies. The goodly and noble Argyll ship is driving on to the rocks. Mark my words, she will go to pieces soon! you will see her ruins strewing the shore."

"I pray heaven to avert your prophecy. I hope not to live to see any such sight."

"How can it be otherwise?" he exclaimed, rising and pacing to and fro through my little room, like a caged elephant. "A spendthrift and a gambler—a man like *that*—about to have the helm put in his hands! But it's none of my business—none of my business; nor much yours, either."

"It is mine!" I cried; "I can not help but make it mine, as if these girls were my sisters, and Mr. Argyll my father. Yet, as you say—it is, indeed, nothing to me. They will not allow it to be!"

I drooped my head on my arms; my own loss and disappointment were receding into the background before the idea

---

* While Mr. Jarndyce does not utter this phrase in Charles Dickens's *Bleak House* (1853), he is continually commenting on the wind's direction.

of their possible discomfiture. I was startled by the detective bringing his clenched hand down upon the table with a blow which shook it; he was standing, looking not at me, but at the wall, as if he saw some one before him, invisible to me.

"James Argyll is a singular man—a *singular* man! A person ought to be a panther in cunning and strength to cope with him. By George, if I don't look out, he'll overreach me yet—with that will of his. I see everybody about me succumbing. He's having the game all in his own hands. By the way, Redfield, I was a little surprised to see Lenore so fond of him."

"Why so, Mr. Barton? James is an attractive, elegant young man; he has never had any lack of admirers. It would rather have been strange if your daughter had *not* fancied him. He has been very good to her."

"He has, indeed; I'm sure I ought to be greatly obliged to all of you. Did I ever tell you that I place great confidence in Lenore's intuitive perception of character? You know that I have a remarkable gift that way myself. When I meet people, I seem to see their minds, and not their bodies—I can't help it. Well, I've remarked the same thing in my child. She is so young and inexperienced that she can not explain her own impressions; she has her instantaneous partialities, and I have noticed that she leans toward true natures like a flower toward the light, and away from the false as if they were shadows. I hardly expected she would be so intimate with young Argyll."

I remembered the curious effect his first address had made upon her; but I did not repeat it to her father. I was sensitive about appearing in any manner jealous of James; if he could win my friends from me, even that little girl whom I had loved for her pure sweetness, let them go! I was too proud to solicit them to reconsider their opinions.

"Do you know," continued my companion, "he is performing

a marvel with my little Lenore? He has gained a great ascendancy over her in these few days. This morning, for a purpose which you will realize I considered highly important, I endeavored, alone with her in my own apartment, to place her in the clairvoyant state. For the first time, I failed. Her mind is no longer a pellucid mirror, reflecting truths without color or refraction. She is under the influence of a counter-will, as strong as my own—and mine moves mountains," he added, with a laugh.

"I shouldn't think you would like it."

"I don't; but she is going home to-morrow. I will tell you why I wished to procure Lenore's aid again. I have succeeded in tracing Leesy Sullivan to this village. She came here the day after we frightened her from Brooklyn—that is, she got off the cars at a little station about six miles from here, not daring to land at this depot, and, I have no doubt, started on foot for Blankville, coming here in the night."

"That aunt of hers is in the work," I exclaimed. "We are justified in taking any step to compel her to own up where she conceals that girl."

"I am convinced that her aunt knows nothing whatever about her. Has Mrs. Scott kept a sharp lookout at the villa?"

"She has not seen her since that first day; and I believe it would be difficult for her to set her foot on the place without being discovered, for the woman has got it into her head that the place is haunted, and she is on guard night and day."

"Haunted?"

Mr. Burton sat down and drew up his chair with an appearance of interest, which led me to recount our experiences at the villa, and my intention of completing my researches that night, in his company, if he had no objection. He said, "Of course; it would give him pleasure; he liked nothing better than an adventure of the kind."

In fact, the idea evidently pleased him immensely; his face brightened, and after that, for the rest of the day, for the first time in our brief acquaintance, I saw him a little flurried and expectant. One of his mottoes was:

"Learn to labor, and to *wait*."

His was one of those minds which would have kept silence seven years, rather than speak a moment too soon; he was seldom in a hurry, no matter what was at stake; but the fancy for lying *perdu** in a haunted house, to "nab" a ghost, was a novelty in his detective experience, which inwardly amused him.

He smiled to himself more than once during the intervening hours. As soon as tea was over, we excused ourselves to the family, kissed Lenore, and, saying that Mr. Burton would stay with me all night, we took our departure. I left the conduct of the proceedings in his hands. When we reached the cottage, we found Mrs. Scott disposed to regard the non-fulfillment of my engagement on the previous night as proof that I was frightened from the pursuit; she accepted my excuse, however, and highly approved of my having a companion in the spiritual dangers which I was about to encounter. She made us, moreover, some of her excellent coffee, to aid us in keeping awake, and gave us her prayers for our protection along with the keys of the house.

"Treat a ghost as you would any other burglar," said my companion, as we approached the villa, in the darkness, by the back entrance. "Steal a march on him if you can."

It was a wild night for an enterprise like ours. It reminded me of that night upon which Henry Moreland was murdered. One of those sudden changes in the weather, common to our climate,

---

* Hidden, concealed.

had been transpiring through the day, and now the warm, wild wind which brings in the "January thaw," was blowing about the place, making every loose board creak, and rubbing the bare branches of the trees against each other with a grating sound. Black clouds, with ragged edges, skurried along the air, with the large stars looking down between, with wide, bright eyes, as of fear. While we stood outside, the great drops began to patter down; and presently it was raining violently, as it rained *that* night. As gently as if he were a robber making a felonious entrance, Mr. Burton turned the key in the lock; we entered the thick darkness of the house, closed the door, and stole noise-lessly, I taking the lead, along the stairs and corridors, until we came to Henry's room. This we entered, and, finding chairs, sat down upon either side the little table in absolute silence. But we might safely have knocked over half the furniture without giving alarm to any inmate—had there been an inmate of the room or villa—such a tremendous uproar was now made by the elements. As the rain dashed fitfully against the windows, and the wind shook the solitary building, I was nearly overpowered with the memories which the place and the storm so vivified. I was in a fit mood to become a convert to a nocturnal spec-ter—in that hour of gloom and tempest, under the roof of the murdered, the material world seemed not so far removed from the awful and shadowy confines of the spiritual, as it appeared in the common routine of daylight life. As my heart thumped loudly with the agitation of feelings almost too powerful for mortal endurance, I was glad to consider that my companion was cool, calm and vigilant. He had no such memories of the wind and rain to overwhelm him as I had; this roof was not the roof of his friend—he did not know Eleanor.

It was rather impressive to the dullest imagination to be sit-ting there at night, in that empty mansion, in the darkness, with the storm beating around it, waiting for—we knew not what. To me, with my ardent temperament, and under the peculiar circumstances, it was exciting in the highest degree.

For a long time there was but one interruption to our silent watch. Mr. Burton leaned over the table, whispering,

"Did you hear some one singing?"

"I heard nothing but the wind, and the creaking of a tree against the side of the house, except the rain, that I would be sure of. Hark!"

I did think I heard a soft, angelic note of music swelling in the air above me, but at that moment the tempest redoubled its clamor, beating out all lesser sounds.

"Unless I am mistaken, there was a human voice," he continued, in the same whisper.

"Or a heavenly one," I murmured.

I believe Mr. Burton said "nonsense!" but I am not certain. Again there was a long interval of waiting; we both leaned over toward each other at the same instant, as the sound of something shoved overhead attracted our attentive ears.

"It is rats in the garret," said I. "Mrs. Scott says they are in the house."

"I hardly think it was rats; but we will wait a while."

Mr. Burton had brought a lamp and matches, so that we could have a light when we wished it: if we heard any thing more overhead, I knew he would examine the attic. There was a lull in the rain; as we sat expectant, the pushing sound was shortly followed by a light, regular patter, as of soft footsteps, along the floor of the garret. I had heard rats make precisely similar sounds traversing a ceiling; and though my heart beat a little faster, I was still quite certain it was these troublesome vermin.

The next thing which fixed our attention was a glimmer of light. I think the most spectral visitant could hardly have affected me as did that sudden ray of light, shooting through the key-hole and under the bottom of the door. Silently it crept along over the carpet, moving as if the object which threw it was carried in the hand of a person walking. I do not know exactly what I did expect when it paused in front of the door, except that the door would open, and I should see—the mystery. An instant of suspense—then the flickering light wavered and moved around to the opposite angle from that at which it had first appeared—it was going through the corridor and down the stairs.

"All right," breathed my companion, in a scarcely audible whisper. "Wait!"

The hand which he laid on my own was cold with excitement. As the last yellow gleam trembled and disappeared, the elements conspired in a grand attack upon our citadel; we could hear nothing but the roar of their artillery—the tramp of their battalions. We waited perhaps five minutes.

"Now," and I arose, following Mr. Burton through the darkness, as he silently opened the door, crossed the corridor, and, leaning over the railing, looked down into the lower hall. We could see nothing, until, as we descended the stairs, a faint effulgence from some distant room penetrated the obscurity. With cautious steps we followed it up through the hall and library, to the family-room, from which, it will be recollected, Mrs. Scott assured me she had heard mysterious noises. The door was open a little distance, but not sufficiently to give us a view of the interior. As we paused on the threshold, we heard a sigh—a deep, long-drawn, tremulous sigh. With a deft hand my companion pushed the door ajar, so that we could step in, and we both silently entered. This room, in summer, was the favorite sitting-room of Mrs. Moreland; and here, upon the walls, she had the portraits, life-size, in oil, of her little family. In front of us, as we stepped in, hung the likeness of Henry Moreland. Before it stood a woman, one hand holding aloft a lighted candle, in a small chamber-candlestick, the other pressed upon her heart, as if to keep down those painful signs. Motionless, rapt, absorbed she stood; we made no sound, and if we had, I do not think she would have heard us; her back was toward us; the light was thrown full on the picture upon which her gaze was bent.

The Portrait.

The woman was Leesy Sullivan. I knew her at once, though her face was turned from us. Here, at last, we had found the fugitive we sought, haunting the home of the man of whose murder my thoughts accused her, standing before his portrait, in the dead of night, unwitting who were the witnesses of her secret, as she betrayed it now. How she had obtained access to the villa, or how long she had been its inmate, I left to future inquiry to develop—the present scene was all-engrossing.

A long—long—long time she stood there; we did not interrupt her; it was probably the expectation that she would utter some soliloquy which would be of importance to us, as revealing what was on her mind, which kept my companion quiet. She said nothing, however; only drawing those deep sighs; until, at the last, she set the light on the little table beneath the picture, and, lifting up both hands with a passionate gesture toward it, sobbed one word—"Henry!"

Then, slowly, as if her eyes refused to leave the object of their attraction, she began to turn away. We had one instant's glance at her face before she discovered us; there was a burning spot upon either thin cheek, and two great tears, frozen, as it were, upon her eyelids; and a tremulous curve to the full, red lips of the tender and beautiful mouth, as if they quivered with grief and love. There was nothing wild or severe about her at that moment. Turning, slowly, she perceived us, standing there in the shadow—two cruel men, hunting her even in this sacred solitude. That was the feeling she gave us by the look which passed over her countenance; I felt ashamed and unjustified until I forced myself to recollect all.

She did not scream; she had passed through too many vicissitudes to betray any fright; she only turned white, and put her hand on the table to steady herself.

"You two men have come here at last, have you? Why do you

interfere with me? It's only a little while I have to stay, and I want peace."

"Peace only comes with a pure conscience," said Mr. Burton, sternly. "What are you doing in this house?"

"I know I have no right here; but where else will you let me stay? Not even by his grave—no, not even by his grave! You want to drag me forth before the world, to expose my foolish secret, which I have hidden from everybody—to put me in prison—to murder me! This is the business of you two men; and you have the power, I suppose. I am so poor and friendless it makes me a fit object for your persecution. Well, if you can justify yourselves, do as you will with me!"

She folded her hands, looking us full in the face with eyes which absolutely blazed.

"If you had no guilty secret, why did you fly from friends and enemies? Why did you not seek an interview and explanation which would have been satisfactory to us?" asked Mr. Burton.

"You would not believe me if I told you the reason," scornfully. "It is not in the minds of men—the gross, suspicious minds of men—to conceive or credit my excuse. I will not make it to such people."

Really, there was a majesty about the girl which quite awed me. As she confronted us, the undaunted spirit sparkling through her slight, wasted face and form, compelled a sort of acquiescence in me. I was not the one to subdue or handle this powerful nature. Mr. Burton was.

"This is not the proper hour, nor the proper place, to enter into explanations, Miss Sullivan. You must go with me to Mrs. Scott's cottage; she will care for you until morning, and then we will have a talk together. You will not find me harsh; nor shall I take any step without good cause. All I want is the truth—and that I am bound to have."

"Let me stay here to-night; I promise you I will not attempt to leave the place. I will wait here until you see fit to come in the morning."

"I can not; there is too much at stake," he said, with determination.

"Then let me go and get the child," she said.

She took up the lamp and we followed her; up and along the garret staircase, mounting the narrow steps which led into the attic. There, upon the pile of mattresses which I have mentioned as lying in the corner, reposed the baby-girl before spoken of, sleeping sweetly, as only infancy can rest.

"We were under this when you paid us a visit the other day," said Leesy, with a sort of bitter smile. "I had hard work to keep baby from crying out. She did make a fuss at last; you said it was a cat."

"How sound the little creature sleeps," said the detective. He had a gentle heart, which shrunk from disturbing the slumbering infant.

"It's too bad to startle her up so," murmured her nurse.

"Yes, it is. I'll tell you what we will do. We will lock you up here, and keep guard in the chamber until morning, if that pleases you."

"I don't care to take Norah out in the storm."

"Tell me one thing," said Mr. Burton, his bright eye fixing itself on her own; "are you the mother of that babe?"

For a moment she answered his look with one of astonishment; then the rosy blood rushed up to neck, cheek and brow—a virgin blush, which showed all the soft and girlish side of her character.

"Am I Norah's mother?" she repeated. "I thought you knew I was not a married woman."

The detective stood, a little embarrassed by the perfect simplicity of her reply.

"It is understood to be your deceased cousin's child—an orphan, I believe," he said. "Well, Miss Sullivan, we will leave you here, undisturbed, for the remainder of the night."

We descended to the second floor, turning the key of the little store-room which inclosed the garret staircase, well satisfied to keep guard until morning, since we had secured the mysterious inmate of the haunted house.

CHAPTER XIII.
THE SHADOW ASSUMES SHAPE.

We now lighted our lamp, and, finding a light cane sofa in the hall, nearly opposite the locked door, we took seats, and kept ourselves awake by talking. The storm had subsided into the monotonous patter of a steady rain.

"I am surprised," said Mr. Burton, "that you did not at once comprehend the secret of this house. The moment you spoke the word 'haunted,' I knew how our investigations would end. It solved a mystery which has bothered me for some time. I knew that Leesy Sullivan was here, in this vicinity; the exact hiding-place was all I wanted to know; and when you mentioned Moreland villa, I said to myself, 'that's it!' All I was then afraid of was, that she would again elude us, before we could lay hands on her. And in fact," he added laughingly, "I hardly feel sure of her now. She may sublime through the ceiling before morning."

"I did not think of her, Mr. Burton; I was quite sure some person was playing some game, either of mischief or worse, about the villa; but how could I be certain, when two thorough daylight examinations failed to reveal any thing? There did not seem to be a place at which a person could enter the house; and as for a woman and child being actual inmates, living and subsisting here for weeks—I think nothing but actual proof could have convinced me of the marvel. I am curious to know how she managed it."

"I ought to have come right here at first," continued my friend, pursuing his train of thought. "Women are like mother-birds, when boys approach the nest. They betray themselves and their cherished secret by fluttering about the spot. If this Miss Sullivan had been a man, she would have been in Kansas or California by this time; being a woman, I ought to have look-ed for her in exactly the place it would seem natural for her to avoid. One thing is certain—she loved young Moreland with an intensity beyond the strength of most women. I have had to do with natures like hers before—where a powerful brain is subservient to a still more powerful emotional force. She was proud, ambitious, discontented, with tastes and perceptions reaching up into a much higher sphere of life. Miss Sullivan would have made a magnificent heiress and pet daughter; yet in love she would be humble, self-abnegating—give all and count it nothing. It's a sad pity such a capacity for happiness should have brought only ruin."

"If she had loved Henry, how could she, under any impulse of jealousy, have injured him? She is terrible to me in any view of the case."

"I do not know that she did injure him, or cause him to be injured. Circumstances are against her. But I am far from believ-ing her the guilty person. Yet I am exceedingly anxious to have a quiet interview with her. I must see her and talk with her alone. She is frightened now, and defiant. I shall soothe her—magnetize her will, as it were—and draw from her the truth. Every atom of knowledge which she has, in any way connected with Henry Moreland, I shall draw from her, and consolidate into one mass, to be used for or against her. If you have the reliance upon my judgment which I flatter myself you have, Richard, you will not object to my seeing Miss Sullivan alone, and deciding, upon that interview, whether there are causes for her arrest, as a party to the murder."

"I shall not object. It is your privilege to see her alone; and I have the utmost confidence in you. I suppose Mr. Argyll and Henry's father would be the proper persons to decide upon the arrest and prosecution."

"Of course. And if, after I have talked with her, I can elicit no facts to warrant her being put on trial for her life, I shall not give her her liberty until I have consulted both families, laying all my evidence before them. They will be loth to begin a prosecution which they can not sustain, even if they have an *impression* of guilt. By the way, Redfield, these *impressions* are curious things! Supposing I should tell you there are persons who, without one particle of proof of any kind, have an impression that *you* are the guilty man."

I arose from the sofa, looking at him, not knowing whether or not to knock him down.

"Don't 'slay me with a look'," he said, laughing quietly. "I don't say that *I* have any such inner revelation. And I did not say this, either, to hurt your feelings. I did it to save them. For, if I mistake not, the same person who confided his impressions to me, has recently been gradually confiding them to others. The very thought, the very possibility, once entertained, or half-entertained and driven away again, as an unwelcome guest, still has its injurious influence. You are standing upon an earthquake, Richard—you may be swallowed up any instant."

"I?"

"Yes. I have detected the premonitory rumblings. I have said this only to warn you, that you may be ready for self-defense."

"I scorn to defend myself! Defend myself, forsooth! against

what? Who has dared to insinuate that thought against me which you have allowed yourself to echo? But I need not ask— it is my natural foe, James Argyll. He hates me as the rattlesnake hates the black-ash tree!"

"Well, the dislike is mutual. Will you deny that you, too, have had a thought—mind, I say a mere, floating thought—that *he* may have instigated the deed?"

My conscious eye sunk before the steel-blue glance which pierced me. God knows, such a fear, such a belief, at times vague and shadowy, again vivid but brief as lightning, had again and again troubled me. I have hinted at it once, when I said that I was glad that if James ever took money, unpermitted, from his uncle, he took it to waste at the gaming-table. Soon I raised my eyes.

"If I have had such a suspicion, I have struggled against it; I have never breathed it into mortal ear. He has sought to injure me in various ways; I have wished to win and conciliate him; to be friendly with him, for the sake of my regard for his relatives. As to taking a step to fix a blasting stigma upon him, without giving him a chance openly to efface it, I am incapable of it. You are at liberty to judge between us, Mr. Burton."

"You know that I do not like him," answered my companion. "But no aversion which I may feel for him shall prevent my weighing all facts which come under my observation, with the utmost impartiality. I am on the right track, in this pursuit, and I shall follow it up to the dark end, though you, yourself, abandon it. Justice shall be meted out! If the bolt strikes the loftiest head in all this aristocratic vicinity, it *shall* fall where it belongs."

He left the sofa, walking up and down the corridor with a stern, thoughtful face. As for me, I sunk back on my seat, overwhelmed by the confirmation of a thousand times more than my worst fears. *Suspicion of me* was creeping like a shadow over the Argyll household. I had felt its approach long ago; now my whole being grew cold, freezing, except one burning spasm of indignation which throbbed in my breast.

As the gray dawn approached, the rain ceased. Morning was long in coming. As soon as it grew light enough to see, I heard the gardener cutting wood for the fire, and shortly after I walked over, at Mr. Burton's request, to ask for some breakfast for the woman and child. I will not describe the garrulous astonishment of the husband and wife upon my announcement that the ghost was cornered, and proved to be Leesy Sullivan. Of course the evil omen of hearing children crying was now explained, as well as the disappearance of a considerable quantity of flour, condiments and apples, which Mrs. Scott had charged to the rats.

It went sorely against the inclination of formal, correct Mrs. Scott, to furnish a comfortable breakfast to "such a jade as that seemed likely to prove; behavin' in this style, which nobody on 'arth could account for;" but the gratification of her feminine curiosity was some reward for the outrage to her sensibilities, and she went with great expedition to carry the desired refreshments to the prisoners.

When we entered the attic, in the light of the rising sun, Miss Sullivan was sitting quietly on the edge of the mattresses, curling little Norah's flaxen hair around her fingers. An obstinate reticence marked her looks and actions; she scarcely replied to any of Mrs. Scott's inquiries—only, when the comfort of the child was concerned. For *her* she took some of the warm food and tea, quietly feeding the eager little girl, while we made a survey of her surroundings.

I now ascertained that a small sky-light, hidden from outside view by the chimneys and ornamental work of the battlements, had given egress to the mysterious brightness which had hovered so frequently over the roof. The tenant of this great house had evidently arranged herself for the winter. She had chosen the attic as a place of greatest safety, in the case of parties entering the deserted dwelling for any purpose; here she had brought a tiny charcoal-furnace, used in the basement in summer-time for the purpose of heating smoothing-irons, which she supplied with fuel from the stock left over in the cellar. The provisions left in the house had served her wants equally well. It was evident that by the exercise of extreme care and vigilance, leaving the house only in the darkness of the night, she might have remained here for a considerable longer time undisturbed in her novel seclusion, had not the light, which she had never ventured to burn until all was dark and silent in the little cottage, by chance first attracted the curiosity which led finally to discovery.

Mr. Burton took a cup of tea and a roll, brought to him there; and then, at his request, he was left alone with the silent woman, who sat there with resolute brows and lips firmly closed, as if locked over her thoughts.

"It will require all his diplomacy to wile her into a communicative mood," was my decision, as I took a parting glance at her face. I was chilled with my night's watching, and chilled more utterly by the words the detective had spoken to me as I watched; I returned to the cottage-fire, sitting there three hours, in a painful reverie, answering almost at random the remarks of the housekeeper.

At the close of the three hours, Mr. Burton came into the little dwelling, carrying Norah in his arms, who was stroking his cheek with her chubby hand, and followed by the sewing-girl, whose cheeks bore traces of tears, and whose hunted, defiant look had given place to a dejected, gentle expression.

"Mrs. Scott, I want you to do me a kindness," he said, in his authoritative, persuasive manner, to which people seldom thought it worth while to object. "I want you to take care of Miss Sullivan and this little cousin of hers, until I send them word they are wanted. It may be to-day, or not for a week. In the mean time, if you have any sewing to be done for yourself or little Johnny, she will be glad to help you."

"She's welcome to stay, I'm sure," said the woman, in a tone not quite so sure.

"Thank you. I knew I could ask a favor of you. Johnny, come here, and make Miss Norah's acquaintance. I'm ready, Richard, if you are, to return to the village. Lenore will wonder what has become of us. Good-morning, all."

We walked away.

"Are you not afraid to leave that girl unguarded, after all the trouble she has given us?"

"She will stay there; she has promised me. If she chooses to run away, now, it is a matter of no consequence. I am perfectly, entirely convinced that she is innocent of any participation in the murder of Henry Moreland; or any knowledge of the murder— except, upon one point, I could use her testimony. I shall give my opinion to Mr. Argyll, with my grounds for it; if he chooses to arrest her, she will be there at the cottage. Richard, this affair has gone as far as it can! I shall tell Mr. Argyll, to-day, that I have withdrawn from it—that I give it up. But I am willing *you* should understand that I have not dropped it entirely—that I shall still retain my interest in it—still secretly pursue my investigations, which I believe I can carry on to the best advantage if all parties believe that I have given the matter up. Are you satisfied?"

"If I am not, what difference does it make? It is not for me to dictate your course. I believe that you think it is the best one."

"I do. So will you some day, if we live to see the termination of this thing. In the mean time, I am your friend, Richard, whether I give any outward signs of friendship very soon or not.

You are at liberty to devote yourself to the cause as ardently as ever—and if ever you wish to consult me, you will find me what you now know me."

I felt strangely as we walked along together. He talked as if he thought some change were coming—as if things were to assume new shapes—as if I were to need friendship, and yet as if he should be compelled to conceal his for me behind a mask of coldness. I did not understand it. I felt half offended with him, and wholly disheartened.

I dined with him at Mr. Argyll's. It was the last time I sat at that table.

In the afternoon he had a private interview with the family, *from which I was excluded*; and in the evening he returned to the city, taking with him Lenore, the last wave of whose hand was for James, her last kiss for Miss Argyll.

The next morning Mr. Argyll informed me that he had resolved to make his nephew his partner in the practice of the law, and that I was at liberty to take advantage of any other opportunity I might have for going into business for myself. His manner was cold; he expressed no regrets for my probable disappointment, caused by his own suggestions; I could feel myself dismissed from his friendship as well as his office. I would not ask why. My tongue grew dry as ashes when I thought of attempting it. Mr. Burton had given me the clue to the feelings which prompted this rupture of a life-long friendship—it was such as to forbid any questions. No explanations could be made—nothing could obliterate the memory of so deadly a wrong as they were committing upon me. The golden bowl of friendship was broken at the fountain—the waters spilled upon the ground.

I told him that I had contemplated a visit to my mother, which I would take this opportunity to make. I might find what

I wished for, in the way of business, in the vicinity of my father's former home; when, with formal thanks for his past kindness (which I was mentally vowing I would find some means to repay), and begging him to trouble himself not at all about my fortunes, I bowed myself from the office where I had spent so much of the last three years of my life.

Blind, dizzy, cold, I went to my boarding-house to pack my trunks.

Before I went to bed, my few arrangements were completed. My clothes, books, the few little articles of taste, or gifts of friends, allowable in one small rented room, were easily put away in their traveling receptacle. But, as for the rest!—for the wealth which my heart had silently garnered during the golden harvest of youth—where was it? Swept away as by a mighty wind.

I slept some, for I was thoroughly worn out by my emotions, no less than by my recent vigils; but the earliest morning found me awake. I was to leave at noon; I had many pleasant acquaintances in the village, from whom I ought not to have parted without a farewell call; but all these small pleasures and courtesies of life were swept aside, as sand upon my path. I had nothing to do, all the tedious morning, save to pretend to eat my breakfast, until the hour which I had set in my thoughts for saying good-by to the girls.

I would not go away without seeing them; if there was any accusation in their eyes I would confront it. And then, I did not believe that Eleanor would do me an injustice. Blue-eyed, just, gentle as was her character, *she*, at least, was grieved for me— believed in me. I did not admit to myself how much comfort I drew from this faith, until I was startled from it. My baggage was dispatched; my watch told eleven; I passed the house on the way to the cars, giving myself a few minutes for this farewell. As I knocked at the door, one of the servants opened it. I sent her to ask Miss Argyll if she would come down to say good-by, before I left on my visit to my mother; and Mary—I would like to see her also.

While I waited for them, I stepped into the dear familiar parlors and library, mutely taking my leave of them, with all their mingled associations. Presently the messenger returned:

"Miss Argyll sent her farewell; she could not see Mr. Redfield that morning."

"Where is she?"

"In the breakfast-room, looking at her flowers."

I started for the room in a wild tumult of anger and passion, resolved to make her confess the reason of this treatment. Surely, three years of an intimacy like ours, gave me the right. In three minutes I confronted her where she stood, in the door between the breakfast-room and conservatory, like a statue draped in crape.

"Eleanor!"

She shrunk back; she held up her hands with an expression of horror. My God! that look in Eleanor's eyes was enough to kill me. I turned away as hastily as I had come. As I stumbled along the passage, half blind with the terrible surging and throbbing of the blood through me, a soft pair of arms fell about my neck, a cheek wet with tears was pressed to mine—it was Mary.

"Never mind what they say about you, Richard," she sobbed. "I don't believe one word of it—not one word! I never shall. I am your friend. I love you; indeed I do. I do not want you to go away," and she kissed me twice or thrice.

I took the sweet face in my cold hands, looked into the brimming eyes, hastily kissed the blushing cheek—"God bless you, Mary," said I, and was gone.

END OF PART ONE.

PART II.

THE DEAD LETTER.

CHAPTER I.
THE LETTER.

The reader can now understand why it was that I turned cold with excitement as I sat there in the dead-letter office, holding the time-stained epistle in my hand. Every word burned itself into my brain. Obscure as it was—non-committal—directed to an unknown person of a neighboring village—I yet felt *assured* that those vague hints had reference to the sinful tragedy which had occurred October 17th, 1857. Here was placed in my hands—at last!—a clue to that mystery which I had once sworn to unravel. Yet, how slender was the clue, which might, after all, lead me into still profounder labyrinths of doubt and perplexity! As I pondered, it seemed to break and vanish in my fingers. Yet, I felt, in spite of this, an inward sense *that I held the key which was surely to unlock the awful secret.* I can never rightly express the feelings which, for the first few moments, overpowered me. My body was icy cold, but my soul stung and stirred me as with fire, and seemed to rise on "budding wings"*of flame with conviction of a speedy triumph which was to come after long suffering. I arose, clutched my hat, and went forth from

---

* A phrase from stanza 27 of Robert Browning's 1850 poem "Christmas-Eve and Easter-Day."

the Department, to return to it no more, for the present. Half the night I sat in my room at my boarding-place, looking at that letter on the table before me.

Before I proceed further with its history, I will give, in a few words, the brief, monotonous record of my life, since I was driven—driven is the word you must use, Richard, haughty and sensitive though you may be—from the friendship and presence of the Argylls, and from my prospects of a long-cherished settlement in life. I made the visit to my mother. She was shocked at the change in me, and grieved that I withheld my confidence from her. But, I did not feel in a confiding mood. The gentleness of my nature had been hardened; I was bitter, sneering, skeptical; not from my own mother would I accept the sympathy which my chilled heart seemed no longer to crave. Only one thing saved me from utter loathing of humanity, and that was the memory of Mary's face, as she had sought me at parting. In those sweet eyes were trust and love; the tears which streamed down and fell upon her bosom, the quiver of her lip, the sobs and fond words, attested to the sorrow with which she had beheld my banishment.

Of course my mother was surprised to hear that I had left Blankville, with no intention of returning to it; that the long-understood partnership was not to be entered into. But, she did not press me for explanations. She waited for me to tell her all, patiently; ministering to my health and comfort, meanwhile, as a widowed mother will minister to an only son—with a tenderness only less than that of heaven, because it is yet, perforce, of earth.

Before I had been at home a fortnight, the unnatural tension of my mind and nerves produced a sure result—a reaction took place, and I fell sick. It was in the softer mood which came over me, as I was convalescing from this illness, that I finally told my mother all the dreadful story of the influences which had broken up my connection with the Argylls. Her grief for me, her indignation against my enemy or enemies, was what might have been expected. I could hardly restrain her from starting at once for Blankville, to stand before her old friend, the friend of my father, and accuse him, face to face, of the wrong he had done her boy. But, out of this I persuaded her. I asked her if she did not see that the wrong was irreparable? I could not forgive it. It did not admit of being talked about; let the cloud drop between them and us; our paths were henceforth apart. To this she finally yielded; and, if there could have been any balm to my wounded pride and still more deeply wounded affections, I should have found it in the enhanced, touching, almost too-perfect tenderness with which my parent sought to make up to me that which I had lost.

For a few weeks I abandoned myself to her healing attentions. Then I set myself resolutely to find work both for hands and mind. My mother was not without influential friends. As I have said, my fortunes were somewhat nipped by my father's untimely death, but our family and associations were among the best. We had a relative in power at Washington. To him I applied for a clerkship, and received, in answer, the situation I was filling, at the time when that dead-letter came so strangely into my hands.

It may be thought improbable that I should abandon the profession for which I had studied with so much zeal. But, the very memory of that zeal, and of the hopes which had stimulated it, now gave me a dislike to the law. I required both change of scene and of pursuits. The blow dealt at my heart had stunned my ambition, also. To one of my temperament, aspirations, acquisitiveness, all the minor passions and pursuits of life are but steps leading up the hillside to the rose-crowned summit, where love sits smiling under the eye of heaven. And I, being for the time at least, blasted prematurely, was no more myself, but was to myself like a stranger within my own sanctuary. I went into the dead-letter office, and commenced my routine of breaking seals and registering contents, as if I had been born for that business. I was a rapid worker, quiet, and well-thought-of by my associates, who deemed me a little cold and skeptical, a trifle reserved, very steady for so young a fellow, and an efficient clerk who thoroughly earned his salary. That was all they knew of Richard Redfield. And in those days I did not know much more about myself. The months had worn away, one after the other, with a dreary coldness. In the summer I struggled through the suffocating dust; in the winter I picked my way through the disgusting mud, to and fro, from my lodgings to the office buildings; that was about all the change which the seasons brought to me, whom once the smell of spring violets filled with pungent delight, and the odor of June roses made happy as a god on Olympus.

Half the night I sat brooding over that brief revelation, so precious to me, yet so loathsome. The longer I pondered its words the less vivid grew my hope of making any triumphant use of it for the detection of the two guilty persons—the one who wrote it, and the one to whom it was addressed. I might lay it before Mr. Argyll, but he might not feel, as I did, that it had any connection with the murder, neither was there anything to prove but that the missive might have been directed to *me*. Indeed, Mr. Argyll might well inquire how I could pretend that it should have reached me through the routine of the Dead-Letter Department, after all this stretch of time—very nearly two years!

This was a matter which puzzled me exceedingly. In the ordinary course of affairs, it would, if not claimed, have been forwarded to Washington three months after its reception at Peekskill, and have long ago been consigned to the waste-basket and the flames. The hand of an overruling Providence seemed to be moving the men in this terrible game. At that hour I recognized it, and felt a solemn conviction that, sooner or later, the murderer would be checkmated. It was this assurance, more than any evidence contained in the letter, which gave me hope that it would eventually be the instrument of punishment to the guilty. I remembered the vow I had once made to my soul, never to rest in the peace of my own pursuits, until I had dragged the slayer of the innocent into the awful presence of Justice. That vow I had neglected to fulfill to the uttermost, partly because of the injury which had been done to my self-love, and also because the circumstance which had attached suspicion to me, in the eyes of those interested, had made it dangerous for me to move in a matter where all my motives were misconstrued. But now that Fate had interposed in this singular manner, in my behalf and in that of Truth, I took fresh courage. I was fully startled from my apathy. That night I wrote my resignation to the Department, gathered up my few effects again, and the next morning found me on the way to New York.

My first purpose was to consult Mr. Burton. I had not seen him since the day when we parted in Blankville; I only knew, by accident, that he was still a resident of New York, having casually heard his name mentioned in connection with a case which had brought some detectives on to Washington only a few weeks previous.

I had never forgiven or understood the part he had played in that last interview with the Argylls. I remembered the assurance he had given me of friendship, but I did not believe that he had shown any friendship for me, in that consultation with the relatives, or the results would not have been so disastrous to me.

Nevertheless, I felt a confidence in him; he was the man for the emergency, and to him I would take the letter. I thought it quite probable, that in the multiplicity of new interests, the circumstances which had once brought us so much together had faded from his mind, and that I should have to reawaken his recollection of the details.

On the morning after my arrival in New York, I consulted the directory, and finding that Mr. Burton still resided in Twenty-third street, I called at the house at the earliest admissible hour.

While I was handing my card to the servant, his master came out of the library at the end of the hall, and hastening forward, shook me heartily by the hand. His joyous tones were better evidence of his pleasure at seeing me, than even his words, which were cordial enough.

"I heard your voice, Richard," he said, "and did not wait for you to be ushered in with the formalities. Welcome, my friend;" his expression was as if he had said—"Welcome, my son."

He led me into the library, and placing me in an armchair, sat down opposite me, looking at me with the well-remembered piercing shafts of those steel-blue eyes. After inquiring about my health, etc., he said, suddenly,

"You have news."

"You are right, Mr. Burton—else I should not have been here. I suppose you are aware that I have been a clerk in the dead-letter office for the last eighteen months?"

"I was aware of it. I never intended to let you slip out of the numbered rosary of my friends, and lose you so entirely as not even to know your whereabouts."

"Day before yesterday this letter arrived at the office, and I chanced to be the clerk who opened it."

I handed him the missive. He examined the envelope attentively, before unfolding the sheet within; and as he continued to hold it in his hand, and gaze at it, one of those wonderful changes passed over his countenance that I had remarked on some previous important occasions. His practical intelligence seized upon the date, the post-office marks, the hasty direction, and made the contents of the letter his own, almost, before he read it. For some moments he pondered the outside, then drew forth the letter, perused it with one swift glance, and sat holding it, gazing at it, lost in thought, and evidently forgetful of my presence. A stern pallor settled gradually over his usually placid face; at last he looked up, and seeing me, recalled his surroundings to his recollection.

"It is sad to be made to feel that such creatures live and flourish," he said, almost despondingly; "but," as his face brightened, "I can not say how glad I am to get hold of this. It partially explains some things which I have already found out. The chance which threw this document into your hands was a marvelous one, Richard."

"However simple the explanation may prove to be, I shall always regard it as Providential."

"All things are Providential," said my companion, "none less, and none more so. Causes will have their effects. But now, as to the writer of this—I am glad I have a specimen of the villain's handwriting; it will enable me to know the writer when I see him."

"How so, Mr. Burton?"

"Because I have a very good picture of him, now, in my mind's eye. He is about thirty years of age, rather short and broad-shouldered, muscular; has dark complexion and black eyes; the third finger of his right hand has been injured, so as to contract the muscles and leave it useless. He has some education, which he has acquired by hard study since he grew up to be his own master. His childhood was passed in ignorance, in the midst of the worst associations; and his own nature is almost utterly depraved. He is bad, from instinct, inheritance and bringing-up; and now, our blessed Redeemer, himself, would hardly find good enough in him to promise a hope of ultimate salvation. It is curious that he should ever have seen fit to study, so as to acquire even the smattering of knowledge which he has. He must have been led into it by some powerful passion. If I could decide what that passion was, I might have a key to unlock the gate into some other matters."

I stared at the speaker in astonishment as he rapidly pronounced the above analysis of the personal appearance and character of the writer.

"Do you know him?" I asked.

"I do not know his *name*, and I have never met him. All the acquaintance I have with him, I have made through the medium of his chirography.* It is sufficient for me; I can not mistake,"— then, observing my puzzled and incredulous look, he smiled, as he added, "By the way, Richard, you are not aware of my accomplishment in the art of reading men and women from a specimen of their handwriting. It is one of my greatest aids in the profession to which I have devoted myself.† The results I obtain some-

---

* Handwriting.

---

† The use of handwriting as an identifier of the author, while historically controversial, is generally accepted today. According to the FBI: "Published research demonstrates the validity of the expertise and supports the principle of handwriting individuality." "Handwriting Examination: Meeting the Challenges of Science and the Law," *Forensic Science Communications* 11, no. 4 (October 2009). As to the idea that handwriting informs the author's character (known as graphology), however, the subject remains controversial. Though there are records of Greek and Roman merchants commenting on a customer's character based on handwriting, it wasn't until 1871 that Rosa Baugham published her seminal essay "Character Indicated by Handwriting." Burton, therefore, was a pioneer in applying the technique to criminology. There is no legal foundation for the admissibility of handwriting analysis as a basis for conclusions regarding the author's character, however, and it is still largely regarded as a pseudoscience.

times astonish my friends. But, I assure you, there is nothing marvelous in them. Patient study and unwearied observation, with naturally quick perceptions, are the only witchcraft I use. With moderate natural abilities, I assert that any other person could equal me in this art (black art, some of my acquaintances regard it,) by giving the same time to it that a musician would to master an instrument."

"I do not know about that, Mr. Burton. I guess it would take a mind of the singular composition of your own to make much out of an art with no rules and no foundations."

"It has its rules, for me. But as proof is better than argument, show me any letters or scraps of writing you may have about you. I would like to satisfy you, before we proceed further, for I do not wish you to feel that you are working with a crack-brained individual, who is riding a hobby at your expense."

I emptied my inside coat-pocket of its contents, among which were several letters—one from my mother, a note from my uncle in Washington, an invitation from an old college-chum to attend his wedding in Boston, and two or three business epistles from casual acquaintances—one, I remember, an entreaty from a young man to get him something to do in that magnetic center of all unemployed particles—Washington. Of these, I revealed only to him the superscription and signature, with, perhaps, some unimportant sentence, which would, in no way, of itself, betray the characters or pursuits of the writers. I need not describe my surprise when, in each instance, he gave a careful and accurate description of the age, appearance, habits, profession and mental qualities of the person whose handwriting he had examined.

I could hardly credit my own senses; there must be some "*hocus-pocus*" about it, as in the tricks which jugglers play with cards. But my respect for the earnestness of my companion's pursuits, and the indubitable nature of his proof, did not allow me to doubt any length of time. I became a believer in *his facts*, and I give these facts to my readers, at the risk of seeing the plain, sensible nose of the majority turned up with an expression of skepticism, mortifying to me. Mr. Burton's character is a real one, and the truth of his wonderful achievements will become history.

The terrible interest of the subject which had brought us together did not permit us to spend much time in these interesting but irrelevant experiments. We discussed the past and present. Mr. Burton assured me that he had never, for a day, lost sight of the case—that his interest in it had deepened, rather than lessened: that he had not been idle during all this long period; but that he had already gathered up a fact or two of some importance, and had been on the point of sending for me, once or twice. He had refrained, waiting for some lights to culminate, and "now, he was glad enough to get hold of that letter."

He informed me that Leesy Sullivan was living quietly in the city, subsisting mostly upon donations from himself, she being too far gone with consumption to exert herself much with the needle. The child was with her, healthy and pretty.

I made no inquiries after James Argyll, but he told me that the young man came frequently to the city; that, for a while, he had seemed dispirited, and gambled desperately, but that lately he was looking and behaving better.

"It is my impression," added he, "that he is about to marry one of his cousins—probably the youngest. And as to his bad habits, I caused him to understand, indirectly, that if they were not reformed, he should be convicted of them, before his uncle. This I did (after I became convinced that he would marry one of the young ladies) out of compassion to the family."

My head drooped on my hand. It was long since I had any

tidings of the Argylls—death could hardly have created a more barren space between us. Yet, now that I heard the names of the girls mentioned, a flood of old emotions broke over me, beneath which I struggled, half-suffocated. Keen pain shot through my heart at the idea of Mary, that innocent, most sweet and lovable girl, becoming the wife of James. I felt as if it ought to be prevented, yet how could I interfere? Why should I wish to? I recalled the hour when she had flown to me—had said, "*I* believe in you, Richard; *I* love you!" and I knew that I had put a construction upon the tearful, passionate words of her last avowal, which was, after all, not warranted. I had feared that she did really love me, and that, in the last moment of sorrow and trouble, her feelings had betrayed themselves to her own comprehension—and I had felt a hope that it was not so. My own unanswered passion—my lonely, unmated life—had taught me sympathy; and I was not so utterly selfish as to have my personal vanity tickled with the idea that this young creature loved me, who did not love her, except truly as a sister.

Yet now, when hearing that James had turned from Eleanor to her, I felt a pang of pity—a wish that she might rather have loved me than him whose cold, deceitful bosom could never be a safe shelter for a woman as affectionate as Mary. With this regret I felt a triumph that Eleanor had remained unassailable on the sublime and solitary hight of her sorrow. It was what I expected of her. I gloried in her constancy to the dead. I had loved her for this noble beauty of her nature, and should have been disappointed had the test found her wanting in any of the attributes with which my worship had invested her. She had done me a wrong too cruel for me to complain about; but I would rather, still, that she would wrong me than herself.

Lastly, Mr. Burton assured me that he had tidings of the five-hundred-dollar bill which had been stolen from Mr. Argyll's desk. This was, indeed, important, and I showed by my looks how deeply I was absorbed in the particulars. That bill had come into the hands of Wells, Fargo & Co., about six months after the robbery, having been sold for specie to their agent in California, and forwarded to them along with the other sums which they were constantly receiving. At least, he had taken it for granted that it was the same bill, it being one of the two which left the city of New York the week of the robbery; the other he had traced to St. Louis, and ascertained that no possible suspicious circumstances attached to it.

Wells, Fargo & Co. had given him every assistance in their power to discover who had sold that bill to the California branch of their house; but an answer had been returned from there that the person who disposed of it was a stranger, on his way to the mining regions, whom they had never seen before or since, and whose name they had not taken. The clerk who transacted the brief business with him, had no distinct recollection of him, except that he was rather a thick-set man, with an unpleasant expression—doubtless one of the "hard cases" so frequent in the precincts of San Francisco.

Of course, it was clear to us two, who sat in company with the dead-letter, that the five-hundred-dollar bill was a part of the sum referred to by the writer; that it had come out of Mr. Argyll's desk, and that it was blood-money paid for a murder; and the receiver was this person who, in the letter, so explicitly declared his intention of fleeing to California. We were much excited in the presence of these bold facts. In our enthusiasm, then, it seemed easy to stretch a hand across the continent and lay it upon the guilty. We scarcely realized the long and wearisome pursuit to which we were doomed—the slight clue which we had to the individual whose deeds were yet so patent to us.

At this revelation of conspiracy, my mind eagerly searched

about for the accessory, and again settled itself upon Miss Sullivan. It did seem to me that she had thrown a glamour over the usually clear sight of Mr. Burton: so that I resolved to keep a separate watch which should not be influenced by his decisions. While I was thinking of this, Mr. Burton was walking about the floor. Suddenly he stopped before me, and looked into mine with those vivid eyes, so full of power, and said, as confidently as if a vision had revealed it to him,

"I have now made out all the meaning of the letter. In the first place, it is written '*by contraries*'—that is, it means just the contrary of what it says. The contract *was* fulfilled. The price was expected, the emigration decided upon. The bright day was a rainy night; the picture taken was a human life. And, don't you see it, Richard?—the old friend was the hiding-place of the instrument of death, after which the accomplice is directed to look. That instrument is the broken toothpick. It was secreted in the pocket of the old friend. Now, who or what is this old friend? Richard, didn't Leesy affirm she saw a man descending from the old oak tree at the right of the Argyll mansion, on the evening of the murder?"

"She did."

"Then *that* is it. I want to know no more. The arms are the arms of that old oak. Unless it has been removed, which is not probable, since this letter was never received, the broken knife or dagger (of which I have the point which was taken from the wound), will be found in some hollow on the left side of that oak."

I gazed at him in astonishment; but he, unconscious of my wonder, sat down, with a relieved, almost happy, expression.

---

* There is an old expression that "dreams go by contraries," meaning that one should interpret events seen in a dream to forebode exactly the opposite—e.g., a dream of a funeral is really about a wedding.

CHAPTER II.

OUR VISITS.

So engrossed were we by our plans, which we were laboring to get into shape, that we forgot the passing hours and the demands of appetite. It was long past the lunch hour when a servant appeared to ask if he should not bring in the tray, having waited in vain for the usual summons. With its appearance Lenore came in, the same lovely, sylph-like little creature, but looking rather less fragile than when I saw her last. At the sight of me, her color went and came—one instant she hesitated, then approached and gave me her hand, with a smile and kiss. Her father had already told of her having made two or three visits to the Argyll mansion within the time of my absence; and I attributed her blushes, upon meeting me, to her frank heart accusing her of the disparaging thoughts she had entertained of me. The subtle influence of James had doubtless, without any necessity for putting the idea into words, warned her against me as a bad man; but now as she looked at me, she was sorry for what she had felt, and disposed to renew her old friendship.

Before lunch was concluded, Mr. Burton fell into a reverie, which he ended by saying,

"We must have the assistance of Lenore, if she can give us any."

I felt reluctant to see the child placed again in that unnatural trance; but other considerations were even weightier than our fears for the shock to her nervous system; and after she had chatted a while with us, and had sung for me, Mr. Burton subjected her to the experiment. It had been so long since he had exercised his power over her, that it required a greater effort than on the former occasion which I witnessed, to place her in the desired condition. He, however, finally succeeded perfectly. The dead-letter was placed in her hands, when we observed her shrink as if a serpent had glided over her lap; but she did not throw it down, as she seemed moved to do.

"What do you see, Lenore?"

"It is too dark to see. A lamp shines across the walk, and I see a man dropping the letter in the box. He is muffled up so that I can not tell about his face; he steals up and goes off again very quickly."

"Follow him, Lenore."

"It is too dark, father. I am lost in the streets. Oh! now I have overtaken him again; he walks so fast—he is short and thick—he looks as if he were afraid of something. He will not pass the police-officer, but crosses the street, and keeps in the shadow. Now we are at the ferry—it is the Fulton Ferry—I know it well. Oh, dear! the water rises and the wind blows—it is getting morning, but it rains so—and the water is so wild I can not make my way on to the boat."

"Don't be discouraged, my child. I would give much to have you follow him across the river, and tell me at what house he stops."

"The wind blows so," continued Lenore, pitifully; "all is dark and uncertain. I have missed him—I do not know him from others."

"Try again, my darling. Look well at the letter."

"All is dark and uncertain," she repeated, in a vague tone.

"It is useless," exclaimed Mr. Burton, in a burst of disappointment; "it has been too long since the letter was penned. The personality of the writer has departed from it. If she had only been able to pursue him to his haunts, our investigations in that vicinity might have richly repaid us."

Finding it impossible to get any more information from the child, she was relieved from her trance, stimulated with a glass of cordial, and sent up to take a siesta before the hour for dinner. Scarcely had she left the library before I sprung to my feet, exclaiming,

"Good heavens, how easy!—and here I have never thought of it."

"What is easy?"

"To ascertain who is the John Owen who calls for these letters at Peekskill. Of course—why, what a fool I am!"

"I am afraid you will not find it so easy. People carrying on a correspondence for such a purpose, do not come forward openly for their letters—and this was a good while ago—and it is quite possible this may be the only missive ever sent, through the mail, to that address—and this, evidently, was never called for."

"At least, it is worth inquiring into," I added, less triumphantly.

"Of course it is. We wish, also, to ascertain how the letter came drawing along to Washington two years, nearly, behind its time. I propose that we start for Peekskill by the early morning train."

To wait, even until morning, seemed too tardy for my mood. But as it was now four o'clock, and I had no right to ask the detective to resign his dinner and evening comfort, I made no objection to the time. And, in truth, the time sped more swiftly than I expected; we had still so much to discuss. Dinner came—and the hour of retiring followed—before we had matured our course of action. We were to go to Peekskill and learn all possible about John Owen. If we gained no important information there, we were to go on, in the evening, to Blankville, to enter, under cover of the darkness, the lawn of the Argyll house, and secure the broken knife or dagger, which, we believed, we should find secreted in a certain oak upon the premises. This we wished to do without the knowledge of the family, for two reasons: the smaller one of which was, that I did not wish my visit to be made known, and the larger, that we both were certain we could prosecute our plans more successfully if the friends knew nothing of our efforts. Then, if we still failed to discover the accomplice, we were to sail for California.

The reader may see that we were set upon the accomplishment of our purposes by the willingness with which we gave time, money and mind to our object. I had first proposed the visit to California, avowing my intention to make it, when Mr. Burton had surprised me by offering to be my companion. This was a sacrifice which I could not have asked or expected of him; but he would not allow me to view it in that light, saying, with pleasant peremptoriness, that Lenore needed a sea-voyage, and he had been thinking of taking one on her account. He would make it a pleasure-tour, as well as one of business, "and then," with a laugh which would have been satirical if it had not been so frank—"he was afraid my mission would not be so successful, if undertaken alone." And I had answered him that I realized my own inefficiency, as compared with his talent and experience— all I had to encourage me was the devotion with which I undertook my work—to *that*, alone, I trusted to insure me some reward. But if he really were willing to go with me, I should feel almost elated.

We were at Peekskill the next day in good season. We found

the same postmaster in service who had been in the office at the time the dead-letter arrived there. When Mr. Burton—I lounging carelessly in the background—showed the envelope and inquired how it had occurred that it had been forwarded to the Department at this late hour, the official showed a little embarrassment, as inferring that he was about to be taken to task for a neglect of duty by some indignant individual.

"I will tell you how it happened, Mr. Owen," said he, "if you're the person addressed on that envelope. You never came for the letter, and before the expiration of the time required by law for forwarding it to Washington, it got slipped into a crack, and was never discovered till about a fortnight ago. You see, our place here wasn't just the thing for an office; it never did suit, and this month, I finally had new boxes and shelves put in, and the room fixed up. In tearing down the old fixings, several letters were discovered which had slipped into a crack between the shelf and wall. This was one of them. I thought, 'better late than never,' though at first I had a mind to throw them into the stove. I hope, sir, the loss of the letter hasn't put you to any very great inconvenience?"

"It was of some importance," answered my companion, in a commonplace tone, "and I'm not sorry, even yet, to have recovered it, as it settles a matter I had been in doubt about. My man must have been very negligent; I certainly sent him for the letter. Don't you remember a young man, a coachman, coming for my letters?"

"He never came but twice, to my knowledge," answered the postmaster, giving a glance of curiosity at the speaker. "I wondered who it was they were for—not being any one that I knew—and I know mostly everybody in the district. Traveling through our town, perhaps?"

"Yes, I was a stranger, who merely passed two or three times through your village, stopping on business. My usual address is New York. That coachman was hired at the next village to drive me about the country a few days. I have nearly forgotten him. I would like to call him to an account for some of his conduct which was not satisfactory. Can you describe his personal appearance?—though, I suppose, you could not have taken any particular notice of him."

"It was evening on both occasions of his calling. He was muffled up about the lower part of the face, and his cap pulled down. I couldn't tell you a thing about him, indeed, except that he had black eyes. If I'm not mistaken, he had black or dark eyes. I think I remember of their looking at me very sharp through the window here. But it was evening, and I shouldn't mind the circumstance at all if I had not wondered, at the time, who John Owen was. It's likely the fellow was a rogue—he looked kind of slippery."

I, listening apart to the conversation, longed to ask if this muffled driver was small and slender, for I was thinking of a woman. While I was studying how to propose the question to Mr. Burton, he continued,

"A smallish fellow, if I remember rightly? I really wish I had his name."

"Can't say any thing more about it," was the reply of the postmaster. "I couldn't answer if he were large or small, white or black, except as to his eyes, which were about all I saw of him. If you want to find out about him, why don't you go to the livery-keeper who furnished your team to you? Of course, his employer could tell you all you want to know."

"That *would* be the most sensible course," answered the detective, with a laugh. "But, my good friend, it is considerably out of my way to go to S—; and I must leave on the train up, in half an hour. After all, the matter is not of so much importance.

I had a curiosity to learn what had kept the letter so long on its travels. Good-day, sir."

It never entered the official's thoughts to inquire how we came in possession of a document which had not been returned from the Dead-Letter Department—at least, not while we remained with him—though he may afterward have puzzled his brains over the affair.

As we did not wish to arrive in Blankville until after dark, we had to leave the cars once again, and to get off at a little intermediate station, with half a dozen houses clustered about it; and here we whiled away, as we best could, several tedious hours, whose dreariness was only partially soothed by the influences of such a supper as could be obtained in the small public-house attached to the depot.

As the sun drew toward setting and the night approached, a fierce restlessness thrilled along my nerves. That peace—if the dullness and sluggishness of my chilled feelings could be called peace—into which I had forced myself for many months, was broken up. The mere fact of my nearness to the spot which had once been so dear to me, overpowered me with strong attractions; the force of habit and of memory was at work; and when, at twilight, the train stopped and took us up, my mind ran on before the iron-horse, and was at the end of the little journey before the commencement. Upon arriving at Blankville, we descended the rear car and walked up toward the village, without approaching the depot, as I was afraid the lamps might betray me to some former acquaintance. It was a mild evening, early in September, and I had no excuse for muffling up; so I pulled my hat down over my eyes, quite sure that I should escape recognition, in the dim moonlight, which, overblown by light, thin clouds, transfused the western sky. We walked about, in quiet parts of the village, until ten o'clock; and then, the moon having set, we approached the Argyll mansion, along the well-remembered street. I know not if my companion guessed my disturbance, as I passed the office and came up in front of the lawn, black beneath the starlight, with the shadows of its fine old trees. The past was not half so dead as I had got in the habit of believing it—life is sweet and strong in the heart of youth, which will endure many blows before it will cease to beat with the tremulous thrill of hope and passion.

A bright light was shining from the windows of the parlor and several of the other rooms, but the hall-door was closed, and every thing was so quiet about the premises that I did not believe I ran any risk in entering the gate and seeking out the monarch oak—a mighty tree, the pride of the lawn, which stood quite to one side from the central avenue which led up to the front portico, and only some thirty feet from the left corner of the mansion, which was, at times, almost touched by the reach of its outermost branches. We advanced together through the darkness, it being the understanding that, should any accident betray our visit, before its purpose was accomplished, I was to retreat, while Mr. Burton would boldly approach and make the excuse of a call upon Mr. Argyll. My familiarity with the premises and my superiority in the art of climbing, made the duty of ascending the tree devolve upon me. While my companion stood on guard beneath, I drew myself up, carefully making my way through the night, out along to the "second branch to the left," feeling for the hollow which I knew existed—for, in my more boyish days, I had left no possible point of the grand old tree unvisited. Not five minutes had elapsed since I began my search, before my fingers, pressing into the ragged cavity of the slowly-decaying limb, touched a cold object which I knew to be steel. My hand recoiled with an instinctive shudder, but returned immediately to its duty, cautiously drawing forth a slender instrument of which I could not make out the precise character. Upon raising my head, after securing the object of our anxiety, my eyes fell upon a scene which held them fascinated for so long a time that the patience of my friend at the foot of the tree must have been sorely tried.

The windows on the side of the parlor looking on the left were both open, the chandeliers lighted, and from my airy eyrie in the tree, I commanded a full view of the interior. For a time I saw but one person. Sitting by a center-table, directly under the flood of light from the chandelier, was one of the sisters, reading a book. At first—yes, for a full minute—I thought it was Eleanor!—Eleanor as she was, when the homage of my soul first went out toward her, like the exhalation of a flower to the sun—as young, as blooming and radiant as she was before the destroyer came—the dew upon the lip, the light on the brow, the glory of health, youth and joy upon every feature and in every flow of her garments, from the luster of her hair to the glimmer of her silken slipper.

"Can it be?" I murmured. "Is there such power of resuscitation in human vitality as this?"

While I asked myself the question, I was undecided. I saw (and wondered how I could have been mistaken for an instant), that this beautiful woman was Mary, grown so like her older sister, during the months of my absence, as to be almost the counterpart of what Eleanor had been. When I left her she was a girl, half-child, half-woman, bright with the promise of rare sweetness; and now, in this brief summer-time of fifteen months—so rapid had the magic culmination been—she had expanded into the perfection of all that is loveliest in her sex. A thoughtfulness, caused, probably, by the misfortune which had befallen the house—a shadow from the cloud which wrapped her sister— toned down the frolicsome gayety which had once characterized her, and added the grace of sentiment to her demeanor. I could not gaze upon the fair, meditative brow without perceiving that Mary had gained in depth of feeling as well as in womanly beauty. She wore a dress of some lustrous fabric, which gleamed slumberously in the yellow light, like water shining about a lily; as she bent above her book, her hair clustered about her throat, softening its exquisite outlines; so near, so vivid, was the unconscious *tableau-vivant*, seen through the open frame of the window, that I imagined I heard her breathe, and inhaled the fragrance lingering in her curls and handkerchief.

While I gazed, another figure glided within range of my vision. Eleanor, as I beheld her in my dreams, colorless, robed in black, young still, beautiful still, but crowned, like a queen, with the majesty of her desolation, which kept her apart from sympathy, though not from adoration. Gliding behind her sister's chair, she bent a moment to see what volume had such attractions, kissed the fair face turned instantly with a smile to hers, and passed away, going out into the hall. I had heard her low "good-night."

Then, almost before she had vanished, came the third figure into the picture. James, approaching as if from some sofa where he had been lounging, took the book from Mary's hand, which he held a little, saying something which brought blushes to her cheeks. Presently she withdrew her hand; but he caught it again, and kissed it, and I heard him say,

"Oh! Mary, you are cruel with me—you know it."

Not until I heard him speak, did it rush upon me that I had no business to be there, spying and eavesdropping. I had looked at first, unconscious of the circumstances, like a wandering spirit lingering by the walls of Eden, gazing upon the beauty which is not within its sphere. No sooner did I realize my position than I began to descend from my eyrie; but James had drawn his cousin from her chair, and the pair approached the window, and stood there, their eyes fixed, apparently, upon that very point in the giant oak where I crouched, suddenly fear-blasted, with the square of light from the window illuminating the limb where I lay concealed. I had crawled from my first resting-place, and was about jumping to the ground, when their presence transfixed me, in the most dangerous possible predicament. I dared not move for fear of being discovered. I was paralyzed by a lightning consciousness that should I then and there be betrayed, I would be the victim of a singular combination of *circumstantial evidence.* Found lingering at night, like a thief, upon the premises of those I had injured; stealthily seeking to remove the evidence of my guilt—the weapon with which the murder was committed, hidden by me, at the time, in this tree, and now sought for in order to remove it from possible discovery—why, I tell you, reader, had James Argyll sprung upon me there, seized the knife, accused me, nothing would have saved me from condemnation. The probabilities are, that the case would have been so *very* conclusive, and the guilt so horribly aggravated, that the populace would have taken the matter in their own hands, and torn me to pieces, to show their love of justice. Even the testimony of Mr. Burton would not have availed to turn the tide in my favor; he would have been accused of seeking to hide my sin, and his reputation would not have saved him from the ban of public opinion. A cold sweat broke over me as I thought of it. Not the fear of death, nor of the horror of the world—but dread of the judgment of the two sisters took possession of me. If this statement of my critical position, when the trembling of a bough might convict an innocent man, should make my reader more thoughtful in the matter of circumstantial evidence, I shall be repaid for the pangs which I then endured.

The young couple stepped out upon the sward.* I did not trouble myself about what had become of Mr. Burton, for I knew that he was in the shadow, and could retreat with safety; he, doubtless, felt more anxiety about me.

"Draw your scarf up over your head, Mary," said James, in that soft, pleasant voice of his, which made me burn with dislike as I heard it—"the night is so warm, it will not harm you to be out a few moments. Do not deny me a little interval of happiness to-night."

As if drawn forward more by his subtle will than by her own wish, she took his arm, and they walked back and forth, twice or thrice, in the light of the window, and paused directly under the limb of the tree, which seemed to shake with the throbbing of my heart. A beam of light fell athwart the face of James, so that I could see its expression, as he talked to the young creature on his arm—a handsome face, dark, glowing with passion and determination, but sinister. I prayed, in my heart, for Mary to have eyes to read it as I read it.

"Mary, you promised me an answer this week. Give it to me to-night. You have said that you would be my wife—now, tell me how soon I may claim you. I do not believe in long engagements; I want to make you mine before any disaster comes between us."

"Did I promise you, James? I really did not know that you considered what I said in the light of a promise. Indeed, I am so young, and we have always been such friends—cousins, you know—that I hardly understand my own feelings. I do wish you would not over-persuade me; we might both be sorry. I never believed in the marriage of cousins; so I do not think you ought to feel hurt, cousin James."

---

* An expanse of grass—a lawn.

In the oak.

He interrupted the tremulous voice with one a little sharper than his first persuasive tone:

"I am surprised that you do not feel that I regard you as already betrothed to me. I did not think you were a coquette, Mary. And, as for cousinship, I have already told you what I think of it. I know the secret of your reluctance—shall I betray it to you?"

She was silent.

"Your heart is still set on that scoundrel. One might suppose that dread and loathing would be the only sentiment you could entertain toward a traitor and—I will not speak the word, Mary. You took up swords in his defense, and persisted in accusing us of wronging him, against the judgment of your own father and friends. I suspected, then, by the warmth of your avowed friendship for him, that he had, among his other *honorable* deeds, gained my little cousin's heart, for the pleasure of flattering his self-love. And I shall suspect, if you persist in putting me off, when you know that your father desires our union, and that my whole existence is wrapped up in you, that he still holds it, despite of what has passed."

"He never 'gained' my heart by unfair means," said the girl, speaking proudly. "I *gave* him what he had of it—and he never knew how large a part that was. I wish he *had* known, poor Richard! for I still believe that you are all wronging him cruelly. I am *his friend*, James, and it hurts me to hear you speak so of him. But that would not prevent my being your friend, too, cousin—"

"You must not say 'cousin,' again, Mary. I'm worn out, now, and half mad with my feelings—and it makes me desperate. One thing is certain: I can not stay any longer where you are, if you continue so undecided. I want a final answer to-night. If it is unpropitious, I shall go away to-morrow, and seek for such poor fortune as may be mine, in some other part of the world."

"But what will father do without you, James?"

There was distress and a half-yielding cadence in Mary's voice.

"That is for you to think of."

"His health is failing so rapidly of late; and he leans so much upon you—trusts every thing to you. I am afraid it would kill him to have all his hopes and plans again frustrated. He has never recovered from the shock of Henry's death, and Richard's—going away."

"If you think so, Mary, why do you any longer hesitate? You acknowledge that you love me as a cousin—let me teach you to love me as a lover. My sweetest, it will make us all so happy."

But why should I try to repeat here the arguments which I heard?—the main burden of which was the welfare and wishes of her father and sister—mingled with bursts of tender entreaty—and, what was more powerful than all, the exercise of that soft yet terrible will which had worked its way, thus far, against all obstacles. Suffice it, that when the cousins at last—after what seemed to me an age, though it could not have been twenty minutes—returned through the window, I had heard the promise of Mary to become the wife of James before the beginning of another year.

Never was a man more glad to release himself from an unpleasant predicament than I was to descend from my perch when the two figures had passed within the house. My fear of discovery had become absorbed in my keen shame and regret at being compelled to play the eavesdropper to a conversation like that which I had overheard. Moving a few paces in the shadow of the trees, I whispered—"Burton."

"Got yourself into a pretty scrape," was instantly answered, in a low tone, as my friend took my arm and we moved forward to the gate. "I didn't know but we should have a tragico-comedy upon the spot, impromptu and highly interesting."

"I almost wonder that you are not too greatly out of patience with waiting to jest about the matter."

"I've told you my motto—'learn to *wait*,' Richard. The gods will not be hurried; but have you the knife?"

"Ay!" was my grim answer; I felt grim, as I grasped the treacherous, murderous thing which had wrought such deadly mischief. The sound of shutters drawn together startled us into a quicker pace; we looked back and saw the lower part of the house dark—hurried forward, and without any molestation, or our presence in Blankville being known to a single acquaintance, took the night-train back to New York, which we reached about two, a. m., and were at Mr. Burton's house, ringing up the surprised servants, shortly after.

It was not until we were in the library, with the doors closed, and the full blaze of a gas-burner turned on, that I took from my pocket the weapon, and handed it to my companion.

Both of us bent curiously forward to examine it.

"This," said the detective, in a surprised and somewhat agitated tone, "is a surgical instrument. You see, it is quite unlike a common knife. It corroborates one of my conclusions. I told you the blow was dealt by a practiced hand—it has been dealt by one skilled in anatomy. There's another link in my chain. I hope I shall have patience until I shall have forged it together about the guilty."

"There is no longer any doubt about the dead-letter referring to the murder. You see the instrument is broken," I remarked.

"No doubt, indeed," and Mr. Burton went to a drawer of a secretary standing in the room, and took out the little piece of steel which had been found in Henry Moreland's body.

"You see it is the very fragment. I obtained this important bit of evidence, and laid it away, after others had given up all efforts to make it available. How fortunate that I preserved it! So, the wedding is to take place within three months, is it? Richard, we must not rest now. A great deal can be done in three months, and I would give all the gold I have in bank to clear this matter up before that marriage takes place. Should *that* once be consummated before we are satisfied with our investigations, I shall drop them for ever. A doctor—a doctor"—he continued, musingly—"I knew the fellow had half-studied some profession—he was a surgeon—yes! By George!" he exclaimed, presently, leaping from his chair as if he had been shot, and walking rapidly across the room and back.

I knew he was very much excited, for it was the first time I had heard him use any expression like the above. I waited for him to tell me what had flashed into his mind so suddenly.

"The fellow who married Leesy's cousin, and ran away from her, was a doctor—Miss Sullivan has told me that. Richard, I begin to see light!—day is breaking!"

I hardly knew whether his speech was figurative or literal, as day was really breaking upon us two men, plotting there in the night, as if we were the criminals instead of their relentless pursuers.

"Three months! There will be time, Richard!" and Mr. Burton actually flung his arms about me, in a burst of exultation.

CHAPTER III.
THE CONFESSION.

In the afternoon we paid Miss Sullivan a visit. It was the first time I had met her since that strange night of watching at Moreland villa; and I confess that I could not meet her without an inward shudder of abhorrence. Unbounded as was my respect and confidence for Mr. Burton, I did think that he had erred in his conclusions as to the character of this woman; or else that he concealed from me his real opinions, for some purpose to be explained at the proper time. If he still had suspicions, it was evident that he had kept them from their object as skillfully as from me, for I saw, by her manner of receiving him, that she regarded him as a friend.

Notwithstanding I had been informed of her rapidly-failing health, I was shocked at the change in Miss Sullivan since I had seen her. It was with an effort that she rose from her easy-chair at our approach; the fullness had all wasted from her naturally queenly figure; her cheeks were hollow, and aflame with the fire of fever; while those black eyes, which had ever seemed to smolder above unfathomable depths of volcanic passion, now almost blazed with light. Something like a smile flitted across her face when she saw my companion, but smiles were too strange there to feel at home, and it vanished as soon as seen. I do not think she liked me any better than I did her; each recoiled from the other instinctively; she would not have spoken to me had I come alone; but out of concession to the presence of her friend, she bowed to me and asked me to be seated. A little child in the room ran to Mr. Burton, as if expecting the package of bon-bons which he took from his pocket; but, as he became engaged in conversation with Leesy, I coaxed her over to me, where she was soon sitting on my knee. She was a pretty little girl, about three years old, in whose chubby little features I could no longer trace any resemblance to her "aunt." She prattled after the fashion of children, and in listening to her, I lost a remark or two of Mr. Burton's; but soon had my attention aroused by hearing Miss Sullivan exclaim,

"Going away! For how long?"

"Three months, at least."

Her hands sunk in her lap, and she became pale and agitated.

"It is presumptuous in me to dare to be sorry; I am nothing to you; but you are much to me. I don't know how we shall get along without you."

"Don't be uneasy about that, my child. I shall make arrangements with this same person who boards you now to keep you until my return, and, if you should fall sick, to take good care of you."

"You are far too good," she responded, tremulously. "You will have the blessing of the friendless. I only wish it had the power to bring you good luck on your journey."

"Perhaps it will," he said, with a smile. "I have a great deal of faith in such blessings. But, Leesy, I think you can assist my journey in even a more tangible way than that."

She looked at him inquiringly.

"I want you to tell me all and every thing you know about the father of little Norah."

"Why, sir?" she quickly asked. "I hope you have not heard from him," looking over toward the child, as if afraid it might be snatched from her.

"Your health is very far gone, Leesy; I suppose you hardly hope ever to recover it. Would you not be glad to see Norah under her father's protection before you were taken away?"

She stretched out her arms for the child, who slid off my knee, ran and climbed into her lap, where she held the curly head close to her bosom for a moment; her attitude was as if she sheltered the little one from threatened danger.

"I know, much more surely than any one else, that my days are numbered. I believe I shall never see your face again, Mr. Burton; and that was what grieved me when you spoke of going away—it was not that I thought of my comfort so much. The winter snow will hide me before you come back from your journey; and my darling will be left friendless. I know it—it is my only care. But I would rather, far rather, leave her to the cold charity of an orphan asylum—yes, I would rather turn her upon the street, with her innocent face only for a protector—than that her father should have aught to do with Norah."

"Why?"

"Because he is a bad man."

"I understand that he is in California; and as I am going to San Francisco, and perhaps shall visit the mining regions before my return, I thought you might wish to send him a message, telling him the child's condition. He may have laid up money by this time, and be able to send you a sum sufficient to provide for little Norah until she is old enough to take care of herself."

She only shook her head, drawing the child closer, with a shudder.

"I have forgotten his name," said Mr. Burton.

"I will not tell you," answered Miss Sullivan, with a return of the old fierceness, like that of a hunted panther. "Why can I never, never, never be let alone?"

"Do you think I would do any thing for your injury or disadvantage?" asked the detective, in that gentle yet penetrating voice which had such power to move people to his will.

"I do not know," she cried; "you have seemed to be my friend. But how do I know that it is not all simply to compass my destruction at last? You have brought into my house that person," looking at me, "who has persecuted me. You promised me that I should be free from him. And now you want to set a bloodhound on my track—as if I must be driven into my grave, and not allowed to go in peace."

"I assure you, Leesy, I had no idea that you regarded Norah's father with so much dislike. I have no object in the world in troubling you with him. I promise you that no word of mine shall give him the clue to your present circumstances, nor to the fact that he has a child living, if he is ignorant of it. You shall be protected—you shall have peace and comfort. What I would like is, that you shall give me a history of his life, his habits, character, where he lived, what was his business, etc.; and I will give you my reasons for wishing the information. A circumstance has come to light which connects him with an affair which I am investigating—that is, if he is the person I think he is—a sort of a doctor, I believe?"

Miss Sullivan did not answer the question so skillfully put; she still watched us with shining, half-sullen eyes, as if ready to put forth a claw from the velvet, if we approached too near.

"Come, Leesy, you must tell me what I want to hear." Mr. Burton's air was now that of a master. "Time is precious. I can not wait upon a woman's whim. I have promised you—and repeat it, upon my honor—that no annoyance or injury shall come to *you* through what you may tell me. If you prefer to answer me quietly to being compelled to answer before a court, all is right. I *must* know what I desire about this man."

"*Man*, Mr. Burton! Call him creature."

"Very well, creature, Leesy. You know him better than I do, and if you say he is a creature, I suppose I may take it for granted. His name is—"

"Or was, George Thorley."

When the name was spoken, I gave a start which attracted the attention of both my companions.

"You probably know something about him, Mr. Redfield," remarked the girl.

"George Thorley, of Blankville, who used to have an apothecary shop in the lower part of the village, and who left the place some three years ago, to escape the talk occasioned by a suspicious case of malpractice, in which he was reported to be concerned?"

"The same person, sir. Did you know him?"

"I can not say that I was acquainted with him. I do not remember that I ever spoke a word with him. But I knew him, by sight, very well. He had a face which made people look twice at him. I think I bought some trifles in his shop once. And the gossip there was about him at the time he ran away, fixed his name in my memory. I was almost a stranger then in Blankville—had lived there only about a year."

"How did he come to have any connection with your family, Leesy?"

Miss Sullivan had grown pale during the agitation of our talk, but she flushed again at the question, hesitated, and finally, looking the detective full in the eyes, answered:

"Since you have promised, upon your honor, not to disturb me any further about this matter, and since I am under obligations to you, sir, which I can not forget, I will tell you the rest of the story, a part of which I told you that morning at Moreland villa. I confessed to you, there, the secret of my own heart, as I never confessed it to any but God, and I told you something of my cousin's history to satisfy you about the child. I will now tell you all I know of George Thorley, which is more than I wish I knew. The first time I ever saw him was over four years ago, a short time after he set up his little shop, which, you recollect, was not far from my aunt's in Blankville. My aunt sent me, one evening, for something to relieve the toothache, and I went into the nearest place, which was the new one. There was no one in but the owner. I was surprised by the great politeness with which he treated me, and the interest he seemed to take in the case of my aunt. He was a long time putting up the medicine, pasting the label on, and making change, so that I thought my aunt would surely be out of temper before I could bring her the drops. He asked our name, and where we lived, which was all, I thought, but a bit of his blarney, to get the good will of his customers." (Miss Sullivan usually spoke with great propriety, but occasionally a touch of her mother's country, in accent or expression, betrayed her Irish origin.) "That was the beginning of our acquaintance, but not the end of it. It was but a few days before he made an excuse to call at our house. I was a young girl, then, gay and healthy; and the plain truth of it is that George Thorley fell in love with me. My aunt was very much flattered, telling me I would be a fool not to encourage him—that he was a doctor and a gentleman—and would keep his wife like a lady—that there would be no more going out to sew and slave for others, if I were once married to him; it was only what she expected of me, that I would at least be a doctor's wife, after the schooling she had given me, and with the good looks I had. It is no vanity in me, now, to say of this clay, so soon to be mingled with the dust of the earth, that it was beautiful—too much so, alas, for my own peace of mind—for it made me despise the humble and honest suitors who might have secured me a lowly, happy life. Yet it was not that, either, and I'll not demean myself to say so—it was not because I was handsome that I held myself aloof from those in my own station; it was because I felt that I had thoughts and tastes they could not understand—that my life was above theirs in hope, in aspiration. I was ambitious, but only to develop the best that was in me. If I could only be a needle-woman all my days, then I would be so skillful and so fanciful with my work, as almost to paint pictures with my needle and thread. But this isn't telling you about George Thorley. From the first I took a dislike to him. I'm not good at reading character, but I understood his pretty thoroughly, and I was afraid of him. I was very cold to him, for I saw that he was of a quick temper, and I did not mean he should say that I had ever encouraged him. I told my aunt I did not think he was a gentleman—I had seen plenty of real gentlemen in the houses where I sewed, and they were not like him. I told her, too, that he had a violent temper, and a jealous disposition, and could not make any woman happy. But she would not think of him in that light; her heart was set on the apothecary's shop, which, she said, would grow into a fine drug-store with the doctor's name in gilt letters on the door of his office.

"George soon offered himself, and was terribly angry when I refused him. I believe he loved me, in his selfish way, better than he loved any other human creature. He would not give me up, nor allow me any peace from his persecutions. He dogged my steps whenever I went out, and if I spoke to any other man, it put him in a rage. I got to feeling that I was watched all the time; for sometimes he would laugh in his hateful way, and tell me of things he had seen when I thought him miles away.

"Twice, in particular, I remember of his being in a savage

passion, and threatening me. It was after"—here the speaker's voice, despite of her efforts to keep it steady, trembled and sunk—"he had seen me riding out in the carriage with Mrs. Moreland. He said those people were making a fool of me— that I was so set up, by their attentions, as to despise him. I told him that if I despised him, it was not for any such reason. It was because he behaved so ungentlemanly toward me, spying around me, when he had no business whatever with my affairs. That made him madder than ever, and he muttered words which I did not like. I told him I was not afraid of any mortal thing, and I didn't think he would frighten me into marrying him. He said he would scare me yet, so that I would never get over it. I think he liked the spirit I showed; it seemed the more I tried to make him hate me, the more determined he was to pursue me. I don't know how it was that I understood him so well, for in those days there had been nothing whispered against his character. Indeed, people didn't know much about him; and he got himself into the good graces of some of the leading citizens of Blankville. He had told me something of his history; that is, that his family were English; that he, like myself, was an orphan; that, by dint of good luck, he had got a place in a doctor's office in one of the towns in this State—one of those humble situations where he was expected to take care of the physician's horse, drive the carriage, put up medicines, attend upon orders, and any thing and every thing. He was smart and quick; he had many hours of leisure when waiting behind the little counter, and these hours he spent in studying the doctor's books, which he managed to get hold of one at a time. By these means, and by observing keenly the physician's methods, his advice to patients who called at the office, and by reading and putting up prescriptions constantly, he picked up a really surprising smattering of science. Making up his mind to be a doctor, and to keep a drug-store (a profitable business, he knew) he had the energy to carry out his plans. How he finally obtained the capital to set up the little business in Blankville, I never understood, but I knew that he attended lectures on surgery, one winter, in New York, and was in a hospital there a short time. All this was fair enough, and proved him ambitious and energetic; but I did not like or trust him. There was something dark and hidden in the workings of his mind, from which I shrunk. I knew him, too, to be cruel. I could see it in his manner of treating children and animals; there was nothing he liked so well as to practice his half-learned art of surgery upon some unfortunate sufferer. The more he insisted on my liking him, the more I grew to dread him.

"Affairs were at this crisis when my cousin came from New York to pay my aunt a visit. Coming to our rooms almost every evening, of course he made her acquaintance immediately. For the purpose of making me jealous, he began to pay the most devoted attention to her. Nora was a pretty girl, with blue eyes and fair hair; an innocent-minded thing, not very sharp, apprenticed to a milliner in the city; she believed all that *Doctor* Thorley told her, and fell in love with him, of course. When she went away, after her little holiday, George found that, instead of provoking me to jealousy, he had only roused my temper at the way he had fooled Nora. I scolded him well for it, and ended by telling him that I never would speak to him again.

"Well, it was just after that the scandal arose about his causing the death of a person by malpractice. He found it was prudent to run away; so he sold his stock for what he could get, and hid himself in New York. I did not know, at first, where he was; but felt so relieved to be rid of him. I had made up my own mind to go to New York, and get employment in a fancy-store. You know, Mr. Burton, for I once laid my heart before you, what wild, mad, but sinless infatuation it was which drew me there. I am not ashamed of it. God is love. When I stand in his presence, I shall glory in that power of love, which in this bleak world has only fretted and wasted my life. In heaven our whole lives will be one adoration." She clasped her thin hands together, and turned her dark eyes upward with an expression rapt to sublimity. I gazed upon her with renewed surprise and almost reverence. Never do I expect to meet another woman, the whole conformation of whose mind and heart so fitted her for blind, absolute devotion as Leesy Sullivan's.

"When I went to the city to see about getting a place, I met my cousin, who told me that she was married to George Thorley, and had been for some weeks; that they were boarding in a nice, quiet place, and that George staid at home a great deal—indeed, he hardly went out at all.

"It was evident that she had not heard of his reasons for leaving Blankville, and that she did not guess why he kept himself so quiet. Of course I hadn't the heart to tell her; but I made up my mind that I'd be better to stay where I was, for the present—so I went back to my aunt, without trying to get a situation in New York.

"It was about six months after this I got word from Nora, begging me to come and see her. I loved my cousin, and I'd felt grieved that she was married to Dr. Thorley. I mistrusted something was wrong; so I went to the city, and found her out in the miserable tenement where she was now stopping, starving herself in a room with hardly a bit of furniture. She burst out a-crying when she saw me; and when I stopped her sobbing, she told me she had not seen George for more than three months; that either he had met with an accident, or he'd run away from her, leaving her without a cent of money, and she in such health that she could hardly earn enough to buy a bit of bread and pay the rent of this room.

"'Do you really think he has left you?' I asked her.

"'Sure, how can I tell?' she answered, looking at me so pitifully with her innocent blue eyes. 'He was a fine gentleman, and it's afraid I am that he's grown tired of his poor Irish Nora.'

"'I warned you, cousin,' I said; 'I knew George Thorley for a villain; but you were taken with his fine words, and wouldn't heed. I'm sorry, sorry, sorry for you—but that won't undo what's done. Are you sure you are his wife, Nora dear?'

"'As sure as I am of heaven,' she cried, angry with me. 'But it's married we were by a Protestant clergyman, to please George— and I've got my certificate safe—ah, yes, indeed.'

"I could never ascertain whether the ceremony had been performed by a legalized minister; I always suspected my poor cousin had been deceived, and it was because my aunt thought so, too, and was sore on the subject, that she got so angry with you two gentlemen when you went to inquire. But, whether my suspicions were or were not correct, Nora was George's wife as certainly, in the sight of the angels, as woman was ever the wife of man. Poor child! I no longer hesitated about coming to New York. She needed my protection, and my help, too. I paid her board till the day of her death, which was but a few days after her poor little baby was born; I saw her decently buried, and then I put out the infant to nurse, and I worked to keep that. It was a comfort to me, sir. My own heart was sad, and I took to the little creature almost as if it was my own. I had promised Nora that I would bring it up, and I have kept my word, thus far. I hated its father for the way he'd treated Nora, but I loved the child; I took pleasure in making its pretty garments and in seeing that it was well taken care of. I knew I should never marry; and I adopted Nora's child as my own.

"Hardly was poor Nora cold in her grave when I was, one evening, surprised by a visit from George Thorley. Where he had been during his absence I did not know. He tried to excuse his conduct toward my cousin, by saying that he had married her in a fit of jealousy, to which I'd driven him by my coldness; that he'd been so tormented in mind he couldn't stay with her, for he didn't love her, and he'd gone out West, and been hard at work, to try and forget the past. But he couldn't forget it; and when he saw his wife's death in the papers, he had felt awfully; but now he hoped I'd forgive it all, and marry him. He said he had a good business started in Cincinnati, and I should want for nothing, and I *mustn't* say no to him again. I stood up, I was so indignant, and faced him till he grew as white as a sheet. I called him a *murderer*—yes, Nora's murderer—and ordered him never to speak to me nor come near me again. I knew he was terribly angry; his eyes burned like fire; but he did not say much that time; as he took up his hat to go, he asked about his baby—if it was living? I would not answer him. He had no right to the child, and I did not wish him to see it, or have any thing to do with it.

"What became of him, after that, for a long time, I don't know. He may have been in the city all the time, or he may have been in Cincinnati. At any rate, one day, as I was going from my boarding-house to the store, I found him walking along by my side. Norah was nigh a year old then. He commenced talking to me on the street, asking me again to marry him; and then, to frighten me, he said what a pretty baby Norah had got to be; and that he should have to find a wife to take care of his child. She was his, and he was going to have her, right away; and if I had any interest in her, I could show it by becoming her step-mother. He said he had plenty of money, and pulled out a handful of gold and showed me. But this only made me think the worse of him. He followed me home, and into my room, against my will, and there I turned upon him and told him that if he ever dared to force himself into my presence again, I would summon the police, and he should be turned over to the Blankville authorities for the crime that had driven him out of the village.

"After he was gone, I sunk into a chair, trembling with weakness, though I had been so bold in his presence. He looked like an evil spirit, when he smiled at me as he shut the door. His smile was more threatening than any scowl would have been. I was frightened for Norah. Every day I expected to hear that the little creature had been taken from her nurse; I trembled night and day; but nothing happened to the child, and from that day to this I have not seen George Thorley. If he is in California, I am glad of it; for that is a good ways off, and perhaps he'll never get track of his daughter. I'd far rather she'd die and be buried with her mother and myself, than to live to ever know that she had such a father.

"It seems a strange lot has been mine," concluded the sewing-girl, her dark eyes musing with a far-away look, "to have been followed by such a man as that, to have set my heart so high above me, and then to have fallen, by means of that love, into such a dreadful pit of circumstances—not only to be heart-broken, but so driven and hunted about the world, with my poor little lamb-kin here."

The pathetic look and tone with which she said this touched me deeply. For the first time, I felt fully the exceeding cruelty I had been guilty of toward her, if she were as innocent as her words averred of that nameless and awful crime which I had written down against her. At that moment, I did believe her innocent; I did pity her for her own melancholy sufferings, which had wasted the fountains of her life; and I did respect her for that humble and perfect devotion, giving all and asking nothing, with which she lavished her soul upon him whose memory called upon his friends for sleepless vigilance in behalf of justice. I did not wonder that she shrunk from me as from one ready to wound her. But this was only when in her presence; as soon as I was away I felt doubtful again.

"Have you any likeness of George Thorley?" asked Mr. Burton.

"No. Poor Nora had his ambrotype,* but after her death I threw it into the fire."

"Will you describe him to us?"

Miss Sullivan gave a description corresponding in all particulars with that given by Mr. Burton, after reading the dead-letter; he asked her about the third finger of the right hand, and she said—"Yes, it had been injured by himself, in some of his surgical experiments."

We now proposed to take leave, the detective again assuring Leesy that he should rather protect her against Thorley than allow him any chance to annoy her; he assured her she should be cared for in his absence, and, what was more, that if little Norah should be left friendless, he would keep an eye on the child and see that it was suitably brought up. This last assurance brightened the face of the consumptive with smiles and tears; but when he gave her his hand at parting, she burst into sobs.

"It is our last meeting, sir."

"Try to keep as well as you are now until I come back," he said, cheerfully. "I may want you very much then. And, by the way, Leesy—one question more. You once told me that you did not recognize the person you saw upon the lawn, at Mr. Argyll's, that night—have you a suspicion who it might be?"

"None. I believe the man was a stranger to me. I only saw him by a flash of lightning at the instant he was descending from the

---

* Ambrotyping was an early photographic process, cheaper and easier that daguerreotyping, and so was popular for portraits.

tree; if he had been an acquaintance I do not know that I should have known him."

"That is all. Good-by, little Norah. Don't forget Burton."

We heard the girl's sobs after the door was shut.

"I'm her only friend," said my companion, as he walked away. "No wonder she is moved at letting me go. I think, with her, that it is doubtful if she lasts until we get back. Still, her disease is a lingering one—I hope I shall see her live to witness the sad triumph of our industry."

"You speak as if the triumph were already secured."

"If he's on the face of the earth, we'll find Doctor George Thorley. It is no longer possible that we should be on the wrong track. You know, Richard, that I have not confided all my secrets to you. There will be no one more astonished than yourself when I summon my witnesses and sum up my conclusions. Oh, that the hour were come! But I forget my motto—'learn to labor and to wait.'"

CHAPTER IV.
EMBARKED FOR CALIFORNIA.

We were on our way to California by the next steamer. By the advice of Mr. Burton I purchased my ticket under an assumed name, for he did not wish to excite the curiosity of the Argylls, who might happen to see the passage-list, and who would be sure to suspect something from the contiguity of our names. To his friends, who chanced to know of his sudden intentions, Mr. Burton represented that the health of his daughter demanded a change of climate, and business matters had led him to prefer California.

It was fortunate, since the expenses of such a trip had become so unexpected a necessity, that I had lived in the plain, retiring manner which I had done in Washington. I had wasted no money on white kids,* bouquets, nor champagne-suppers; I had paid my board and washing-bills, and a very moderate bill to my tailor; the rest of my salary had been placed in a New York bank to my account. My scorched soul and withered tastes had demanded no luxurious gratification—not even the purchase of new books; so that now, when this sudden demand arose, I

---
* White kidskin gloves, worn by men with formal evening wear.

had a fund sufficient for the purpose. Mr. Burton bore his own expenses, which, indeed, I could not help, for I had not the means of urging a different course upon him.

We had a very definite object, but no definite plans; these were to be formed according to the circumstances we had to encounter after our arrival in El Dorado. Of course our man was living under an assumed name, and had traveled under an assumed one; we might have every difficulty in getting upon his track. At the time the detective had discovered the return of the five-hundred-dollar bill from San Francisco, he had, with great perseverance, gained access to, and "made a note of" the passengers' lists of all the steamers which sailed at or about the time of the murder, for California. These he had preserved. Out of the names, he had chosen those which his curious sagacity suggested were the most likely to prove fictitious, and, if no quicker method presented itself, he intended to trace out one and all of those passengers, until he came upon *the man*. In all this I was his assistant, willing to carry out his directions, but trusting the whole affair to his more experienced hand.

During the long, monotonous days of our voyage, I seemed to have

> *"Suffered a sea-change"**

into something quite different from the wooden sort of being into which I had gradually been hardening. With the dull routine of my office-life were broken up also many of the cynical ways of thinking into which I had fallen. I felt as if the springs of youth were not quite dried up. The real secret of this improvement was in the eager hope I entertained that the real criminals

---

* From act 1, scene 2, of Shakespeare's *The Tempest* (1611).

were soon to be brought to light, and the Argylls made to realize the cruel wrong they had done me. Already, in imagination, I had accepted their regret and forgiven them their injustice. It seemed as if every breath of the sea-breeze, and every bound of the sparkling waves, swept away a portion of the bitterness which had mingled with my nature. The old poetry of existence began to warm my chilled pulses and to flush the morning and evening sky. For hours most melancholy, yet most delicious, I would climb to some lonely post of observation—for I was a perfect sailor among the ropes—and there, where the blue of heaven bent down to meet the blue of the ocean, making an azure round in which floated only the ethereal clouds, all the sweetness of the past would come floating to me in fragments, like the odor of flowers blown from some beloved and distant shore.

The most vivid picture in my sea-dreams, was that of the parlor of the old Argyll mansion, as I had seen it last, on the night of my excursion to the oak tree. Mary, in the rosy bloom of young womanhood, the ideal of beauty to the eye of a young and appreciative man, whose standard of female perfection was high, while his sensitiveness to its charm was intense—Mary, reading her book beneath the rich light of the chandelier—I loved to recall the vision, except always that it was marred by that shadow of James coming too soon between me and the light. But that flitting vision of Eleanor was as if a saint had looked down at me out of its shrine. I saw, then, that she was no longer of this world, as far as her hopes were concerned. My once strong passion had been slowly changing into reverence; I had grieved with her with a grief utterly self-abnegating, and when I saw that her despair had worked itself up to a patient and aspiring resignation, I now felt less of pity and more of affection-ate reverence. I would have sacrificed my life for her peace of heart; but I no longer thought of Eleanor Argyll as of a woman to be approached by the loves of this world. Still, as I mused in my sea-reveries, I believed myself to have exhausted my wealth of feeling upon this now dead and hallowed love. I had given my first offering at the feet of a woman, peerless amid her compeers, and since she had chosen before me, I must needs live solitary, too honored by having worshiped a woman like Eleanor, to ever be satisfied with a second choice. For Mary I felt a keen admiration, and a brother's fondest love. The noble words she had spoken in my favor had thrilled me with gratitude, and increased the tenderness I had always cherished toward her. When I thought of her approaching marriage, it was not with jealousy, but with a certain indefinable pang which came of my dislike to the motives and character of James. I did not believe that he loved her. Eleanor he *had* loved; but Mary was to him only the necessary means of securing the name, property, respectability, etc., of his uncle's family. As I recalled that visit to the gaming-table, I felt, at times, as if I *must* get back from this journey in time to interfere, and break up the marriage. I would run the risk of being again treated as before—of being misunderstood and insulted—I would run *any* risk to save her from the unhappiness which must come from such a partnership! So I thought one hour, and the next I would persuade myself that I could not and must not make such a fool of myself; and that, after all, when once "married and settled," James might make a very good husband and citizen.

Little Lenore was the light and glory of the steamer. People almost fancied that, with such a good angel aboard, no harm could come to the ship. And indeed we had a speedy, prosperous voyage.

Yet it was tedious to Mr. Burton. I had never seen him so restless. I used to tell him that he made the hours a great deal longer by counting them so often. It was evident that he had some anxiety which he did not share with me. A feverish dread of delays was upon him.

After we had crossed the isthmus, and were fairly embarked on the Pacific, his restlessness abated. Yet it was just then that a small delay occurred, which threatened to irritate him into new impatience. It was found that the captain had taken on board quite a company of passengers whom he had promised to land at Acapulco. It was a beautiful, sunny day early in October, that our ship steamed into the little bay. Nearly all the passengers were on deck, to take a look at the country and harbor as we approached. I was upon the hurricane-deck with Lenore, who was delighted with the warm air and green shores, and whose hair streamed on the fresh yet delicious breeze like a golden banner. She observed the distant mountains, the sunny haze, the glimmering water of the bay, with all the intelligence of a woman; while I could not but be more pleased with the roses blowing on her cheeks and the trick the wind was playing with her hair, than with all the scenery about us. The child's attendant, a steady, careful matron, who had long had the charge of her, was likewise on deck, chatting with some of her new acquaintances, and she could not refrain from coming to us, presently, on the pretext of wrapping Lenore's shawl closer about her.

"Do look at her, Mr. Redfield," said the good woman, "did you ever see her looking so bright and healthy, sir? The master was right, sure enough—it was a sea-voyage she needed, above all things. Her cheeks are like pinies, and, if I do say it, who shouldn't, it's the opinion of the company that you're the best-lookin' couple on the decks. I've heard more'n one speak of it this past half-hour."

"That's half true, anyhow," I answered, laughing, and looking at Lenore, whose modest, quiet mind was never on the alert for compliments. She laughed because I did, but remained just as unconscious of her pretty looks as hitherto.

"There's papa coming," she said; "something has happened to him."

With her marvelous quick discernment, so like her father's, she perceived, before I did, that he was excited, although endeavoring to appear more calm than he really felt.

"Well, Richard, Lenore," he began, drawing us a little apart from the others, speaking in a low voice, "what do you say to my leaving you?"

"Leaving us!" we both very naturally exclaimed.

"It would be rather sudden, that is true."

"Where would you go? Walk off on the water, or betake yourself to the valleys and mountains of Mexico?"

"There's no jest about it, Richard. Information, which has come to me in the strangest, most unexpected manner, renders it imperative that I should stop at Acapulco. I am as much surprised as you are. I have not even time to tell you the story; in twenty minutes the ship will begin to send off her passengers in a small-boat; and if I decide to remain here, I must go to my state-room for some of my clothes."

"Are you in earnest, father?" asked Lenore, ready to cry.

"Yes, my darling. I am afraid I must let you go on to San Francisco without me; but you will have Marie, and Richard will take as good care of you as I would. I want you to enjoy yourselves, to have no cares, to take the second return steamer, which will give you a fortnight in San Francisco, and *I will meet you at the isthmus.* As you will have nothing to do, after your arrival, I will advise you to explore the country, ride out every pleasant day, etc. The time will soon pass, and in five weeks, God willing, we shall meet and be happy, my dear little girl. Run, run to Marie, and tell her what I am to do; she will come and get my orders."

Lenore moved away, rather reluctantly, and Mr. Burton continued to myself, who was standing silent from mere stupidity
of astonishment:

"By the merest chance in the world I overheard a conversation between the people about to land, which convinces me
that George Thorley, instead of being in California, is not thirty
miles from Acapulco. If I were not positive of it, I should not run
the risk of experiment, now, when time is worth every thing.
But I am so certain of it, that I do not see as there is any thing
for you to do in San Francisco but to help little Lenore pass the
time pleasantly. I have thought, as calmly as I could under the
pressure of much haste, whether you had better stop with me,
and await, at some hotel in Acapulco, the result of my visit into
the interior, or go on to the end of your journey, and returning,
meet me at the isthmus. On the child's account, I think you had
better finish the voyage as expected. The sea-air is benefiting
her greatly; and, unless you fret too much, there is nothing to
prevent your enjoying the trip."

"I shall do just as you advise, Mr. Burton; but, of course, I
shall be intolerably anxious. For my own part, I would rather
keep with you; but that must be done which is best for all."

"You could do me no good by remaining with me; the only
thing to be gained is, that you would be out of your suspense
sooner. But, I assure you, you ought to rejoice and feel light-
hearted in view of so soon learning the one fact most important
to us—the hiding-place of that man. Think you I would wish
delay? No. I'm sure of my man, or I should not take this unexpected step. How curious are the ways of Providence! It seems
as if I received help outside of myself. I was vexed to hear that
we were to be delayed at Acapulco, and now this has proven our
salvation."

"God grant you are in the right, Mr. Burton."

"God grant it. Do not fear that I shall fail, Richard. You have reason to be doubly cheerful. Don't you trust me?"

"As much—more, than any person on earth."

"Be true to your part, then; take good care of my child— meet me at the isthmus—that is your whole duty."

"But, Mr. Burton, do you not place yourself in danger? Are you not incurring risks which you ought to share with others? Can I go on, idle and prosperous, leaving you to do all the work, and brave all the dangers of a journey like yours?"

"I wish it. There may be a little personal risk; but not more, perhaps, than I incur every day of my life. Perhaps you do not know," he added, gayly, "that I lead a charmed life. Malice and revenge have followed me in a hundred disguises—six times I have escaped poisoned food prepared for me; several times, infernal machines, packed to resemble elegant presents, have been sent to me; thrice I have turned upon the assassin, whose arm was raised to strike—but I have come unscathed out of all danger, to quietly pursue the path to which a vivid sense of duty calls me. I do not believe that I am going to fail in this, one of the most atrocious cases in which I have ever interested myself. No, no, Richard; I enjoy the work—the sense of danger adds to its importance. I would not have it otherwise. As I said, God willing, I will meet you at the isthmus. If I do not keep my appointment, *then* you may know that harm has come to me; and, after providing for the safe passage home of my little family, you may, if you please, come back to look after the threads of the history which I have dropped. The steamer has cast anchor; I must get my luggage in shape to go ashore."

He turned away; but presently paused and returned, with an air of perplexity.

"There *will* be something for you to do, Richard. I had forgotten about that five-hundred-dollar bill, which certainly went to California within a short time after the robbery. If I should be mistaken, after all—but no! my information is too conclusive—I *must* take the course, now, and if I am on the wrong track, it will be a bad business. However, I will not allow myself to think so," he added, brightening again; "but it will do no harm for you to take a lesson in my art, by exercising your skill in tracing the fortunes of that bank-note. In doing that, you may come upon evidence which, if I fail here, may be turned to use."

With a foreboding of evil I looked after him as he descended the ladder to the lower deck—form, face and manner expressing the indomitable energy which made him the man he was.

When the sun sunk, that night, into the molten waves of the Pacific, Lenore and I paced the deck alone; and as she quietly wiped away the tears which fell at the sense almost of desertion which her father's sudden departure caused, I could hardly cheer her, as he had bidden me; for I, too, felt the melancholy isolation of our position—voyaging to a strange land in the wake of an awful mystery.

CHAPTER V.
ON THE TRAIL.

I need not dwell at much length upon our visit to San Francisco, since nothing important to the success of our enterprise came of it. From the hour we entered the Golden Gate till we departed through it, I was restless with a solicitude which made me nervous and sleepless, destroyed my appetite, and blinded me to half the novelties of San Francisco, with its unparalleled growth and hybrid civilization. I gave the most of my time to two objects—looking, by night, into all the bad, popular, or out-of-the-way dens, haunts, saloons, theaters and hotels, scanning every one of the thousands of strange faces, for that one sinister countenance, which I felt that I could know at a glance—and in the endeavor to identify the man who had disposed of the Park Bank bill to the Express Company.

I was rewarded, for days of research, by ascertaining, finally, and beyond doubt, that a gentleman of respectability, a Spaniard, still residing in the city, had offered the bill to be discounted at the time it had been accepted by the company. I made the acquaintance of the Spanish gentleman, and, with a delicacy of address upon which I flattered myself, I managed to learn, without being too impertinent, that he had obliged a fellow-passenger, two years previously, who was getting off at Acapulco, and who desired gold for his paper money, with the specie, and had taken of him some two or three thousand dollars of New York currency, which he had disposed of to the Express Company.

Burton was right, then! My heart leaped to my throat as the gentleman mentioned Acapulco. From that moment I felt less fear of failure, but more, if possible, intense curiosity and anxiety.

It had been my intention to proceed to Sacramento in search of the haunting face which was forever gliding before my mind's eye; but, after this revelation, I gladly yielded to the belief that Mr. Burton would find the face before I did; and, in the relief consequent upon this hope, I began to give more heed to his injunction, to do my part of the duty by taking good care of his child.

Lenore was in rising health and spirits, and when I began to exert myself to help her pass away the time, she grew very happy. The confiding dependence of childhood is its most affecting trait. It was enough for her that her father had given her to me for the present; she felt safe and joyous, and made all those little demands upon my attention which a sister asks of an older brother. I could hardly realize that she was nearly thirteen years of age, she remained so small and slender, and was so innocently childlike in her manners and feelings. Her attendant was one of those active women who like nothing so much as plenty of business responsibility; the trip, to her, was full of the kind of excitement she preferred; the entire charge of the little maiden intrusted to her care, was one of the most delightful accidents that ever happened to her; I believe she rejoiced daily in the absence of Mr. Burton, simply because it added to the impor-tance of her duties.

But I was glad when the fortnight's long delay was over, and we were reëmbarked upon our journey. My mind lived in advance of the hour, dwelling upon the moment when I should either see, awaiting us on the dock, where he had promised to meet us, at the isthmus, the familiar form of the good genius of our party, or—that blank which would announce tidings of fatal evil.

We glided prosperously over the rounded swells of the Pacific, through sunshiny days, and nights of brilliant moonlight. Through the soft evenings, Lenore, well wrapped in shawls and hood by her faithful woman, remained with me upon deck, sometimes until quite late, singing, one after another, those delicious melodies never more subtly, understandingly rendered, than by this small spirit of song. Rapt crowds would gather, at respectful distances, to listen; but she sung for my sake, and for the music's, unheeding who came or went. Sometimes, even now, I wake at night from a dream of that voyage, with the long wake of glittering silver following the ship, as if a million Peris,* in their boats of pearl, were sailing after us, drawn on by the enchantment of the pure voice which rose and fell between stars and sea.

The last twenty-four hours before reaching the isthmus witnessed a change in the long stretch of brilliant weather common at that season of the year. Torrents of rain began to fall, and continued hour after hour, shutting us in the cabin, and surrounding us with a gray wall, which was as if some solid world had closed us in, and we were never more to see blue sky, thin air, or the sharp rays of the sun.

Lenore, wearied of the monotony, at length fell asleep on one of the sofas; and I was glad to have her quiet, for she had been

---

* In Persian mythology, fallen angels, beautiful, fairylike beings.

restless at the prospect of seeing her father early the next morning. It was expected the steamer would reach her dock some time after midnight. As the hours of the day and evening wore on, I grew so impatient as to feel suffocated by the narrow bounds of the ship, and the close, gray tent of clouds. Lenore went early to her state-room. I then borrowed a waterproof cloak from one of the officers of the vessel, and walked the decks the whole night, in the driving rain, for I could not breathe in my little room. It was so possible, so probable, that harm had befallen the solitary detective, setting forth, "a stranger in a strange land," upon his dangerous errand, that I blamed myself bitterly for yielding to his wishes, and allowing him to remain at Acapulco. In order to comfort myself, I recalled his ability to cope with danger— his physical strength, his unshaken coolness of nerve and mind, his calmness of purpose and indomitable will, before which the wills of other men were broken like reeds by a strong wind. The incessant rain recalled two other memorable nights to me; and the association did not serve to make me more cheerful. There was no wind whatever, with the rain; the captain assured me, after I had asked him often enough to vex a less question-inured officer, for the twentieth time, that we were "all right"—"not a half-hour after time"—"would arrive at the isthmus at two o'clock, a.m., precisely, and I might go to bed in peace, and be ready to get up early in the morning."

I had no idea of going to bed. The passengers were not to be disturbed until daylight; but I was too anxious to think of sleep; I said to myself that if Mr. Burton was as impatient as myself, he would, despite the storm and the late hour, be upon the dock awaiting our arrival; and if so, he should not find me slumbering. As we neared our landing, I crowded in among the sailors at the forward part of the boat, and strained my eyes through the gloom to the little twinkle of light given out by the lamps along the quay. As usual, there was considerable stir and noise, upon the arrival of the steamer, shouts from the ship and shore, and a bustle of ropes and swearing of sailors. The passengers generally were snug in their berths, where they remained until morning. In a few moments the ropes were cast ashore and we were moored to our dock. I leaned over the gunwale and peered through the mist; the rain had kindly ceased descending, for the time; various lamps and lanterns glimmered along the wharf, where some persons were busy about their work, pertaining to the arrival of the ship; but I looked in vain for Mr. Burton.

Disappointed, despondent, I still reconnoitered the various groups, when a loud, cheery voice called out,

"Richard, halloo!"

I experienced a welcome revulsion of feeling as these pleasant tones startled me to the consciousness that Mr. Burton had emerged from the shadow of a lamppost, against which he had been leaning, and was now almost within shaking-hands distance. I could have laughed or cried, whichever happened, as I recognized the familiar voice and form. Presently he was on the vessel. The squeeze I gave his hand, when we met, must have been severe, for he winced under it. I scarcely needed to say— "You have been successful!" or he to answer; there was a light on his face which assured me that at least he had not entirely failed.

"I have much, much to tell you, Richard. But first about my darling—is she well—happy?"

"Both. We have not had an accident. You will be surprised to see Lenore, she has improved so rapidly. My heart feels a thousand pounds lighter than it did an hour ago."

"Why so?"

"Oh, I was so afraid you had not got away from Acapulco."

"You do look pale, that's a fact, Richard—as if you had not slept for a week. Let your mind rest in quiet, my friend. *All is right.* The trip has not been wasted. Now let God give us favoring breezes home, and two years of honest effort shall be rewarded. Justice shall be done. The wicked in high places shall be brought low."

He always spoke as if impressed with an awful sense of his responsibility in bringing the iniquities of the favored rich to light; and on this occasion his expression was unusually earnest.

"Where is my little girl? What is the number of her stateroom? I would like to steal a kiss before she wakes; but I suppose that careful Marie has the door bolted and barred; so I will not disturb them. It is three whole hours to daylight yet. I can tell you the whole story of my adventures in that time, and I suppose you have a right to hear it as soon as possible. I will not keep you in suspense. Come into the cabin."

We found a quiet corner, where, in the "wee sma' hours,'"* by the dim light of the cabin-lamps, now nearly out, I listened, it is needless to say with what painful interest, to the account of Mr. Burton's visit in Mexico. I will give the history here, as he gave it, with the same reservations which, it was evident, he still made in talking with me.

These reservations—which I could not fail to perceive he had frequently made, since the beginning of our acquaintance, and which, the reader will recollect, had at times excited my indignation—puzzled and annoyed me; but there was soon to come a time when I understood and appreciated them.

On that day of our outward voyage, when the ship was detained to land a portion of her passengers at Acapulco, Mr. Burton, restless at the delay, was leaning over the deck-rails, thrumming impatiently with his fingers, when his attention became gradually absorbed in the conversation of a group of

---

* An old Scottish expression for the early (postmidnight) hours of the day.

Mexicans at his elbow, several of whom were of the party about to land. They spoke the corrupted Spanish of their country; but the listener understood it well enough to comprehend the most of what was said.

One of their number was describing a scene which occurred upon his landing at this same port some two years previous. The ship, bound for San Francisco, met with an accident, and put into Acapulco for repairs. The passengers knowing the steamer would not sail under twenty-four hours, the most of them broke the monotony of the delay by going on shore. A number of rough New Yorkers, going out to the mines, got into a quarrel with some of the natives, during which knives, pistols, etc., were freely used. A gentleman, named Don Miguel, the owner of a large and valuable *hacienda* which lay about thirty miles from Acapulco, and who had just landed from the steamer, attempted, imprudently, to interfere, not wishing his country-men to be so touchy with their visitors, and was rewarded for his good intentions by receiving a severe stab in the side from one of the combatants. He bled profusely, and would soon have become exhausted, had not his wound been immediately and well dressed by a young American, one of the New York passen-gers, who had landed to see the sights, and was standing idly to one side, viewing the *mêlée* at the time Don Miguel was injured. The Don, exceedingly grateful for the timely attention, con-ceived a warm liking for the young man, whose "Yankee" quick-ness and readiness had attracted his attention while on board the steamer. Having given such proof of his fitness for the place as he had done by dressing the Don's wound, that gentleman, in the course of the two or three hours in which the young stranger remained in attendance upon him, offered him the situation of physician upon his immense estates, with the plain prom-ise that he should receive benefits much more important than his salary. This offer, after a short hesitation, was accepted by the doctor, who stated that he was out in search of his fortune, and it made no difference to him where he found it, whether in Mexico or California, only that he should be assured of doing well. This Don Miguel, in his sudden friendship, was prompt to promise. The Don, besides vast grazing farms, had extensive interests in the silver mines which bordered upon his *hacienda*. Doctor Seltzer was deeply interested in an account of these, and returned to the ship for his baggage, bidding his fellow-passengers good-by, in excellent spirits. "And well he might consider himself fortunate," continued the narrator, "for there are none of us who do not feel honored by the friendship of Don Miguel, who is as honorable as he is wealthy. For my part, I do not understand how he came to place such confidence in the 'Yankee' doctor, who had to me the air of an adventurer; but he took him to his home, made him a member of his family, and before I left Acapulco, I heard that Don Miguel had given him for a wife his only daughter, a beautiful girl, who could have had her choice of the proudest young bloods in this region."

It may be imagined with what interest Mr. Burton listened to the story thus unconsciously revealed by the chatty Mexican. He at once, as by prescience, saw his man in this fortunate Dr. Seltzer, who had registered his name Mr., not Dr., on the passenger-list, and which name was among those that the detective had selected as suspicious.

(I interrupted my friend's narrative here to explain the matter of the bank-notes which he had exchanged for specie with a passenger, but found that Mr. Burton already knew all about them.)

Edging gradually into the conversation, Mr. Burton, with his tact and experience, was not long in drawing from the group a description of the personal appearance of Dr. Seltzer, along with all the facts and conjectures relating to his history since his connection with Don Miguel. Everything he heard made "assurance doubly sure;" and there was no time to be lost in deciding upon the course to be pursued in this unexpected doubling of the chase. To get off at Acapulco was a matter of course; but what to do with the remainder of his party he could not at first determine. He knew that I would be eager to accompany him; yet he feared that, in some way, should we all land and take rooms at any of the hotels, the wily Doctor Seltzer, doubtless always on the alert, might perceive some cause for alarm, and secure safety by flight. To go alone, under an assumed name, in the character of a scientific explorer of mines, seemed to him the surest and most discreet method of nearing the game; and to this resolve he had come before he sought us out to announce his intention of stopping at Acapulco, while leaving us to pursue our voyage without him.

CHAPTER VI.

AT LAST—AT LAST.

As our ship steered away out into the open sea, Mr. Burton walked up into the ruinous old Spanish town, and stopped at the hotel, in whose breezy corridor he found several of his traveling companions, who had preceded him. These persons had been somewhat surprised at his desertion of the rest of his party for a visit to their decayed city; but when he explained to them his desire of visiting some of their deserted mines, and examining the character of the mountainous region, a little back, before proceeding to similar investigations in California, their wonder gave place to the habitual indolence of temperaments hardly active enough for curiosity. There were two or three persons from the United States stopping at the hotel, who quickly made his acquaintance, eager for news direct from home, and while he conversed with these the four o'clock dinner was announced. He sipped his chocolate leisurely, after the dessert, chatting at ease with his new friends; and upon expressing a desire to see more of the old town, one of them offered to accompany him upon a walk. They strolled out among cool palm groves, and back through the dilapidated streets, made picturesque by some processions of Catholics, winding through the twilight with their torches, until the moon arose and glimmered on the restless ocean.

Most persons, on business similar to Mr. Burton's, would have gone at once to the American consul for his assistance; but he felt himself fully equal to the emergency, and desired no aid in the enterprise which he was about to prosecute. Therefore he refused the invitation of his companion to call upon the consul; and finally returned to his hotel, to sit awhile in the open, moonlit corridor, before retiring to his room, where he lay long awake, pondering upon the steps to be taken next day, and somewhat disturbed by the open doors and windows, which were the order of the establishment.

He was awakened from his first slumber by the cold nose of a dog rubbed in his face, and from his second by a lizard creeping over him; but not being a nervous man, he contrived to sleep soundly at last. He was served, early in the morning, with a cup of coffee in his apartment, and before the late breakfast was ready, he had been abroad and concluded his arrangements for a visit to the estates of Don Miguel. Everybody knew that gentleman by reputation; and he had no difficulty in securing the services of two half-naked, lazy-looking native Indians, to act as guides, who, with three forlorn mules, destined to carry the party, were at the door when he finished his repast. He was warned to go well armed, as, though the route to Don Miguel's was an old one, often traveled, there was always more or less danger in that country. A pistol or two would not be out of place, if only to keep his shiftless guides in order. Mr. Burton thanked his advisers, told them he feared nothing, and set out upon his long, hot and tedious ride—thirty miles on muleback, under a southern sun, being something more of a task than he had ever known a journey of that length to be hitherto. At noon he took a rest of a couple of hours at a miserable inn by the wayside, and a dinner of fried tortillas, rendered tolerable by a dessert of limes, bananas and oranges. With a supply of this cooling fruit in his pockets, he braved the afternoon sun, determined to reach the *hacienda* before dark. As he neared his destination, the character of the country changed. The broad road, cut through groves of palm, and fields of corn, with orchards of figs and peaches, grew more narrow and uneven, and the surface of the ground more broken. Before him loomed up hills, growing higher as they retreated, some of the glittering peaks seeming to glisten with snow. A cool, refreshing air swept down from them; the scenery, although wilder, was beautiful and romantic in the extreme. Wearied as he was with the conduct of a mule which was no disgrace to the reputation of its species, Mr. Burton enjoyed the magnificent scene which opened before him, as he approached the *hacienda* of Don Miguel. It lay at the foot of a low mountain, first of the brotherhood which overtopped it, and stood looking over its shoulder. Rich plains, some of them highly cultivated, and others covered with the grazing herds of a thousand cattle, lay at the foot of the hill, which was heavily timbered, and down which leaped a sparkling cascade, not more beautiful to the eye than promising of freshness to the pastures below, and of "water-privileges" to the mines understood to lay somewhere in the cañons of the mountain.

Before entering upon the estates which he had now reached, Mr. Burton secured a night's lodging for his *peons*, at a hovel by the roadside, and having abundantly rewarded them, dismissed them from his service, riding forward alone along the private carriage-way, which, through groves of flowering trees and fragrant peach-orchards, led up to the long, low, spacious mansion of Don Miguel.

By the servant who came forth to receive him he was informed that the master of the place was at home, and was soon shown into his presence, in the cool, tile-floored sitting-room, in which he was lounging, waiting for the supper-hour.

Mr. Burton's powers of pleasing were too great, and his refinement too real, for him to fail in making the impression he desired upon the gentleman into whose house he had intruded himself. The cold courtesy with which he was at first received, soon took a tinge of warmth, and it was with sincere cordiality that Don Miguel offered him the hospitalities of his home, and full liberty to make all the researches he might desire upon his estate. The habitual dislike of the Spaniard for "los Yankees," seemed quite overcome in the case of Don Miguel, by his friendship for his son-in-law, of whom he soon spoke, anticipating the pleasure it would give Dr. Seltzer to meet a gentleman so recently from his old home, New York. On this account he made the stranger doubly welcome. Mr. Burton was interested in his host, and liked him, perceiving him to be intelligent, generous and enthusiastic; his heart rebuked him when he thought of the mission upon which he had come into this little retired Paradise, so remote from the world and so lovely in itself that it did seem as if evil ought to have forgotten it.

The two had conversed nearly an hour, when Don Miguel said,

"It is now our supper-hour. Allow a servant to show you to your apartment, where we will give you time to at least bathe your face and hands after your weary ride. I was so entertained with the news that you bring me from the States that I have neglected your comfort. Dr. Seltzer went up on the mountain, to-day, to look after our mining interests a little, but I expect his return every moment. He will be charmed to meet a countryman."

This last assertion Mr. Burton doubted, for he knew that the remorse of a guilty conscience stung the possessor into a restlessness which made any unexpected event a matter of suspicion.

As the door closed upon him in the large, airy chamber into which he was ushered, he sunk, for a few moments, into a chair, and something like a tremor shook his usually steady nerves. He stood so close upon the probable accomplishment of the object he had kept in view for two years, that, for an instant, excitement overcame him. He soon rallied, however, and at the end of fifteen minutes, when the *peon* came in again to announce supper, he had toned up his courage with a plentiful dash of cold water, and was never more his own peculiar self, than when he set foot in the supper-room. A glance told him that the absent member of the family had not yet returned; only two persons were present, his host, and the beautiful woman whom he introduced as his daughter, Mrs. Seltzer. The three sat down to the table, which was covered with an elegant repast, the first dish of which was a fine-flavored roast wild-turkey.

There was a plentiful supply of porcelain and silverware; it did not take five seconds for the guest to decide that the quondam* druggist of Blankville—if this were indeed the person, as he assumed with such certainty—had gotten himself into enviable quarters.

As his penetrating glance rested on the exquisite face which confronted him across the "pale specter of the salt," he kept asking himself, with inward anguish, why it was that he had not circumvented this adventurer sooner, before the young, girlish creature he saw before him had involved her fate with that of the guilty.

Beautiful as our dreamiest fancies of Spanish women she was, according to the report of Mr. Burton, and he was no enthusiast. He saw that she was as uneasy as a bird which misses its mate, her black eyes constantly wandering to the door, and her ear

---

* Former.

so preoccupied with listening for the expected step as scarcely to take note of the remarks made to her by the stranger. Once she asked him, with much interest, if he had known Dr. Seltzer in New York, but upon his answering in the negative, he could guess that he had fallen in her esteem, for she immediately withdrew her attention from him.

The senses of the guest were all keenly on the alert; but it was by the sudden fire which leaped and melted in the eyes of the Donna, and the rich color which shot into her hitherto olive cheek, that he was informed of the approach of her husband. She had heard the rapid gallop of his horse afar off, and now sat, mute and expectant, until he should arrive at the gate, cross the veranda and enter the room. In three minutes he stood in the supper-room. The visitor met him just in the manner he would have most desired—when the man was entirely unwarned of company, and had no chance to put on a mask. Outwardly Mr. Burton was serene as a summer day, but inwardly his teeth were set upon each other to keep his tongue from crying out—"*This is the man!*" When Dr. Seltzer first perceived a stranger in the room, and heard his father-in-law say, "A countryman of yours, from New York, doctor," his slight start of surprise would, to most persons, have appeared no more than natural; but the person whose courteous eye met his, saw in it the first impulse of an ever-ready apprehension—an alarm, covered instantly by a false warmth of manner which caused him to greet the stranger with extreme friendliness.

The new-comer retired for a moment to his room to prepare for the meal; upon his taking his place at table, hot dishes were brought in; the Donna seemed also to have recovered her appetite, which had been spoiled by his absence; a gay and social hour followed.

Dr. Seltzer might have been good-looking had his eyes not

possessed the shifting, uncertain glance that plays before a soul which dares not frankly meet its fellows, and had not an evil expression predominated on his features. His face was one which would have been distrusted in any intelligent company of our own people; but the Spaniards, with whom he was now associated, were so accustomed to treachery and untruth among their race, and so familiar with kindred features and subtle black eyes, that he, doubtless, had never impressed them unfavorably.* A Spaniard he was at heart, and he had found, in his present life, a congenial sphere. Not that all Spaniards are necessarily murderers—but their code of right and wrong is different from ours. Don Miguel was an excellent gentleman, honorable, to an unusual degree for a Mexican, real and sanguine in his feelings, and thoroughly deceived as to the character and acquirements of the person to whom he had confided so much. It was the bitter flavor in the cup of his assured triumph that Mr. Burton, in bringing the villain to bay, must shock this amiable host, and ruin the happiness of his innocent child.

After supper, they sat on the veranda a couple of hours. The half-filled moon sunk down behind the groves of fragrant trees; the stars burned in the sky, large, and, to a Northern eye, preternaturally bright; the wind was luscious with warmth and sweetness; and the beautiful woman, whose soft eyes dwelt ever on the face of her husband, looked yet more lovely in the clear moonlight. (Through all the earnestness of his story, my friend

---

* Discrimination against Mexicans and other persons of Spanish and Indian descent (who were largely conflated in the minds of non-Hispanic Americans) was widespread in the mid-nineteenth century, especially in parts of the country near Mexico where border disputes continued. Although Hispanics were not enslaved per se, many were also victims of the peonage system, crushed with debt to their employers. A large influx of Hispanic miners in the California Gold Rush, many of whom were highly successful, increased resentment that nonwhites were reaping disproportionate rewards. Lynchings of Hispanics were common occurrences, though the numbers are vague because the victims were classed as "white" for statistical purposes.

dwelt on these details, because he observed them at the time, and they became a part of the narrative in his mind.)

The conversation was principally upon mining. Mr. Burton had sufficient scientific knowledge to make it apparent that his exploring expedition was for the purpose of adding to that knowledge. Before they separated for the night, Dr. Seltzer had promised to escort him, on the following day, over all the mountainous portion of the ranch.

The visitor retired early, being fatigued with his journey; but he did not sleep as quietly as usual. He was disturbed by the onerous duty to which he had devoted himself. Visions of the Donna, pale with grief and reproach, and of the interview which he had resolved upon with the murderer, alone on the mountainside, when, by the force of will, and the suddenness of the accusation, he expected to wring from him the desired confession—kept him long awake. Once, he half rose in his bed; for, lying in that feverish condition when all the senses are exalted, he heard, or fancied he heard, the handle of the door turned, and a person step silently into the apartment. Knowing the thievish propensities of the Spanish servants, he had no doubt but one of these had entered for purposes of robbery; he therefore remained quiet, but ready to pounce upon the intruder should he detect him approaching the bed. The room was entirely dark, the moon having set some time before. Whether he made some sound when rising on his couch, or whether the visitor gave up his purpose at the last moment, he could only conjecture; after some moments of absolute silence he heard the door drawn softly together again, and was conscious of being alone. Soon after this he dropped asleep, and awoke in the dawn to find his purse and garments undisturbed.

He was summoned to an early breakfast, which was partaken of by the two excursionists alone; his companion was, if possible, more social and friendly than on the previous evening. It was yet hardly sunrise when they arose from the table to mount the horses which awaited them at the door. A basket of lunch was attached to the pummel of Dr. Seltzer's saddle, whose parting injunction to the servant was to have dinner at four, as they should stand in need of it upon their return. Then, through a world of dew, coolness and perfume, glittering with the first rays of the sun, the two men rode off toward the mountains.

After following a good road some five or six miles, they commenced climbing the first of the series of hills of which mention has been made. The road here was still tolerable; but when they advanced into the immediate region of the mines they were compelled to abandon their horses, which were left at a small building, belonging to the ranch, and to proceed on foot into the mountain gorges.

The scenery now became wild beyond mere picturesqueness—it was startling, desolate, grand. Traces of old mines, once worked, but now deserted, were everywhere visible. Finally they came to a new "lead," which was being successfully worked by the *peons* of Don Miguel. There were some forty of these men at work, under an overseer. Dr. Seltzer showed his companion the recent improvements which had been made; the machinery which he himself had introduced, and a portion of which he had invented; stating that, under the system which he himself had introduced, Don Miguel was growing a rich man faster than he previously had any idea was possible. The mountain-stream, spoken of as being visible at a great distance, glittering from hight to hight, was here made to do the unromantic work of washing the ore and grinding it. The overseer was called upon by the host to give every desirable information to the traveler, and here a long visit was made. Lunch was partaken of under the cool shadow of a ledge of rock; and then Dr. Seltzer proposed, if his visitor was not already too much fatigued, to take him higher up, to a spot which he had discovered only the day before, and which he had every reason to believe contained a richer deposit of silver than any vein heretofore opened—in fact, he thought a fortune lay hidden in the wild gorge to which he referred, and he anxiously invited the scientific observation of his guest.

This was just the opportunity for being alone with his man that Mr. Burton desired. It may seem strange that he proposed to confront the murderer with his guilt in this solitary manner with no witnesses to corroborate any testimony he might wring from the guilty; but the detective knew enough of human nature to know that the confronted criminal is almost always a coward, and he had no fear that this person, if guilty, accused of his false name and falser character, would refuse to do what he demanded of him. Again, his principal object, more important by far than the discovery of the actual hired assassin, was to gain from the frightened accomplice a full, explicit confession of *who had tempted him to the crime*—who was really the most guilty murderer—whose money had paid for the deed which his own dastardly hand had shrunk from. Strong in resources which never yet had failed him, Mr. Burton was anxious for the singular encounter he had devised.

Leaving all traces of man behind them, the two climbed a rugged path, and entered a cañon, through the center of which roared a foaming torrent, and which was so deep and sheltered that even at this noon-hour the path was cool and the sunlight tempered. As they walked or clambered on, both men gradually grew silent. Of what Dr. Seltzer might be thinking Mr. Burton did not know—his own mind was absorbed in the scene which he was awaiting the earliest fitting moment to enact. The doctor, who should have acted as guide, had, somehow, chanced to lag behind.

"Which direction shall I take?" asked Mr. Burton, presently.

"Ascend the narrow defile to the right," called out his companion, pressing after him, "but be cautious of your footing. A misstep may hurl you upon the rocks below. In three minutes we shall be in a safe and beautiful region, with our feet, literally, treading a silver floor."

As he spoke thus, he drew nearer, but the path was too narrow to allow him to take the advance, and Mr. Burton continued to lead the way.

The subtle perceptions of the detective, a magnetism which amounted almost to the marvelous, I have so frequently referred to, that my reader will understand how it was that Mr. Burton, thus in the van, and not looking at all at his companion, felt a curious, prickly sensation run along his nerves. He came to the narrowest part of the dangerous path. An immense rock reached up, a mighty wall, upon the right, and to the left, far below the uneven, stony and brier-grown ledge along which he was picking his steps, foamed and roared the torrent, over rocks which thrust themselves here and there above the yeasty water. Directly in front arose an obstacle in the shape of a projection of the rock some three or four feet in hight, covered with tough little bushes, one of which he took hold of to draw himself up by.

However, instead of pulling himself up, as his action seemed to indicate that he was about to do, he turned and grasped the arm of Dr. Seltzer. His movement was rapid as lightning, but it was not made a moment too soon. The arm which he held in a clasp of steel was raised to strike, and a Spanish dirk was in the hand.

A stealthy, murderous light, almost red in its intensity, burned in the eyes which now sunk before his. An instant the foiled assassin stood surprised; then commenced a struggle between the two men. Dr. Seltzer made desperate efforts to hurl his antagonist into the torrent beneath; but, though frantic with rage and hate, his violent exertions did not effect their object. On the contrary, Mr. Burton, calm and self-possessed, despite an instant's astonishment, pressed his adversary backward along the narrow path until they were both on safe ground, in the middle of a little grassy plateau, which they had lately traversed, where he held him, having disarmed him of his knife.

What had caused his momentary astonishment was the fact that Dr. Seltzer knew him and suspected his object, which truth he instantly comprehended, upon turning and reading the murderous eyes that met his. Now, as he held him, he remarked,

"Another stab in the back, George Thorley?"

"Well, and what did you come here for, you accursed New York detective?"

"I came to persuade you to turn State's evidence."

"What about?"—there was a slight change in the voice, which told, against his will, that the adventurer felt relieved.

"I want you to give your written and sworn testimony as to who it was hired you, for the sum of two thousand dollars, to murder Mr. Moreland, at Blankville, on the 17th of October, 1857."

"Who said I murdered him? Humph! you must think I'm decidedly simple to be coaxed or frightened into committing myself."

"We'll not waste words, Thorley. I know you, all your history, all your bad deeds—or enough of them to hang you. I have a warrant for your arrest in my pocket, which I brought from the States with me. I could have brought an escort from Acapulco, and arrested you at once, without giving you any chance for explanation. But I have my own reasons for desiring to keep this matter quiet—one of which is that I do not wish any premature report to alarm your accomplice, man or woman, whichever it is, until I can put my hand on the right person."

"What makes you think that I did it?"

"No matter what makes me *think* so—I don't think, I *know*. I have the instrument with which you committed the act, with your initials on the handle. I have the letter you wrote to your accomplice, claiming your reward. In short, I've proof enough to convict you twice over. The only hope you have of any mercy from me is in at once doing all that I ask of you—which is to give a full written statement, over your real name, of all the circumstances which led to the murder."

"I'm not such a fool as to tie the rope around my own neck."

As he made this answer, he gave a powerful jerk to extricate himself from the unpleasant position in which he was held. Mr. Burton drew a revolver from his breast-pocket, remarking,

"I will not hold you, Thorley; but just as sure as you make an attempt to get away, I will shoot you. Supposing you succeeded in getting free from me—what good would that do you? Your prospects here would be ruined; for I should expose you to Don Miguel. You would have to flee from wife, country and fortune; all you would preserve would be your rascally life, which I do not propose, at present, to take."

"A man's life is his best possession."

"A truth you would have done well to remember before you took away the life of another. I can't talk to such a scoundrel as you, Thorley; I fairly ache to inflict upon you the punishment you deserve. It is for the sake of others, in whom I am interested, that I give you this one chance of mercy. Here is paper, pen and ink; sit down on that stone there, and write what I asked of you."

"What security do you offer me against the consequences of criminating myself? I want you to promise I shall be none the worse off for it."

"You are too fully in my power to demand promises of me. Yet this I will consent to, as I said before, for the sake of others—to let you go imprisoned by the warrant I hold against you, and never to put the officers of justice on your track. One thing, however, I must and shall do. I can not leave this Paradise, into which you have crept like the serpent, without warning Don Miguel what manner of creature he is trusting and sheltering."

"Oh, don't do that, Mr. Burton! He'll turn me off on the world again, and I shall be exposed to the same temptations as ever—and here I was leading a better life—I was indeed—reformed, quite reformed and repentant."

"So reformed and repentant, so very excellent, that you were only prevented, but now, from killing me and tumbling me into this convenient ravine, by my own prudence."

"Every thing was at stake, you know. I was desperate. You must forgive me. It would not be natural for me to submit to see all I had gained snatched away from me—my life periled. I recognized you within five minutes after sitting down to the supper-table last night."

"I had no idea you had ever seen me," said Mr. Burton, willing to hear how it was that this man knew him, when he had never met Thorley until yesterday.

"I was interested, once, in a forgery case in which you were employed to detect the criminals, by the examination of several handwritings which were given you. You accused a highly respectable fellow-citizen, to the astonishment of everybody, and convicted him, too. I, whom he had employed as an agent in some transactions, but who did not appear in any manner in the case, saw you in the court-room once or twice. I *accidentally* found out that you were a secret agent of the detective-police. When I saw you here, playing the scientific gentleman, my conscience was not so easy as to blind me. I saw the game, and what was at stake. I had the choice between my own safety or yours. I wasn't so self-denying as to decide in your favor, and so—"

"You visited my room last night."

"Yes. But, on second thought, I decided that to-day would give me the better opportunity. Had you waited a second longer, your friends would have had a hard time tracing your fate. An excuse to my father-in-law, that you had returned to Acapulco without stopping, by a nearer route, would have ended inquiry here." He set his teeth, as he concluded, unable to conceal how much he regretted that this convenient *dénouement* had been interrupted. "Was it chance caused you to turn?" he continued, after a moment's silence.

"It was watchfulness. I thought I saw murder in your eyes once before, to-day, when I met them suddenly; but as I believed myself unknown to you, I could hardly credit my own impression. It grew upon me, however, as we proceeded, and 'by the pricking of my ribs,'* I turned in time to prevent the compliment you were about to pay me. But this is wasting time. Write what I expect of you. I shall permit no lies. I can tell when I see one, or hear one. If you say any thing which is not true, I shall make you correct it."

Coerced by the eye which never ceased to watch his slightest movement, and by the revolver held in range of his breast, the reluctant doctor took the sheet of paper and the fountain-pen which were offered him, sat down on the stone, and, with the top of his sombrero for a desk, wrote slowly for ten or fifteen minutes. Then he arose and handed the document, which was signed with his real name, to the detective, who, with one eye on his prisoner, and one on the paper, continued to read the evidence without giving his companion a chance to profit by any relaxation of his vigilance.

"You have told the truth, for once in your life," was his

---

* A misquotation? "By the pricking of my thumbs" is the explanation for a witch's prophecy in Shakespeare's *Macbeth*, act 4, scene 1 (1606).

remark, as he finished reading the paper. "I had found this out myself, fact for fact, all but one or two facts which you give here; but I preferred having your testimony before I brought the matter before the proper parties, therefore I came here after it"—speaking as if a trip to Acapulco were one of the easiest and most commonplace of things.

"You're d——d cool about it," remarked the adventurer, eying his adversary with a glance of hate, with which was mingled a forced admiration of a "sharpness" which, had he himself possessed it, he could have used to such advantage. "And now, maybe you'll be good enough to tell me if the affair kicked up much of a row."

"I can not talk with you. I want you to lead the way back to our horses, for, since my business with you is finished, I may say that I do not fancy your company. You must go with me before Don Miguel, and we will enlighten him as to your true character, since with him to be 'forewarned may be forearmed.'"

"Oh, don't do that! I beg you to spare me for my wife's sake—it would kill her, she loves me so much!" and the creature dropped on his knees.

"I would, indeed, rather than blast her innocent heart with such knowledge, allow you still to play your part in that little family; but I know that, sooner or later, you will contrive to break the heart of that confiding woman, and it might be worse in the future than even now. She has yet no children; she is young, and the wound may heal. It is an unpleasant duty, which I must perform."

Then followed a scene of begging, prayers, even tears upon one side, and relentless purpose on the other.

CHAPTER VII.

NOW FOR HOME AGAIN.

Dr. Seltzer and his scientific friend returned down the mountain, reaching the flowery carriage-way which led up to the mansion about four P. M.; but here the former suddenly whirled his horse and set off toward Acapulco, at his utmost speed. Mr. Burton did not fire at him, to stop him; if he wished to run away from the horrible exposure which he had not the courage to face, it was no longer any business of the detective. This very flight would prove his guilt the more incontestably. It was with a pang of pity that he noticed the Donna, coming forth on the piazza with a face illumined with expectation of meeting her husband; he replied to her inquiry, that the doctor had gone down the road without saying how long he expected to be gone; and asking a private interview with Don Miguel, he at once, without circumlocution, laid before him the painful facts.

Of course the Don was shocked and grieved beyond expression, more on his daughter's account than on his own; and blamed himself severely for having introduced a stranger, without proper credentials, into his confidence. If the murder had been committed from jealousy, anger, or upon any impulse of passion, he would not have thought so badly of the young man;

but that it should have been done for *money* was to him an irreparable crime and disgrace.

Mr. Burton had thought of returning to Acapulco that afternoon and evening, considering that his presence could not be welcome to the family under such circumstances; but Don Miguel positively forbade him to attempt the journey at that late hour, as it might be dangerous at any time, and now, if the doctor wished to revenge himself upon his betrayer, a better opportunity could not occur than on this lonely road, where he might linger in the expectation of his passing. From the interview which followed between the father and his child, Mr. Burton was absent; he saw no more of the beautiful young wife, for he left the *hacienda* early the following morning; but her father informed him that she bore the news better than he expected—simply because she refused to believe in the guilt of her husband!

Don Miguel and two of his servants accompanied Mr. Burton all the way back to town; the Don affirming that he had some business requiring a visit to the city sooner or later; though his guest knew very well that his real object was to protect him from any danger which might threaten. For this he was grateful, though his courage did not shrink, even from the idea of secret assassination.

He was detained in Acapulco several days before he had an opportunity of leaving for the isthmus. During that time he learned, by a messenger whom Don Miguel sent him, that, during the Don's absence from the house in the two days of his journey to town and back, Dr. Seltzer had returned there, possessed himself of every article of value which he could carry away upon his person, including the Donna's jewels, which she had inherited from her mother, and a large sum in gold, and had persuaded his wife to accompany his flying fortunes to some unknown region. In the letter which Don Miguel wrote to the stranger, he expressed himself as one robbed and left desolate. It was not the loss of money or jewels, but the loss of his poor, confiding, loving child, that he dwelt upon. The Donna's was one of those impulsive, impassioned natures which must love, even if it knows the object unworthy. No deed which her husband could commit could make him otherwise to her than the man with whose fate her own was linked for "better or worse." Mr. Burton folded up the letter with a sigh; no power of his could amend the fate of this young creature, which promised to be so sad.

While he remained in the ruinous old place he used extraordinary precautions to insure his own safety; for he believed that Dr. Seltzer, or George Thorley, would seek revenge upon him, not only for the sake of the revenge, but to silence the accusation which he might carry back to the States. It was well that he was thus careful, as, among other proofs that he was thus pursued, was the following. One afternoon, as he sat in the great, breezy corridor of the hotel, an old woman came in with a basket and offered to sell him some particularly fine oranges. He bought a couple of the largest, and was about to eat one, when he observed that she did *not* offer the fruit to any other customer; upon this, he regarded her more closely, and was satisfied that all was not right. When she had lingered a time to notice if he ate the fruit, he strolled out to the street, and in her presence called up a stray pig, to which he fed pieces of the orange. When she saw this, the old hag, who was an Indian, quickly disappeared, and shortly after the pig died.

It was, therefore, with feelings of satisfaction that the detective finally bade farewell to Acapulco on a return steamer. He had waited some time at the isthmus, where the days had hung heavily, but he had comforted himself with his motto about patience; and now, as he assured me at the close of his narrative,

"If heaven would give us a propitious passage home we should be *in time*—all would be right."

Day was breaking when Mr. Burton finished his narrative; the rain had ceased, but a thick fog hung over the sea and land, making every thing gloomy and disagreeable.

"I must go now, and awaken my little girl," he said, rising.

"But you have not read me the written confession of that Thorley."

"Richard, you must forgive me if I do not see fit to allow you to read it at present. I have a purpose in it, or I should not keep back from you any of my own information. That confession did not surprise me; I knew the murderer long ago, but I could not prove it. You shall soon be at rest about this affair. I only pray, now, for a speedy voyage, and that Leesy Sullivan may be alive when we reach New York. Richard!" he added, with a passionate gesture, "you do not dream what a constant fever I am in—I am so afraid we shall be *too late*. I can not bear the horror which that would be to me."

And indeed it did seem, at that time, as if my own engrossing interest was scarcely equal to that of my companion, who yet had nothing at all at stake, while I had so much. Not only then, but at various other times during the remainder of our voyage, he expressed so much anxiety lest Miss Sullivan should be dead before we arrived home, that I, who was always torturing myself with conjectures, again revived my suspicions that she was connected with the murder.

In the mean time, the sun arose upon the bustle of disembarking from the steamer to the cars. Fortunately, the fog lifted by eight o'clock, and we could enjoy the magnificent scenery through which the cars whirled us—scenery so at variance, in its wildness and the exuberance of its foliage, and the secluded aspect of its beauty, with this noisy wonder of civilization which scattered its fiery deluge of sparks along the path of gorgeous tropical flowers waving at us, sometimes, in long streamers of bloom from the topmost branches of gigantic trees.

Nothing occurred to mar the tranquillity of the passage home. On the expected day, we landed at the dock in New York, and I stepped upon the earth with a curious, excited feeling, now that we drew so near to the close of our efforts, which made me almost lightheaded. We took a carriage and drove to Mr. Burton's; he was expected by the housekeeper, so that we found the house prepared for our reception. A fine dinner was served at the usual hour—but I could not eat. Appetite and sleep fled before my absorbing anticipations. My host, who noticed my intense, repressed excitement, promised me, before I retired for the night, that tomorrow, God willing, the secret places of the wicked should be laid bare—that myself and all those interested should witness the triumph of the innocent and the confusion of the guilty.

CHAPTER VIII.
THE RIPE HOUR.

I arose from my sleepless bed to face this, the most memorable day of my life. Whether I ate or drank, I know not; but I noticed that Mr. Burton's countenance wore a peculiar, illuminated look, as if his soul was inwardly rejoicing over a victory gained. However, there was still preoccupation in it, and some perplexity. Immediately after breakfast, he proposed to go out, saying,

"Richard, remain here a couple of hours with Lenore, until I find out whether Miss Sullivan is dead or alive. I should not have gone to bed last night without knowing, had I not been troubled with a severe headache. This is now the first step in the day's duties. As soon as possible I will report progress;" and he went out.

The time of his absence seemed very long. Lenore, sweet child, with much of her father's perception, saw that I was restless and impatient, and made many pretty efforts to entertain me. She sung me some of the finest music, while I roamed about the parlors like an ill-bred tiger. At the end of two hours my friend returned, looking less perplexed than when he went out.

"God is good!" he said, shaking my hand, as if thus congratulating me. "Leesy Sullivan is alive, but very feeble. She is scarcely able to undertake a journey; but, since I have explained the object, she has consented to go. She says she is so near death's door, that it matters not how soon she passes through; and she is willing, for the sake of others, to endure a trial from which she might naturally shrink. So far, then, all is well."

Was this trial, of which he spoke, that pang which she must feel in confessing herself implicated in this matter? Did he think, and had he persuaded her, since she was too far gone for the grasp of the law to take hold of her, she might now confess a dangerous and dark secret?

I could not answer the questions my mind persisted in asking. "It will be but a few hours," I whispered to myself.

"We are to go up to Blankville by the evening train," he continued. "Leesy will accompany us. Until that time, there is nothing to do."

I would rather have worked at breaking stones or lifting barrels than to have kept idle; but, as the detective wished me to remain in the house as a matter of caution against meeting any prying acquaintance upon the streets, I was forced to that dreariest of all things—to wait. The hours did finally pass, and Mr. Burton set out first with a carriage, to convey Miss Sullivan to the depot, where I was to meet him in time for the five o'clock train. When I saw her there, I wondered how she had strength to endure the ride, she looked so wasted—such a mere flickering spark of life, which a breath might extinguish. Mr. Burton had almost to carry her into the car, where he placed her on a seat, with his overcoat for a pillow. We took our seats opposite to her, and as those large, unfathomable eyes met mine, still blazing with their old luster, beneath the pallid brow, I can not describe the sensations which rushed over me. All those strange scenes through which I had passed at Moreland villa floated up and shut me in a strange spell, until I forgot what place we were in, or that any other persons surrounded us. When the cars moved rapidly out of the city, increasing their speed as they got beyond the precincts, Leesy asked to have the window open.

The air was cold and fresh; her feverish lips swallowed it as a reviving draught. I gazed alternately at her and the landscape, already flashed with the red of early sunset. It was a December day, chill but bright; the ground was frozen, and the river sparkled with the keen blueness of splintered steel. The red banner of twilight hung over the Palisades. I lived really three years in that short ride—the three years just past—and when we reached our destination, I walked like one in a dream. It was quite evening when we got out at Blankville, though the moon was shining. A fussy little woman passed out before us, lugging a large bandbox; she handed it to the town express, telling the driver to be very careful of it, and take it round at once to Esquire Argyll's.

"I suppose it contains the wedding-bonnet," he said, with a laugh.

"That it does, and the dress, too, all of my own selection," said the little woman, with an air of importance. "Just you carry it in your hand, sir, and don't you allow nothing to come near it."

When I heard these words, a hot flush came to my face. That Mary Argyll was already married, or expected to be very soon, I knew; but I could not hear this reference to the wedding, nor see this article of preparation, without keen pain. Yet what business was it of mine?

Mr. Burton had also heard the brief colloquy, and I noticed his lips pressed together with a fierce expression as we passed under the lamp which lighted the crossing. He took us into the hotel by the depot. Oh, how suffocating, how close, became memory! Into this building poor Henry had been carried on that wretched morning. It seemed to be but yesterday. I think

Leesy was recalling it all, for when a cup of tea was brought in for her, at Mr. Burton's bidding, she turned from it with loathing.

"Leesy," he said, looking at her firmly, and speaking in a tone of high command, "I don't want you to fail me now. The trial will soon be over. Brace yourself for it with all the strength you have. Now, I am going out a few moments—perhaps for half an hour. When I return, you will both be ready to go with me to Mr. Argyll's house."

I was nearly as much shaken by this prospect as the frail woman who sat trembling in a corner of the sofa. To go into that house from which I had departed with such ignominy—to see Eleanor face to face—to meet them all who had once been my friends—to greet them as strangers, for such they were—they must be, to me!—to appear in their midst under such strange circumstances—to hear, I knew not what—to learn that mystery—my heart grew as if walled in with ice; it could not half beat, and felt cold in my breast.

Both Leesy and myself started when Mr. Burton again appeared in the room.

"All is right thus far," he said, in a clear, cheery voice, which, nevertheless, had the high ring of excitement. "Come, now, let us not waste the golden moments, for now the hour is ripe."

We had each of us to give an arm to Miss Sullivan, who could scarcely put one foot before the other. We walked slowly along over *that* path which I never had trodden since the night of the murder without a shudder. A low moan came from Leesy's lips, as we passed the spot where the body of Henry Moreland had been discovered. Presently we came to the gate of the Argyll place, and here Mr. Burton again left us. "Follow me," he said, "in five minutes. Come to the library-door, and knock; and, Richard, I particularly desire you to take a seat by the bay-window."

He went up the walk and entered the house, without seeming

to ring the hall door-bell, leaving the door open as he passed in. I looked at my watch by the moonlight, forcing myself to count the minutes, by way of steadying my head, which was all in a whirl. When the time expired, I helped Leesy forward into the dim hall, on to the library-door, where I knocked, according to directions, and was admitted by Mr. Argyll himself.

There was a bright light shining from the chandelier, fully illuminating the room. In the midst of a flood of recollections, I stepped within; but my brain, which had been hot and dizzy before, grew suddenly calm and cool. When Mr. Argyll saw that it was me, he slightly recoiled, and gave me no greeting what-ever. A glance assured me that every member of the family was present. Eleanor sat in an arm-chair near the center-table; Mary and James occupied the same sofa. Eleanor looked at me with a kind of white amazement; James nodded as my eye met his, his face expressing surprise and displeasure. Mary rose, hesitated, and finally came forward, saying,

"How do you do, Richard?"

I bowed to her, but did not take her outstretched hand, and she returned to her place near James. In the mean time, Mr. Burton himself placed Leesy Sullivan in an easy-chair. I walked forward and took a seat near the window. I had time to observe the appearance of my whilom* friends, and was calm enough to do it. Mr. Argyll had grown old much faster than the time warranted; his form was somewhat bent, and his whole appear-ance feeble; I grieved, as I noticed this, as though he was my own father, for I once had loved him as much. Mary looked the same as when I had seen her, three months since, in that sur-reptitious visit to the oak, blooming and beautiful, the image of what Eleanor once was. Eleanor, doubtless, was whiter than

---

* Former.

her wont, for my appearance had startled her; but there was the same rapt, far-away, spiritual look upon her features which they had worn since that day when she had wedded herself to the spirit of her lover.

Mr. Burton turned the key in the lock of the door which opened into the hall; then crossed over and closed the parlor-door, and sat down by it, saying as he did so,

"Mr. Argyll, I told you a few moments ago, that I had news of importance to communicate, and I take the liberty of closing these doors, for it would be very unpleasant for us to be intruded upon, or for any of the servants to hear any thing of what I have to say. You will perhaps guess the nature of my communication, from my having brought with me these two persons. I would not agitate any of you by the introduction of the painful subject, if I did not believe that you would rather know the truth, even if it is sad to revive the past. But I must beg of you to be calm, and to listen quietly to what I have to say."

"I will be very calm; do not be afraid," murmured Eleanor, growing yet feebler, for it was to her he now particularly addressed the injunction.

I was so occupied with her that I did not notice the effect upon the others.

"Mr. Argyll," continued the detective, "I have never yet abandoned a case of this kind until I have unraveled its mystery to the last thread. Nearly two years have passed since you supposed that I ceased to exert myself to discover the murderer of Henry Moreland. But I have never, for a day, allowed the case to lie idle in my mind. Whenever I have had leisure, I have partially followed every clue which was put in my hands at the time when we first had the matter under discussion. It was not alone the sad circumstances of the tragedy which gave it unusual interest to me. I became warmly attached to your family, and as, from the first—yes, from the very first hour when I heard of the murder—I believed I had discovered the perpetrator, I could not allow the matter to sink into silence. You remember, of course, our last interview. Some ideas were there presented which I then opposed. You know how the discussion of all the facts then known ended. Your suspicions fell upon one who had been an honored and favored member of your family—you *feared*, although you were not certain, that Richard Redfield committed the deed. You gave me all the reasons you had for your opinions—good reasons, too, some of them were; but I then combated the idea. However, I was more or less affected by what you said, and I told you, before parting, that, if you had such feelings toward the young man, you ought not to allow him to be, any longer, a member of your family. I believe he came to understand the light in which you regarded him, and shortly after left the place, and since has been most of the time, in Washington, employed there as a clerk in the dead-letter office. I believe *now*, Mr. Argyll, that you were not far wrong in your conjectures. *I have discovered the murderer of Henry Moreland, and can give you positive proof of it!*"

This assertion, deliberately uttered, caused the sensation which might be expected. Eleanor, with all her long habit of self-control, gave a slight shriek, and began to tremble like a leaf. Exclamations came from the lips of all—I believe James uttered an oath, but I am not certain; for I, perhaps more than any other in the room, was at that moment confounded. As the idea rushed over me that Mr. Burton had been acting a part toward *me*, and had taken these precautions to get me utterly in his power, where I could not defend myself, I started to my feet.

"Sit still, Mr. Redfield," said the detective to me, sternly. "There is no avenue of escape for the guilty," and rising, he took the key of the door and put it in his pocket, giving me a look difficult to understand.

I did sit down again, not so much because he told me, as that I was powerless from amazement; as I did so, I met the eyes of James, which laughed silently with a triumph so hateful that, at the moment, they seemed to me the eyes of a devil. All the feelings which, at various times, had been called up by this terrible affair, were nothing to those which overwhelmed me during the few moments which followed. My thought tracked many avenues with lightning rapidity; but I could find no light at the end of any of them. I began to believe that George Thorley, in his confession, had criminated *me*—who knew him not—who never had spoken with him—and that *this* was the reason why Mr. Burton had withheld that document from me—falsely professing friendship, while leading me into the pit! If so, what secret enemy had I who could instruct him to lay the murder at my door? If he *had* accused me, I was well aware that many little circumstances might be turned so as to strengthen the accusation.

I sat there dumb. But there is always strength in innocence— even when betrayed by its friends! So I remained quiet and listened.

"When a crime like this is committed," proceeded the detective, quite calm in the midst of our excitement, "we usually look for the *motive*. Next to avarice come the passions of revenge and jealousy in frequency. We know that money had nothing to do with Henry Moreland's death—revenge and jealousy had. There lived in Blankville three or four years ago, a young fellow, a druggist, by the name of George Thorley; you remember him, Mr. Argyll?"

Mr. Argyll nodded his head.

"He was an adventurer, self-instructed in medicine, without

principle. Shortly after setting up in your village, he fell in love with this woman here—Miss Sullivan. She rejected him; both because she had a dim perception of his true character, and because she was interested in another. She allows me to say, here, what she once before confessed to us, that she loved Henry Moreland—loved him purely and unselfishly, with no wish but for his happiness, and no hope of ever being any thing more to him than his mother's sewing-girl, to whom he extended some acts of kindness. But George Thorley, with the sharpness of jealousy, discovered her passion, which she supposed was hidden from mortal eyes, and conceived the brutal hate of a low nature against the young gentleman, who was ignorant alike of him and his sentiments. So far, no harm was done, and evil might never have come of it, for Henry Moreland moved in a sphere different from his, and they might never have come in contact. But another bosom was also possessed of the fiend of jealousy. An inmate of your family had learned to love your daughter Eleanor—not only to love her, but to look forward to the fortune and position which would be conferred by a marriage with her as something extremely desirable. He would not reconcile himself to the engagement which was formed between Miss Argyll and Mr. Moreland. He cherished bad thoughts, which grew more bitter as their happiness became more apparent. Once, he was standing at the gate of this lawn, when the young couple passed him, going out for a walk together, he looked after them with a dark look, speaking aloud, unconsciously, the thought of his heart; he said, '*I hate him! I wish he were dead!*' Instantly, to his surprise and dismay, a voice replied, '*I'm with you there—you don't wish it so much as I do!*' The speaker was Thorley, who, passing, had been arrested by the young couple going out of the gate, and who had remained, also, gazing after them. It was an unfortunate coincidence. The first speaker looked at the second with anger and chagrin; but he had betrayed himself, and the other knew it. He laughed impudently, as he sauntered on; but, presently, he returned and whispered, 'I wouldn't object to putting him out of the way, if I was well paid for it.' 'What do you mean?' inquired the other, angrily, and the response was, 'Just what I say. I hate him as bad as you do; you've got money, *or can get it*, and I can't. Pay me well for the job, and I'll put him out of your way so securely that he won't interfere with your plans any more.' The young gentleman affected to be, and perhaps was, indignant. The fellow went off, smirking; but his words left, as he thought they would, their poison behind. In less than a month from that time, the person had sought Thorley out, in his lurking-place in the city—for he had, you recollect, been driven from Blankville by the voice of public opinion—and had conferred with him upon the possibility of young Moreland being put out of the way, without risk of discovery of those who had a hand in it. Thorley agreed to manage every thing without risk to any one. He wanted three thousand dollars, but his accomplice, who was aware that you were about to draw two thousand from a bank in New York, promised him that sum, with which he agreed to be satisfied. It was expected and planned that the murder should be committed in the city; but, as the time drew nigh for accomplishing it, opportunity did not present. Finally, as the steamer upon which Thorley wished to flee to California was about to sail, and no better thing offered, he concluded to follow Mr. Moreland out in the evening train, and stab him, under cover of the rain and darkness, somewhere between the depot and the house. This he did; then, afraid to take the cars, for fear of being suspected, he went down along the docks, took possession of a small-boat which lay moored by a chain, broke the chain, and rowed down the river, completely protected by the storm from human observation. The next morning found him in New York, dress, complexion and hair changed, with nothing about him to excite the least suspicion that he was connected with the tragedy that was just becoming known. However, he wrote a letter, directed to John Owen, Peekskill, in which he stated in obscure terms, that the instrument with which the murder was committed would be found secreted in a certain oak tree on these premises, and that it had better be taken care of. I have the letter and the broken instrument. The way it came to be concealed in the tree was this: After the murder, being so well sheltered by the storm, he was bold enough to approach the house, in hopes of communicating with his accomplice, and receiving the money directly from his hands, which would prevent the latter from the necessity of making a trip to Brooklyn to pay it. He saw nothing of him, however; perceiving that he could look into the parlor through the open upper half of the shutter by climbing the large oak at the corner, he did so; and was looking at you all for some minutes on that evening. Perceiving by the light which shone from the window that the instrument was broken at the point, he at once comprehended how important it was to get rid of it, and chancing to discover a hollow spot in the limb he stood on, he worked it well into the rotten heart of the wood. He it was whom Miss Sullivan detected descending from the tree, on that awful night when she, alas! led by a hopeless, though a pure love, passing the house on her way to her aunt's, could not deny herself a stolen look at the happiness of the two beings so soon, she thought, to be made one. She never expected to see them again until after their marriage, and a wild, foolish impulse, if I must call it so, urged her into the garden, to look through the open bay-window—a folly which came near having serious consequences for her. Well, George Thorley escaped, and fulfilled the programme so far as to sail for San Francisco; but the boat stopping at Acapulco, he received an offer there, from a Spanish gentleman, of the position of doctor on his immense estates. It was just the country for a character like that of Thorley to prosper in; he accepted the proposition, wormed himself into the esteem of the Spaniard, married his daughter, and was flourishing to his heart's content, when I came suddenly upon him and disturbed his serenity. Yes! Mr. Argyll, I started for California after the villain, for I had traces of him which led me to take the journey, and it was by a Providential accident that I ascertained he was near Acapulco, where I, also, landed, sought him out, and wrung a confession from him, which I have here in writing. He has told the story plainly, and I have every other evidence to confirm it which a court of law could possibly require. I could hang his accomplice, without doubt."

At the first mention of the name of George Thorley I chanced to be looking at James, over whose countenance passed an indescribable change; he moved uneasily, looked at the closed doors, and again riveted his gaze on Mr. Burton, who did not look at him at all during the narrative, but kept steadily on, to the end, in a firm, clear tone, low, so as not to be overheard outside, but assured and distinct. Having once observed James, I could no longer see any one else. I seemed to see the story reflected in his countenance, instead of hearing it. Flushes of heat passed over it, succeeded by an ashy paleness, which deepened into a sickly blue hue, curious to behold; dark passions swept like shadows over it; and gradually, as the speaker neared the climax of his story, I felt like one who gazes into an open window of the bottomless pit.

"Have I told you *who* it was that hired George Thorley to murder Henry Moreland?" asked Mr. Burton, in the pause which followed.

It had been taken for granted who the person was, and as he asked the question the eyes of all turned to me—of all except

James, who suddenly sprung with a bound against the door opening into the parlor, which was not locked. But another was too quick for him; the powerful hand of the detective was on his shoulder, and as he turned the attempted fugitive full to the light, he said, in words which fell like fire,

"It was your nephew—James Argyll."

For a moment you might have heard a leaf drop on the carpet; no one spoke or stirred. Then Eleanor arose from her chair, and, lifting up her hand, looked with awful eyes at the cowering murderer. Her look blasted him. He had been writhing under Mr. Burton's grasp; but now, as if in answer to her gaze, he said,

"Yes—I did it, Eleanor," and dropped to the floor in a swoon.

CHAPTER IX.

JOINING THE MISSING LINKS.

The scene which transpired in the next few minutes was harrowing. The revulsion of feeling, the shock, the surprise and the horror were almost too much for human nature to bear. Groan after groan burst from Mr. Argyll, as if his breast were being rent in twain. Mary tottered to her sister and threw herself at her feet, with her head buried in her lap; if she had not been so healthily organized, and of such an even temperament, I know not how she would have survived this frightful check to her hopes and affections. It seemed as if Eleanor, who had lived only to suffer for so many weary months, had now more self-possession than any of the others; her thin, white hand fell softly on her sister's curls with a pitying touch; and after a time, she whispered to her some words. My own surprise was nearly as much as any one's; for, although many times I had *felt* that James was the guilty one, I had always tried to drive away the impression, and had finally almost succeeded.

In the mean time no one went to the unhappy man, who found a temporary relief from shame and despair in insensibility. All recoiled from him, as he lay upon the floor. Finally, Mr. Burton forced himself to raise him; consciousness was returning, and he placed him on the sofa, and gave him a handkerchief wet with cologne.

Presently Mary arose from her kneeling position, and looked around the room until her glance fell on me, when she came toward me, and grasped both my hands, saying,

"I never accused you."

"Richard, *I* never accused you—I always felt that you were innocent, and always said so. You must forgive the others for my sake. My father and sister will bear me witness that I always defended you from the accusations of one who, it is now proved, sought with double, with inconceivable baseness, to divert suspicion from himself to another"—her voice trembled with scorn. "I never wanted to marry him," she added, bursting into tears, "but they overpersuaded me."

"Quiet yourself, sister," said Eleanor, gently, arising and approaching us. "We have all wronged you, Richard—I fear beyond forgiveness. Alas! we can now see what a noble enemy you have been!"

In that moment I felt repaid for all I had suffered, and I said with joy,

"Never an enemy, Miss Argyll; and I forgive you, wholly."

Then there was another stir; James had risen to slip away from the company, now so distasteful to him; but Mr. Burton again stood between him and egress; as he did so, he said,

"Mr. Argyll, it is for you to decide the fate of this miserable man. I have kept all my proceedings a secret from the public; I even allowed George Thorley to remain in Mexico, for I thought your family had already suffered enough, without loading it down with the infamy of your nephew. If you say that he shall go unpunished by the law, I shall abide by your wish; this matter shall be kept by the few who now know it. For *your* sakes, not for his, I would spare him the death which he deserves; but he must leave the country at once and for ever."

"Let him go" said the uncle, his back turned upon the murderer, toward whom he would not look. "Go, instantly and for ever. And remember, James Argyll, if I ever see your face again, if I ever hear of your being anywhere in the United States, I shall at once cause you to be arrested."

"And I, the same," added Mr. Burton. "God knows, if it were not for these young ladies, whose feelings are sacred to me, I would not let you off so easily."

He opened the door, and James Argyll slunk out into the night, and away, none knew whither, branded, expatriated, and alone—away, without one look at the fair, beautiful girl who was so soon to have been his bride—away, from the home he had periled his soul to secure.

When he had gone, we all breathed more freely. Mr. Burton had yet much to say, for he wished to close this horrible business for ever. He took the surgical instrument which we had found in the tree, and fitted it to the piece which had been extracted from the body of the murdered man, and showed the family the initials of George Thorley upon it. He then produced the written confession of Thorley, which we all read for ourselves; but as it contained only, in a plain statement, the facts already given, I will not repeat them here. He then proceeded with the history of the DEAD LETTER, which, also, he had with him, and which proved to be in the same handwriting as the confession. In speaking of the curious manner in which this document had been lost, to be recovered in the right time by the right person, he seemed to consider it almost awfully providential.

From this he went on with a minute history of all the steps taken by both of us, our journey over the ocean, the wonderful success which waited upon patience, perseverance and energy, securing the final triumph of justice; and, to conclude with, he said,

"I owe, still, a good many explanations both to you, Mr. Argyll, and to Mr. Redfield. I can not lay before you the thousand subtle threads by which I trace the course of a pursuit like this, and which makes me successful as a detective; but I can account for some things which at times have puzzled both of you. In the first place there is about me a power not possessed by all—call it instinct, magnetism, clairvoyancy, or remarkable nervous and mental perception. Whatever it is, it enables me, often, to *feel* the presence of criminals, as well as of very good persons, poets, artists, or marked temperaments of any kind. The day on which this case was placed before me, it was brought by two young men, your nephew and this person now present. I had not been ten minutes with them when I began to perceive that *the murderer was in the room with me*; and before they had left me, I had decided which was the guilty man. But it would have been unpardonable rashness to denounce him without proof; by such a course I would throw him on the defensive, defeat the ends of justice, and overwhelm myself with denunciation. I waited and watched—I put him under surveillance. That night upon which he crossed the Brooklyn ferry to pay the money to the hired assassin, I was upon his track; I heard the angry dismay with which he accused Richard of following him, when the other met him upon this side. It was not very long after I began to investigate the case before he cautiously approached me, as he did you, with hints of the might-be-guilty party; he made me see how much to the interest of his friend Richard it would be if rivals were out of the way, and how desperately that person loved Miss Argyll. (Forgive me, friends, for using plain language—the whole truth must be told.) But I need not dwell on his method, for you must be familiar with it. I confess that he used consummate tact; if I had not read him from the first, I, too, might have been misled. He was not over-eager in the search for suspected persons, as the guilty almost always are. He did *not* suspect Miss Sullivan, as Richard did. I favored the pursuit of Miss Sullivan for two reasons; the first was to conceal my real suspicions; the next was, after finding her handkerchief in the garden, after the flight, and all those really strong grounds for supposing her connected with the murder, I began to think that she *was* connected with it, through some interest in James Argyll. I did not know but that she might have been attached to him—that the child she cared for might be his—you see I was totally in the dark as to all the details. I only took it for granted that James was guilty, and had to gather my proofs afterward. It was not until after my interview with Leesy, at Moreland villa, that I became convinced she had nothing to do with the murder, and that all her strange proceedings were the result of the grief she felt at the tragic death of one whom she secretly loved. When I had an interview with you on that same afternoon, I saw that James had poisoned your mind with suspicions of Mr. Redfield; for the same reason which had kept me silent so long—that is, that I should eventually undeceive you—I did not defend him, as I otherwise should. Apparently, I allowed the case to drop. It was only that I might follow it undisturbed. I had already fixed upon California as the retreat of the accomplice, and was about to start off in search of him when Richard appeared upon the scene with the dead-letter in his hand.

"From that hour I felt sure of perfect success. My only anxiety was that the marriage should not be consummated which would seal my mouth; for, if Mary had been married on my return, I should have considered it too late to reveal the truth. This made me very uneasy—not only for her sake, but because then I could not clear Mr. Redfield's character to those friends who had cruelly wronged him. I kept my suspicions from him, although he was the partner of my investigations, for I was afraid that his impetuosity might cause him to do something indiscreet, and I did not want the guilty one alarmed until the net was spread for his feet. To-night, when I came here, I still further carried on my plan of allowing you to remain undecided until the last moment, for I counted on the sudden, overwhelming accusation having the effect to make the murderer confess—which it did. I wished Miss Sullivan to be present, not only to corroborate any points of my testimony in which she might be concerned, but that reparation might also be done her, for we have troubled and frightened her a great deal, poor thing, when her only fault has been too keen a perception of the nobility of that departed martyr, whose memory his friends cherish so sacredly. She has but a brief space to dwell on earth, and I thought it would comfort her to know that no one blames her for the pure devotion which has lighted her soul and consumed it like oil which burns away in perfume."

Mr. Burton never meant to be poetical, but his perceptions were of that refined kind that he could not withhold from poor Leesy this little tribute to her noble folly. His words touched Eleanor; she was too high-minded to despise the fruitless offering of another and a humbler woman at the shrine before which *she* was privileged to minister; I believe in that hour she felt a sister's interest in poor, lowly, but love-exalted Leesy Sullivan. She crossed over, took the wasted hand in her own, and pressed it tenderly. We all now perceived how much this dreadful evening had fatigued the invalid.

"She must go to bed at once," said Eleanor; "I will call Norah, and have her placed in the room which opens out of ours, Mary."

The young ladies retired to give their gentle attention to the sick girl; and both, before they went out, pressed my hand as they said good-night.

We three men remained long, talking over each particular of our strange story, for we could not feel like sleeping. And before we parted for the night, Mr. Argyll had humbled himself to confess that he was led to condemn me without sufficient cause.

"I loved you as a son, Richard," he said, in a broken voice, "better than I ever loved James, for I was aware that he had many faults of heart and head. And when I was induced to believe you the author of the crime which had broken all our hearts, I was still further downcast. My health has failed, as you see; and I was urgent upon Mary to marry her cousin, for I felt as if she would soon be left friendless, and I wanted the girls to have a protector. I might better have left them to the care of a viper," he added, with a shudder. "Poor Mary, dear girl! she was right all the time. She never did love that man—though, of course, she had no idea of the truth. Thank God, it is no worse!"

I knew he was thinking of the marriage, and I, too, murmured, "Thank God."

"Mr. Argyll," said Mr. Burton, laying his hand on that of the other, "this terrible affair is now brought to a close, as far as it can be. Let me advise you to brood over it as little as possible. Your health is already affected. I acknowledge it is enough to shake one's reason; but, for that, I would bid you to drop it all from your mind—to banish the thought of it—never to refer to it again. You can yet be tolerably happy. A fair future lies before all of you, except dear Miss Eleanor. Adopt Richard as your son, make him your partner, as you first intended. I will give you my warrant for what it is worth, that he will relieve you both of business and household cares—and that you will feel, during your declining years, as if you, indeed, had a son to comfort you."

"But I do not believe that Richard would take such a place, after what has passed," said Mr. Argyll, doubtfully.

I hesitated; for a moment pride rebelled; but since all is forgiven, ought it not to be forgotten? When I spoke it was with heartiness.

"If you need a partner in your office, and wish me to take the place, I will do so."

"Then the compact is signed," said Mr. Burton, almost gayly. "And now I will try to find a bed at the hotel."

"Of course you will not," said our host; "this house is yours as much as mine, Mr. Burton, always. How much I thank you for all the time, money and thought you have lavished in our behalf, I will not try to say to-night. Our gratitude is unspoken because it is boundless."

"Don't thank me for following out the instincts of my nature," said the detective, affecting carelessness; and with that we shook Mr. Argyll's hand, and retired to the rooms assigned us.

In the morning Miss Sullivan was found to be much worse; the journey and the excitement had made her very ill, so that it was impossible for her to return to the city with Mr. Burton. A physician was sent for who said that she could not live over two or three days. She heard the sentence with apparent joy; only she begged Mr. Burton to send little Norah up to her, on the evening train, that she might see the child before she died. This he promised to do, and to have always an interest in her welfare. She was much affected when he bade her farewell, for he had gained her love and confidence by his manner of treating her.

The child came, and was tenderly received by the sisters. They were unwearied in their attentions to the sufferer, whose last hours were soothed by their earnest words of hope and comfort. Leesy died with a smile on her face, going out of this world, which had been so cold to one of her impassioned nature, with joy. When I looked at the wasted corpse, I could hardly realize that the fire was out for ever which had so long burned in those wonderful eyes—it was not quenched, it had only been removed to a purer atmosphere. She was buried, very quietly, but reverently, on a beautiful winter day. Her little charge was much petted by the young ladies; and as a lady who chanced to see her, learning that she was an orphan, took a fancy to adopt her, they, with Mr. Burton's consent, resigned her to a new mother. I have seen little Norah lately; she is a pretty child, and well cared for.

CHAPTER X.
THE NEW LIFE.

The winter passed away quietly. The sudden absence of James Argyll caused much harmless gossip in the village. It was reported, and generally believed, that he had gone abroad, on a tour to Egypt, because Miss Argyll had jilted him. Fortunately, the arrangements for the wedding were known to but few, the feelings of the family having inclined toward a very quiet affair. The little woman who had prepared the wedding-dress was a New York milliner, who probably never learned that the wedding was not consummated.

I was very busy in the office. Mr. Argyll's health was poor, and business had accumulated which took the most of my time. He wished me to board in his house, but I declined doing so; though, as in the old, happy times, I spent nearly all my evenings there.

Beyond the first shock, Mary did not seem to suffer from the abrupt termination of an engagement into which she had entered reluctantly. I even believed that she felt very much relieved at not being compelled to marry a cousin for the sake of securing a protector. Her gay laugh soon resumed its sweetness; her bright loveliness bloomed in the midst of winter, making

roses and sunshine in the old mansion. Eleanor seemed to love
to see her sister happy, gently encouraging her efforts to drive
away the shadow which lingered about the house. Her own sad
life must not be permitted to blight the joy of any other. I have
said that my feelings toward her had changed from passionate
love, through intense sympathy, into affectionate reverence.
I think, now, that I felt toward her a good deal as Mary did—
that nothing we could do for her, to show our silent love and
sympathy, could be too much—a tender regard for her wishes
and habits—a deep respect for the manner in which she bore
her loss. We did not expect that she would ever again be gay or
hopeful; so we did not annoy her with trying to make her so.

In the mean time a great change was taking place in my
own nature, of which I was but faintly aware. I only knew that
I enjoyed my hard work—that I felt resolute and strong, and
that my evenings were pleasant and homelike. Further, I did not
question. I wrote to my mother a guarded account of what had
occurred; but I was obliged to pay her a flying visit to explain all
the facts, for I dared not trust them on paper. Thus the winter
glided away into sunshine and spring again.

It was the first day which had really seemed like spring. It
was warm and showery; there was a smell of violets and new
grass on the air. I had my office-window open, but as the afternoon wore away, and the sun shone out after an April sprinkle,
I could not abide the dullness of that court of law. I felt those
"blind motions of the spring," which Tennyson attributes to
trees and plants.* And verily, I was in sympathy with nature. I
felt *verdant*—and if the reader thinks that to my discredit, he
is at liberty to cherish his opinion. I felt young and happy—
years seemed to have dropped away from me, like a mantle of

---

* Another phrase from Tennyson's "The Talking Oak" (see note on page 19).

ice, leaving the flowers and freshness to appear. Not knowing whither my fancy would lead me, I walked toward the mansion, and again, as upon that autumn afternoon upon which I first saw Eleanor after her calamity, I turned my steps to the arbor which crowned the slope at the back of the lawn. Thinking of Eleanor, as I saw her then, I entered the place with a light step, and found Mary sitting, looking off on the river with a dreamy face. She blushed when she perceived who had intruded upon her reverie; I saw the warm color sweep, wave after wave, over the lovely cheek and brow, and I knew instantly the secret it betrayed. I remembered the arms which had once fallen about my neck, the tears which had rained upon my cheek from the eyes of a young girl, the eager voice which had said, "*I love you Richard! I* will believe nothing against you!"

Oh, how sweetly the revelation came to me then! My own heart was fully prepared to receive it. Through months I had been transferring the wealth of young, hopeful love, which craves the bliss of being shared, from the sister who was raised so far above mortal passion, to this dear semblance of her former self. My face must have expressed my happiness, for when I stood over Mary, as she sat, and turned her sweet face up toward my own, she gave but one glance before her eyes fell to hide their thought.

I kissed her, and she kissed me back again, shyly, timidly. She loved me; I was no longer mateless, but drank the cup of joy which is filled for youth. What happy children we were, when, late enough after sunset, we strolled back to the house and went to receive the paternal blessing!

I believe that hour when our betrothal was known was the best which had blessed the household since the shadow descended upon it.

In June we were married; there was no excuse for delay, and

all the friends expressed themselves urgent to have the matter settled. We went, on our wedding-tour, to see my mother, with whom we had a long, delightful visit. Three years have passed since then, and in that time there have been changes—some of them very sad. Mr. Argyll died about two years since, his health never rallying from the shock which it received during those trying times. Since then, we have resided in the old mansion, and Eleanor lives with us. She is a noble woman—one of Christ's anointed, who puts aside her own sorrow, to minister to the griefs and sufferings of others. Both Mary and myself defer a great deal to her judgment, which is calm and clear, never clouded by passion, as ours will sometimes be. We feel as if nothing evil could live where Eleanor is; she is the light and blessing of our household.

The saddest affliction which has fallen upon us since the loss of our father, is the death of Mr. Burton. Alas! he has fallen a victim, at last, to the relentless pursuit of enemies which his course in life raised up about him. The wicked feared him, and compassed his destruction. Whether he was murdered by some one whom he had detected in guilt, or by some one who feared the investigations he was making, is not known; he died of poison administered to him in his food. It wrings my heart to think that great and good soul is no more of this world. He was so active, so powerful, of such a genial temperament, it is hard to conceive him dead. We all loved him so much! Oh, if we could discover the cowardly assassin! Sometimes I wonder if it may not have been the man whom he once so mercilessly exposed. God knows—I do not. Attempts upon his life were many times made, but his acute perceptions had always, hitherto, warned him of danger.

Lenore is with us. We shall keep her until some lover comes in the future to rob us of her. She is a rare child—almost a woman now—as talented as her father, and exceedingly lovely. At present she is overwhelmed with grief, and clings to Eleanor, who is her best comforter. In our love for her we try to repay some of the debt we owe her father.

THE END

READING GROUP GUIDE

1. Do you think that this book should be called "crime fiction"?

2. At what point were you certain of the murderer's identity?

3. Are you bothered by the coincidences and "psychic" elements of the book?

4. Is Eleanor a realistic young woman? What about Leesy Sullivan?

5. Is Mr. Burton impressive as a detective? How do you think he compares to Poe's Auguste Dupin or Conan Doyle's Sherlock Holmes?

6. If you've read *The Leavenworth Case* or *That Affair Next Door* by Anna Katharine Green, how does Mr. Burton compare to Ebenezer Gryce?

7. How do you think crime fiction has changed since Victor's time?

8. What do you like about contemporary crime fiction that is different from *The Dead Letter*?

FURTHER READING

BY METTA VICTOR

Maum Guinea, and Her Plantation "Children;" or, Holiday-Week on a Louisiana Estate: A Slave Romance. New York: Beadle, 1861. An abolitionist dime novel.

The Figure Eight; or, The Mystery of Meredith Place. New York: Beadle, 1869. Written as Seeley Regester.

The Dead Letter & The Figure Eight. Edited, with an introduction, by Catherine Ross Nickerson. Durham, NC: Duke University Press, 2003.

BY OTHER WRITERS

Braddon, Mary Elizabeth. *The Trail of the Serpent*. London: Ward, Lock, 1861. First published as *Three Times Dead*, London: W. M. Clark, 1860.

———. *Lady Audley's Secret*. London: William Tinsley, 1862.

Collins, Wilkie. *The Woman in White*. Serialized in *All the Year Round* magazine, 1859; first book publication, New York: Harper & Bros., 1860.

Felix, Charles. *The Notting Hill Mystery*. Serialized in *Once-A-Week* magazine, 1862–63; first book publication, London: Saunders Otley, 1865.

Wood, Ellen (Mrs. Henry). *East Lynne*. London: Richard Bentley, 1861.

CRITICAL STUDIES

Foxwell, Elizabeth. "Metta Fuller Victor: A Sensational Life," *Mystery Scene* 81 (Fall 2003).

Janik, Erika. *Pistols and Petticoats: 175 Years of Lady Detectives in Fact and Fiction*. Boston: Beacon Press, 2016.

Knight, Stephen. *Towards Sherlock Holmes: A Thematic History of Crime Fiction in the 19th Century World*. Jefferson, NC: McFarland, 2017.

Nickerson, Catherine Ross. *The Web of Iniquity: Early Detective Fiction by American Women*. Durham, NC: Duke University Press, 1998.

Sussex, Lucy. *Women Writers and Detectives in Nineteenth-Century Crime Fiction: The Mothers of the Mystery Genre*. New York: Palgrave Macmillan, 2010.

Watson, Kate. *Women Writing Crime Fiction, 1860–1880: Fourteen American, British and Australian Authors*. Jefferson, NC: McFarland, 2012.

ABOUT THE AUTHOR

Metta Victor. (Collection of Leslie S. Klinger)

Metta Victoria Fuller Victor (1831–1885) was born in Erie, Pennsylvania, the third of five children of Adonijah Fuller and Lucy (Williams) Fuller. At the age of eight, she moved to Wooster, Ohio, with her family. She began writing quite early, with her first poetry published at age thirteen and her first novel,

The Last Days of Tul: A Romance of the Lost Cities of the Yucatan,
published when she was fifteen. She relocated briefly with her
older sister Frances to Ypsilanti, Michigan, in 1850, where, in
November, Metta married a Dr. Richard E. Morse (his fate is
unknown). In 1851, she and Frances traveled to New York and
entered the literary circles there. She published a book of poetry
with Frances that year, but Metta was apparently more interested
in producing fiction.* Her novel *The Senator's Son; or, The Maine
Law, A Last Refuge,* appeared the same year, and reportedly the
book went through ten editions and sold thirty thousand copies.

Orville J. Victor. (Collection of Leslie S. Klinger)

In July 1856, Metta married Orville J. Victor, the editor
of the Sandusky, Ohio, *Daily Register.* In the same month, he

---

* Frances (1826–1902), the oldest of the Fuller children, married Jackson Barritt
in 1853 in Pontiac, Michigan, and after moving to New York, wrote a few novels for
Beadle under her married name, Mrs. Frances F. Barritt. She published nothing thereafter until she married Henry Clay Victor, the brother of her sister's husband, Orville
Victor, and moved to California. There, she began to write again and took up journal-
ism and historical works.

became the editor of the quarterly *Cosmopolitan Art Journal*, and not long after, Metta gave birth to the first of the couple's nine children. In the summer of 1858, they moved to New York City, where both began contributing to leading periodicals. Orville became publisher of the newspaper-sized *Illuminated Western World*, and Metta published several longer stories in it. Metta became the editor of *The Home* for the firm of Beadle & Adams (later Beadle & Company) in 1859, and she began to write contributions to Beadle's nonfiction "dime book" series. In 1860, she wrote *Alice Wilde: The Raftsman's Daughter*, Dime Novel No. 4, for Beadle, and more followed. Orville too had written at least one book for the firm, and in 1861 he became Beadle's general editor. Together, the Victors were instrumental in making the publishing house a force. Metta became the editor of *Beadle's Monthly* as well[*] and helped to oversee the growth of Beadle's vast empire of books and magazines.

A prolific writer, Metta Victor had great success in writing romance, westerns, temperance novels, and rags-to-riches tales, many of them dime novels, under a dizzying variety of pseudonyms. According to Albert Johannsen's monumental *The House of Beadle and Adams and Its Dime and Nickel Novels: The Story of a Vanished Literature*,[†] she wrote more than one hundred books, and her work appeared under the names Corinne Cushman, Elanor Lee Edwards, Walter T. Gray, Rose Kennedy, Louis Legrand, M.D. (probably together with Orville), Mrs. Mark Peabody, Seeley Regester, and the Singing Sybil.

Metta also wrote a number of fictional and editorial works under her own name, in which she promoted temperance and the abolition of slavery, and opposed Mormon polygamy. In

---

[*] Catherine Ross Nickerson, "Introduction," *The Dead Letter & The Figure Eight* (Durham, NC: Duke University Press, 2003), 2.

[†] Norman: University of Oklahoma Press, 1950.

1861, Metta published her best-known work: *Maum Guinea, and Her Plantation "Children;" or, Holiday-Week on a Louisiana Estate: A Slave Romance.* The book was a tale of slave life. According to critic Charles Harvey, writing in 1907, "It was spirited and pathetic, and had a good deal of 'local color'; its sales exceeded 100,000 copies, and it was translated into several languages. 'It is as absorbing as *Uncle Tom's Cabin*' was the judgment which Lincoln was said to have passed on it...and it had a powerful influence in aid of the Union cause [in England].""*

In 1864[†] Metta took her place in the history of American crime fiction with her authorship of *The Dead Letter: An American Romance*, the first American crime novel. Beadle reprinted it numerous times, and it was pirated in England by the *Illustrated Family Paper* with the locations changed to England so that it was passed off as an original English story. Metta wrote several other mysteries as Seeley Regester, notably, "The Skeleton at the Banquet" (1869) and *The Figure Eight; or, The Mystery of Meredith Place* (1869, also published by Beadle).

Yet *The Dead Letter* is not even mentioned in Charles Harvey's paean to the dime novel and his encomium of Beadle.[‡] As late as 1941, Howard Haycraft, in writing the sweeping

---

* "The Dime Novel in American Life," *Atlantic Monthly*, July 1907, 39, 43.

---

† According to Johannsen, *The Dead Letter* was published in 1864 and *re*-published in *Beadle's Monthly* in 1866. His source for this information is the "Notes, Notices and Gossip" column of the February 1867 issue of *Beadle's Monthly* in which the editor expressly states: "Nor was [*The Dead Letter*] written, as assumed, especially for this magazine, but was, in fact, produced two years previous to the issue of our first number [in 1866]" (III, 195). It is unclear whether the "editor" who wrote this column was Erastus Beadle, Orville Victor, or Metta Victor. No scholar has found where the novel was previously published. Johannsen, *House of Beadle and Adams*, 2:279.

---

‡ Similarly, while Frank W. Chandler's important two-volume tome *The Literature of Roguery* (Boston and New York: Houghton Mifflin, 1907) recognizes a few American writers in the second half of the nineteenth century, he fails to mention Victor.

Murder for Pleasure: The Life and Times of the Detective Story,[*]
describes the field of American crime writing between Edgar
Allan Poe and Anna Katharine Green as "fallow" and was apparently unaware of Victor's work. Victor's place in history seems
to have gone largely unmarked by scholars of crime fiction until
Allen J. Hubin, founder-editor of *The Armchair Detective* magazine, reported in the July 1974 issue that he had discovered "the
first American detective novel." "Detective story this is, without
doubt," Hubin wrote. "The identity of the real villain is scarcely
hidden at all, but this reflects only the limited skill of the author
and not ineligibility for inclusion in the detective fiction genre.
In spite of this, the book is quite readable, and should assume
considerable importance in the history of American detective
fiction."[+]

Metta Victor continued to write extensively, including
an exclusive series of stories that she wrote for *New York
Weekly,* beginning October 20, 1870, for which she received
$25,000. She died in 1885, survived by Orville and all but one of
her children.[‡] She is buried in Valleau Cemetery in Ridgewood,
New Jersey. Orville continued on at Beadle until 1895, when
it folded. He died in 1910 and is buried together with his wife.

---

[*] London: Peter Davies.

[+] Allan J. Hubin, *Armchair Detective,* July 1974, 216. However, the book would have
been unobtainable by all but the most assiduous collectors until Michele Slung edited a
new edition in 1979, published by Gregg Press. Slung, in private correspondence with
the editor, credits the inclusion of *The Dead Letter* in the Gregg Press series of reprints
to the renowned book dealer/collector/publisher Otto Penzler, with whom she worked
on the series.

[‡] Her third child, Lucy, died only three years earlier, at the age of twenty-nine. Her
youngest two children were twins, age thirteen, and one of them, Florence, was still
alive in 1950, when Johannsen wrote his biographical sketch of Victor.

THE SILENT BULLET

Twelve tales of intrigue and suspense, featuring
Craig Kennedy, the "American Sherlock Holmes"

Readers of classic crime fiction will delight in this collection of twelve short
stories featuring Craig Kennedy, a university professor who uses science to
help catch criminals. Like the famous British consulting detective with whom
he is often compared, Kennedy applies his impressive knowledge—and the
wide array of instruments available in his university laboratory—to gather evidence and solve cases. He even has his own Watson, namely, his friend Walter
Jameson, a journalist who relates the lively tales.

Set in and around the boroughs of New York City in the early 1900s, these
stories offer fascinating glimpses of city life at the bustling turn of the century.
The crimes themselves are highly imaginative, featuring deaths by apparent
but inexplicable means, including asphyxiation, spontaneous combustion, and
vengeful spirits, along with less fatal crimes involving kidnapping, safe-cracking,
stolen wills, and a missing fortune in diamonds. Kennedy's use of cutting-edge
technology of the day—such as seismographs, lie detectors, artificial respira-
tors, and hidden microphones—makes his investigations unorthodox and
entertaining in equal measure.

Arthur B. Reeve's Craig Kennedy stories were so popular in his time that he
went on to publish twenty-six books featuring the professor, who also appeared
in comic strips and a number of films. Fans of Sherlock Holmes will especially
appreciate Kennedy's insistence on logic and science over brawn.

For more Library of Congress Crime Classics, visit:
SOURCEBOOKS.COM